LEISURE MANAGEMENT

LEISURE MANAGEMENT
Issues and Applications

Edited by

M.F. Collins

*Department of Physical Education, Sports Science
and Recreation Management
Loughborough University, UK*

and

I.S. Cooper

*Director of Leisure Services
Cambridge City Council
Cambridge, UK*

CAB INTERNATIONAL

CAB INTERNATIONAL
Wallingford
Oxon OX10 8DE
UK

Tel: +44 (0)1491 832111
Fax: +44 (0)1491 833508
E-mail: cabi@cabi.org

CAB INTERNATIONAL
198 Madison Avenue
New York, NY 10016-4314
USA

Tel: +1 212 726 6490
Fax: +1 212 686 7993
E-mail: cabi-nao@cabi.org

A catalogue record for this book is available from the British Library, London, UK

Library of Congress Cataloging-in-Publication Data
Leisure management : issues and applications / edited by Ian S. Cooper and
  M.F. Collins.
        p.   cm.
    Includes index.
    ISBN 0–85199–215–3 (alk. paper)
      1. Leisure – – Management – – Case studies.   I. Cooper, I.S. (Ian Stuart)
  II. Collins, Michael F. (Michael Frank)
  GV181.5.L44   1997
  790'.06'9 – – dc21   97–22231
                                                                            CIP

ISBN 0 85199 215 3

Typeset in 10/12pt Melior by Wyvern 21 Ltd, Bristol
Printed and bound in the UK by Biddles Ltd, Guildford and King's Lynn

Contents

Contributors

Antônio Carlos Bramante, State University of Campinas, Rua Alemanha, 522, 18045-150 Sorocaba, São Paulo, Brazil

Chris Bull, Centre for Tourism and Leisure Studies, Department of Geography, Canterbury Christ Church College, North Holmes Road, Canterbury, Kent CT1 1QU, UK

Thomas Burton, Faculty of Physical Education and Recreation, University of Alberta, Edmonton, Alberta T6G 2H9, Canada

Claude Cousineau, Department of Leisure Studies, University of Ottawa, 550 Cumberland, Ottawa K1N 6N5, Canada

Graeme Evans, Centre for Leisure and Tourism Studies, University of North London, Stapleton House, 277–281 Holloway Road, London N7 8HN, UK

Steve Frosdick, IWI Associates Ltd, Hounslow TW3 2PR, UK

Troy Glover, Faculty of Physical Education and Recreation, University of Alberta, Edmonton, Alberta T6G 2H9, Canada

Ian Henry, Department of Physical Education, Sports Science and Recreation Management, Loughborough University, Loughborough, Leicestershire LE11 3TU, UK

Dominic Irvine, Leisure Management Unit, University of Sheffield, Hicks Building, Hounsfield Road, Sheffield S3 7RH, UK

Guy Jackson, Department of Physical Education, Sports Science and Recreation Management, Loughborough University, Loughborough, Leicestershire LE11 3TU, UK

Rob Lynch, School of Leisure and Tourism Studies, University of Technology, Sydney, PO Box 222, Lindfield, NSW 2070, Australia

Heather MacGowan, Ministry of Sport and Recreation, Western Australian Government, PO Box 66, Wembley, Western Australia 6014, Australia

Dan Morgan, Bolton Business School, Deane Road, Bolton BL3 5AB, UK

Juan Paramio Salcines, Department of Physical Education, Sports Science and Recreation Management, Loughborough University, Loughborough, Leicestershire LE11 3TU, UK

Neil Ravenscroft, School of Management Studies for the Service Sector, University of Surrey, Guildford GU2 5XH, UK

Martin Reeves, Cheltenham and Gloucester College of Higher Education, Francis Close Hall, Swindon Road, Cheltenham GL50 4AZ, UK

Leigh Robinson, Leisure Management Unit, University of Sheffield, Hicks Building, Houndsfield Road, Sheffield S3 7RH, UK

Frans Schouten, National Institute for Tourism and Transport Studies, Department of Tourism and Leisure, PO Box 3931, 4800 DX Breda, The Netherlands

Roger Sidaway, Research and Policy Consultant, 4 Church Hill Place, Edinburgh EH10 4BD, UK

Peter Taylor, Leisure Management Unit, University of Sheffield, Hicks Building, Hounsfield Road, Sheffield S3 7RH, UK

George Torkildsen, Rosemont, Hare Street, Harlow, Essex CM19 4AY, UK

Anthony Veal, School of Leisure and Tourism Studies, University of Technology, Sydney, PO Box 222, Lindfield, NSW 2070, Australia

Mike Weed, Centre for Leisure and Tourism Studies, The Business School, University of North London, Stapleton House, 277–281 Holloway Road, London N7 8HN, UK

Christine Williams, Lancashire Business School, University of Central Lancashire, Preston PR1 2HE, UK

List of Tables

List of Figures

Introduction

Michael F. Collins[1] and Ian S. Cooper[2]

[1]Department of Physical Education, Sports Science and Recreation Management, Loughborough University, Loughborough LE11 3TU, UK; [2]Department of Leisure Services, Cambridge City Council, Cambridge CB4 4YQ, UK

This collection of papers is but part of those submitted to the World Leisure and Recreation Association's (WLRA) fourth World Congress on 'Leisure and the Quality of Life in the 21st Century', held in Cardiff, Wales, UK, in July 1996.

At the Congress, the Management Commission, the newest of WLRA's Commissions, attracted 78 papers in the Management and Access theme, from 16 countries in five continents – 35 from UK, 18 from USA, six from Australia, four from Canada, two each from The Netherlands, Poland and South Africa, and single papers from Belgium, Brazil, Finland, France, Greece, India, South Korea, Mexico and Slovenia. For this volume it would have been good to have had more papers from women and from non-white contributors, but these will come as the subject develops beyond its current infancy, both in academia and in public and private practice, in Africa, Asia and Latin America.

Given the very different stages of development of facility provision, legislation for access, the evolution of voluntary and commercial systems and public policy, the professional styles and standards of delivery, and customer/participant responses, it is not surprising in a subject area still in its adolescence worldwide that the nature, approaches, styles and coverage varied widely. For example, the methods used by the authors whose contributions we edited ranged from five who drew on professional practice, four who used qualitative and often very long and probing interviews, five using questionnaires, four who undertook detailed documentary analysis and four who used old-fashioned scholarship and critical observation.

© CAB INTERNATIONAL 1998. *Leisure Management: Issues and Applications* (eds M.F. Collins and I.S. Cooper)

Issues and Applications

Of the many ways we could have grouped them, we have chosen two themes: issues and applications of different theories and approaches to managing leisure resources and customers.

After reviewing these, we take an overview of the chapters.

Issues theme

Access is a vital issue for participation; it can depend on national laws as representing the will of people and government for inclusion, as **MacGowan's** chapter shows in relation to aboriginals in Australia; it can depend on the breadth of policy approaches, as **Cousineau** argues for Exercise for All rather than Sport for All; even with limited investment, take-up can depend on good information and an intention to involve citizens and customers, as **Bramante** argues for recreation in Brazil, and **Schouten** for European museums; it can be controlled by élites despite other intentions in introducing grant aid programmes for managing dramatically changing landscape husbandry regimes, as **Ravenscroft** suggests is happening in England.

Individual approaches are contingent on the political and social history and structures of a particular polity, but are pressed by increasing numbers of international and even global trends. So, since the Rio conference and local approaches to Agenda 21, sustainable development is a watchword and, despite the slowing of economic growth and leisure time and consumption, there are still great debates in developed countries about whether rural landscapes can cope with the volume of aspiring visitors and, more significantly, their cars. **Sidaway** shows that the British Members of Parliament are convinced that sport has a minor and manageable impact relative to sightseers and picnickers, given the will to allocate resources to visitor or habitat management. Meanwhile, in 'rust belt' cities throughout the world, politicians and city managers are seeking new jobs in leisure activity for their unemployed, and new images for their towns and new brands for their tourism products, often with a strong sporting element. **Henry and Paramio Salcines** use Bilbao to show that this is a tense, protracted and uncertain process when the actors in a regime are divided politically and geographically. Throughout the Western world also (both in countries with lots of undeveloped space and weaker planning systems, and even in countries with a dense population and strong planning systems) there are economic forces pushing shopping, sport, and entertainment operations to the edge of towns – to a new 'leisure periphery', which **Evans** vividly illustrates from England, but which has a deleterious effect on the vitality and coherence of the city centre, which in the extreme example of Los Angeles barely exists.

Throughout the Organization for Economic Cooperation and Development the cost of local government and its leisure services is under scrutiny and fiscal limitation. One means of meeting such demanding objectives is to shift some of the delivery and its costs out of direct public management, of which the most common mechanism is contracting out, and **Glover and Burton** reflect on the types of contracting in Canada. Another means is to encourage the commercial sector – by tax rebates, inducements and favourable environmental planning policies – about which leisure students have written very little; **Irvine and Taylor** seek to make a start by a current valuing of the sector in Britain. One booming form of commercial leisure is gambling, and **Lynch and Veal** show that its growth through casinos in Australia – and specifically currently in Sydney – is raising not only moral concerns but also worries about its impact on local communities and existing social-club culture, in very similar ways to concerns about building sports stadia.

Applications theme

Within this framework, there are many applications to management but common principles.

Every manager has safety as a top priority, but there is little written about it outside regulations; **Frosdick** argues for a risk analysis approach that is as valid in Samoa as in Saskatchewan or Stratford-upon-Avon. **Robinson** shows how, in a professionalizing system in England, different approaches are being taken to quality assurance systems which are meant to reassure both customers and local authorities seeking competent contractors, while **Williams** seeks to show the strengths and weaknesses manifest in a variety of leisure facilities when using a much-vaunted business analysis tool, the SERVQUAL index. **Morgan** shows how, in a mixed public–voluntary–commercial delivery system for instruction and competitive climbing new technology and new customers can bring a crisis of philosophy and competition for both natural and man-made resources. 'Forming partnerships' and 'alliances' are new buzzwords for means of gathering scattered resources in difficult times, and in the rapidly developing area of sport–tourism **Weed and Bull** go searching for a network between the two sets of individual and organizational actors in the sport and tourism spheres, and find only a few links, let alone a system. **Jackson and Reeves** argue for a continuum of sport–tourism relationships embracing both spectators and participants from the holiday novice or happy duffer to the full professional, and at the latter end of this spectrum interview in depth some élite athletes to look at their expenditures of time and cash.

Overviewing all this, **Torkildsen** asks in his keynote chapter, who needs leisure managers? He argues that we all do, as students/trainees or participants or consumers, and as societies whose leaders promise their citizens improved quality of life, or as providers who wish to keep their customers and earn income or profits. Despite the falling public confidence in the 'old' professions of the church, the law, the military and, to a lesser degree, medicine, he believes that leisure professionals can be credible if they have strong ethics, clear and coherent philosophy and demonstrate competence, insight and confidence. These are visionary leaders and mentors to their staff, and imaginative and responsive providers to their customers, and effective advocates to resource providers and legislators – much more than administrators, Torkildsen argues, in all three sectors.

Chapters on issues

The downside of democracy – the tyranny of the majority – has been overturned in many societies as the need for equal opportunity or affirmative action policies for minority interests have been identified as a need, fought for and adopted. Australian governments were attacked heavily throughout the 1970s for a legacy of neglect of Aboriginal peoples, and the Sports Commission has a remit to contribute to overcoming this through providing culturally specific forms of sport and recreation, though many programmes are adaptations of those used for groups in the majority population. **MacGowan** describes the efforts of the Western Australian government in both maintaining indigenous forms of sport and sustaining access to imported, modern forms. It is too early to make a judgement as to whether a strategic breakthrough in disadvantage has been made, but they identify that the successful programmes have been those where Aboriginal people have been fully involved in developing, delivering and owning the programmes.

Cousineau has been involved in several Canadian projects to help Third World states, notably in South-east Asia, to get more of their people involved in exercise programmes. The Canadian government has also been a partner in numerous projects to spread the Sport for All ethic through sports programmes since the International Olympic Committee adopted this approach. He argues that the Active Living approach is both more efficient and more effective. It is more effective because it appeals to more segments of the population, and can link directly with the World Health Organization and national health campaigns to prevent or slow down the spread of 'social diseases' from the West (cancers, coronary heart disease and strokes), which arise from eating too fatty or sugary a diet, smoking or drinking too much and becoming too sedentary. It is more efficient, he argues, because it requires little or less expensive equipment and built facilities than sport, and because its exercise forms extend participation in those activities that are already popular – walking, running, swimming, dancing and cycling (and the bike is a basic form of transport for a growing number of workers and their families). The Active Living approach dissociates itself from the Sport for All concept of a continuum or pyramid culminating in excellence which puts off many 'ordinary', unfit people, and often becomes the focus of government support. This was discussed by Roberts and Kamphorst (1989), and seen in the recent British White Paper *Raising the Game* (DNH, 1995), an approach criticized by Collins (1995) and Cooper (1995b) for transferring all the burden of meeting the needs of many groups to local government whose resources are now mostly controlled (85%) by Whitehall, and have been progressively reduced as a main aim of fiscal and political policy. It is also an approach, says Cousineau, that depends on a local, bottom-up approach, whereas many Sport for All programmes are driven top-down, though **MacGowan** stressed that the Western Australian approach specifically guarded against this by involving Aboriginal people.

Bramante examined the activity patterns and facility use of a sample of 455 families living within the catchment areas of 11 urban leisure facilities in Sorocaba City, a town of 450,000 people some 60 miles south-east of São Paulo, Brazil. He suspected that, given its fairly high socio-economic status as a university town, there was substantial under-use of existing sports provision. He used Godbey's (1984) model of non-use of public leisure services. Some of his team's major findings were that: (i) there was an unequal distribution of opportunities; (ii) there was no detailed planning process for leisure facilities related to need; (iii) most sports facilities were under-used, notably on weekdays; (iv) municipal operations policies were fragmented and discontinuous; (v) users were not effectively involved in either the planning or operating policies; and (vi) there were no effective user profiles to aid a marketing policy to reduce the under-use. His interviews confirmed that it was much more consumer ignorance than dislike of the available programmes that underlay this poor management performance.

The lack of planning for municipal leisure services has long been a problem in many countries. At the time of writing, the requirement for all United Kingdom local authorities to create a Local Leisure Plan through consultation and need-related planning is being advocated by one of the authors (Cooper, 1995a, 1997). This concept has received support nationally from local government and leisure agencies as well as the Labour Party and is due to be tested through national consultation.

Schouten attacks a management shortcoming in much longer established and widespread facilities which are a major form of tourist destination for both day trippers and long-stay visitors – western European museums. He argues that too many museum managers see themselves as curators and educators first, treating their visitors as passive receivers, a role that TV and computers are increasingly by-passing in terms of involvement. Not only must they take account of this turn of technology, but, he argues, museums must be pleasurable places like other leisure attractions, and must combine myth, magic and mystery into dreams about past, present *and* future.

Ravenscroft looks at the long-established arrangement for public access free of charge over an overwhelmingly privately owned English countryside, and detects an undercurrent in recent events. With the growth of crop and animal surpluses as a result of scientifically driven productivity, and declining European agricultural production subsidies, new national payments for overall landscape maintenance have included a modest element for access. But this, he claims, is a pseudo-market payment carefully negotiated by the landowning interest, which has been very strong since King John's time, and is replacing a law-based public right, particularly on privatized land as with former Forestry Commission holdings and on the hundreds of thousands of acres now under the Ministry of Agriculture's Stewardship scheme. This is now run by the Ministry which has no tradition of managing access or recreation, having been transferred on the grounds of simplifying access to grants, especially for small landowners, from the Countryside Commission, which does have such a tradition. There is evidence that some of this negotiated access has never been publicized to, or used by, the taxpayers who are paying for it.

There are widespread claims that sport has deleterious effects on the countryside, notably by trampling or wearing away vegetation and by disturbing wildlife; **Sidaway** has been one of the foremost British researchers to work on this issue, not only in the UK but also in North America and The Netherlands, and as advisor to the recent Parliamentary select committee he was able to bring this experience to a review of management practice. Its report and his chapter show that the concern dates back nearly 40 years, but that there has been more debate and rhetoric than action on what is, for the most part, a set of issues which can be handled by: zoning; seasonal and confined bans on activity to protect wildlife while breeding or migrating, or to allow vegetation to regenerate; and by investment in landscape or visitor management at 'honey pot' sites. It also recognizes that the nub of many of these problems is often a cultural and socially constructed one of power or powerlessness between recreation and amenity groups sharing or competing for access, not one of dissipating or remedying a measurable physical impact. What has not yet been faced is the much more ubiquitous issue and sustained long-term trend of rising car use for informal visits to the countryside which the Countryside Commission reckon may increase by 150–200% over the next 15 years.

Henry and Paramio Salcines deal with a new but rapidly spreading trend, of using sport deliberately as a part of the regeneration of city economies and townscapes, and this progress report on the attempts of opposing city and region regimes to restructure the old industrial city of Bilbao is part of a study making transnational comparisons with one of England's current Cities of Sport, Sheffield. Progress is slow and often tangential or crabwise when such political tensions exist, rather than the neat picture of rapidly moving public–private partnerships often portrayed by the American pioneers of sport and recreation regeneration strategies. In Bilbao too, the bulk of the resources put behind the strategy are public rather than private.

Evans describes another widespread trend in current planning, of the pressure to develop on the urban fringes of towns where ring roads intersecting with intercity motorways create great accessibility to markets, yet land is cheaper and there are fewer development constraints than in the central cities; so retail, wholesale and office parks have flourished there, sucking custom and vitality out of traditional town centres, and providing venues for many new forms of restaurant, and the revival of tenpin bowling and cinema. But in 1990 the Department of the Environment ruled out the building of stadia, thereby stultifying what undoubtedly would have been a major geographical restructuring of English professional football, most of whose top teams are redeveloping their Victorian and Edwardian inner-city stadia.

More recently (1996), the Department's revised Guidance Note 6 advised against any more urban-fringe retail development, and it remains to be seen whether this will take the steam out of the urban-fringe development, which has often comprised what Evans calls a new 'Leisure Periphery', or whether there can only be slow recovery of confidence in the old multi-purpose city centre, if sustained by fiscal incentives and improved public transport.

In many countries, governments are encouraging different models of service delivery from the traditional, in an attempt to reduce costs, and perhaps to improve the quality of offering. **Glover and Burton** use Peston's (1972) four types of goods and services, and Burton's own (1982) classification of five roles of government jointly, and suggest that municipalities should consider three significant variables when choosing methods of delivery: the level of competition, the nature of the goods or services and the degree of governmental control. This provides four forms of delivery: the traditional direct provision, and three which entail degrees of privatization – cross-sector alliances, regulated monopolies,

and divestiture. In fact, there has been relatively little complete divestiture in the form of sales, and contracting has been the most common
form; often by negotiation, as in The Netherlands (Snape, 1995), but
sometimes by compulsion, as in Britain. One of the editors has written
elsewhere of the benefits that have accrued to recreation in the sale of
the Water Authorities in England and Wales (Collins, 1996) and of the
impact that has been made on municipal leisure management
structures as well as policies by compulsory competitive tendering
(Collins, 1997). The other editor has commented on many occasions on
local government leisure services in *Leisure Management* magazine
(Cooper, 1995a,b, 1997).

Some modest facilities and contracts are run in England by volunteers, but a much larger part of the system comprises single-sport clubs
run by volunteers, many for recreation but many also for performance
and excellence levels of sport. Surprisingly, this system has only now
received a major measurement exercise as the Sports Council sought to
identify what types and numbers of people were involved and what
forms of support they might need to continue operating in a field that
demands ever higher quality and safety standards. In this, the Sports
Council was following a lead given by the Australian Sports Commission and Sport Canada in their volunteer support programmes.

Governments also look to commerce for an increasing proportion of
leisure provision, yet even fewer studies of the commercial sector exist
than for the voluntary; **Irvine and Taylor** are members of a new centre
shared by the two Sheffield Universities to study the operation of the
commercial sector and attempt to update the earliest attempt, by
Roberts (1977), to measure the size and contribution to GDP, which
they calculate at 1990 values as £84bn or 17.5%. They also looked at
the concentration ratio for firms in 15 sectors, i.e. the proportion of
turnover taken by the top five firms in each sector. In British industry as
a whole, with many takeovers and mergers since 1960, the figure was
83% in 1983; in airlines and photography in 1990 the ratio was over
70%; and in the least concentrated, book publishing and sports equipment, it was only 27%.

A specific sector in which commerce has an overwhelming hold,
but the state takes much care and effort to regulate, is gambling. Outside sociology, few studies have been made of the queen of gambling
forms, the casino, but some are now appearing (see Stokowski, 1996,
for a study of two casino towns in Colorado). With the growth of the
demand to gamble some governments have been seeking to develop
depressed and poor rural areas; for example, in one of the poorest
counties in the USA – Tulane, Mississippi – land values and employment have been transformed by the establishment of 24 casinos, a
concentration second only to Las Vegas. But in Australia the casino is a

major city phenomenon, and **Lynch and Veal** describe the possible political, social and economic benefits, costs and resulting tensions in the establishment phase of the most high profile case, on Sydney's famous harbourside. As with sports stadia, there are inner-city communities whose lives will be drastically changed, if not threatened, by the new monster building for city and out-of-town 'high rollers' leisure.

Chapters on applications

The need for adequate precautions for the safety of leisure customers has been heightened in Britain recently, sadly by disasters, for example, the deaths of spectators at Hillsborough football stadium and of young people while canoeing off the Dorset coast; other examples include deaths in a burning night-club in Germany and a burning cinema in Eastern Europe. The example of the litigious Americans should arouse managers' concerns about the extent of their civil and criminal liabilities. **Frosdick** argues that the secure foundation to good practice is a proper risk evaluation, and draws on his own professional experience to spell out the principles of assessment.

To lure customers back, service delivery must not only be safe but satisfying and of high quality; **Robinson** examines the reasons for adopting or not adopting one of the major forms of quality assurance systems now in widespread use in the UK – BS 5750/ISO 9002, Investors in People, and Charter Marks. She then goes on to evaluate the role and appropriateness of such programmes, which many authorities are beginning to see as a means of ensuring minimum competence in delivery and staff training of both their client-side work forces and of direct service organizations and private contractors bidding to manage facilities.

Williams uses the SERVQUAL indices to look at the performance of a theatre, museum, art gallery, leisure centre, amusement park and golf course in the eyes of their managers and customers. She identifies some methodological limitations of the approach, including the fact that customers' perceptions are coloured by the fact that many have pre-existing differences of expectation of private and public providers. She also felt that none of her six site managers was unequivocally committed to quality; compromise with short-term financial pressures on budgets was widespread, and this led her to conclude that often they were serving the system first and the customer second. She suggests that there should be an investigation of whether a generic performance model is feasible; direct comparison of results generated by other indicators systems, such as that used widely in Australia by the Centre for Recreation in Adelaide, would be instructive.

Morgan takes perhaps the narrowest focus of this collection, on climbing, but shows how a technological innovation can dramatically change a leisure market; climbing is one of the claimants for the title of Britain's fastest growing sport. Be this as it may, the advent of a much better designed, more flexible and more challenging generation of climbing walls has undoubtedly contributed to this growth, made climbing much more visible to the sporting public, and introduced a controlled competitive element into it reminiscent of much other sport, while removing some of the mystique surrounding the sport cultivated by the traditional climbing fraternity. Such developments have brought the strains not just of coping with rapid growth but also of philosophical divides and implications for nature, as some of the new breed of wall climbers take to natural rock and seek to introduce bolts and other artificial aids to what the traditionalists see as the essence of mountaineering, the challenge of nature to the skill and nerve of the individual with as little help as possible, not the artificial evening-up of odds. In a paper to the conference, Ewart and Henderson (1996) mentioned similar impacts in rafting, scuba diving, mountaineering and mountain biking in North America.

As we have already seen, sport provides some major attractions for tourists, spectating amateur adventure sport in the countryside – climbing, hang-gliding, water-skiing and parascending, for example – and spectating professional games; but we must also consider the tourism aspect of both individuals and clubs participating in their chosen activities. **Jackson and Reeves** describe one of their case studies along this continuum of activity, that of the dedicated top amateur athlete; perhaps for the first time, these interviews document the amount of time (up to one-third of the year) and money that these highly professional players expend. Their money has a local multiplier effect, even when they are fed up with 'being on the road', and looking forward to going home. Despite the developing relationship between sport and tourism, **Weed and Bull** sought to identify the policy community on both the sport and tourism arms, and found it no better developed in Britain than when Glyptis in 1982 went looking for its basis in this and five other European countries. They suggest that five factors – ideology, government policy (including its absence), organizational structure, organizational culture and, perhaps particularly, key staff interests – influence this position.

This collection of chapters is diverse in topic, focus and geography but demonstrates the vigour and developing nature of management studies in leisure, both of an applied and theoretical nature. Chapters like that of Bramante show that mistakes from the past in developed countries can easily be repeated in developing ones 20 years later, and Cousineau demonstrates that such countries do have choices but need alerting to them. The World Leisure and Recreation Organization sees as one of its goals the free flow and dissemination of information and experience in leisure and recreation across the globe; this Congress achieved that and future WLRA gatherings will seek to do so more effectively.

References

Burton, T.I. (1982) The roles of government in the leisure services delivery system. Paper to VIIth Commonwealth and International Conference on Sport, Physical Education, Recreation and Dance, Brisbane.

Collins, M.F. (1995) Raising the game: sights on sport. *Leisure Management* 15.9, 26–29.

Collins, M.F. (1996) Riding on the crest of a wave; water recreation on public and privatised resources. In: *Proceedings of the LSA/VVS Conference Accelerating Time and Leisure, Wageningen, September 1996.* Leisure Studies Association, Eastbourne (in press).

Collins, M.F. (1997) Does a new philosophy change the structures? Leisure and CCT in local government in Midland England. *Managing Leisure* 3 (in press).

Cooper, I.S. (1995a) Statutory plans are the best way forward. *Leisure Management* 15.7, 9.

Cooper, I.S. (1995b) Summer musings. *Leisure Management* 15.9, 11.

Cooper, I.S. (1997) Analysis: local plan aesthetics. *Leisure Management* 17.4, 32–34.

DNH (1995) *Raising the Game.* Department of National Heritage, London.

Ewart, A.W. and Henderson, S.J. (1996) Extreme leisure: the status and impacts of adventure. Recreation paper to 4th WLRA Congress 'Free Time and the Quality of Life for the 21st Century', Cardiff, 15–19 July.

Glyptis, S.A. (1982) *Sport and Tourism in Western Europe.* British Travel Educational Trust, London.

Godbey, G. (1984) Nonuse of public leisure services: a model. *Journal of Leisure Research* 16(1), 1–12.

Peston, M. (1972) *Public Goods and the Public Sector.* Macmillan Press, London.

Roberts, J. (1977) *The Commercial Sector in Leisure.* Sports Council/ESRC, London.

Roberts, K. and Kamphorst, T. (1989) *Sport: International Perspectives.* Giordano Bruno, Culembourg.

Snape, S. (1995) Contracting out local government services in Western Europe: lessons from the Netherlands. *Local Government Studies* 21.4, 642–658.

Stokowski, P.A. (1996) *Riches and Regrets: Betting on Gambling in Two Colorado Mountain Towns.* University of Colorado Press, Niwot, Colorado.

'Who Needs Leisure Managers?'   1

George Torkildsen

Rosemont, Hare Street, Harlow, Essex, CM19 4AY, UK

'Who Needs Leisure Managers?'

I don't. I have mountains to climb and rivers to cross and peace in the countryside. And my television.

I don't. I'm secretary of the golf club. Greenkeepers maintain the course. The club runs itself. I administer.

I don't. I'm an experienced teacher and coach and run a successful Sports Development Programme.

I don't. I'm a commercial manager. I have to hit the bottom line. People flock to our cinema, tenpin bowling centre and catering and bars.

Introduction

In the context of leisure and recreation across the world, the use of the word 'manager' is relatively recent. In public and institutional settings, even today, we are more likely to encounter 'supervisor', 'officer', 'organizer' and, most of all, 'administrator'. Managership, however, encompasses a far broader portfolio and it becomes alive and more potent when good leadership is present.

My thesis is that leisure managers are needed in all organizations that provide resources, services, facilities and opportunities for people's leisure outside the home, whether in the public, voluntary, commercial or institutional sectors. Why? Are we not capable enough to provide

© CAB INTERNATIONAL 1998. *Leisure Management: Issues and Applications*
(eds M.F. Collins and I.S. Cooper)

and manage our own leisure? And, if not, surely an administrator will be sufficient?

This chapter will present a rationale and suggest that managers are different from administrators and that, without good management, there will be less choice, many people will be deprived opportunity, organizations will be less efficient, resources will be under-used, and programmes will be less effective. Yet the juxtaposition of 'leisure' with 'management' appears ambiguous. What is the relationship?

'All Work and No Play'

Sounds like the motto of leisure managers!!

The word 'leisure' is bonded with words like 'play' and 'recreation', and the word 'leisure' is used here as a shorthand to encompass this wider and deeper context. Human beings play as well as work, captured in the rhyme: 'all work and no play makes Jack a dull boy' (and presumably Jill a dull girl!). Play for children and leisure for adults can help build self-esteem, develop skills, expand interests and provide opportunity for personal, educational, emotional and social growth.

'Leisure' is interpreted variously (as blocks of time, as activities, as a state of being) and is also described, idealistically, as a way of life, a philosophy of living. Leisure was thought to be the opposite of work, but, increasingly, leisure is being fused into a holistic concept, a central element in a culture, with intricate ties to work, family, institutions and 'free' time. My perception of leisure is that it has to do with 'activities' (of almost any kind), usually chosen for their own sake, in relative freedom, which bring intrinsic satisfactions. The personal and social orientations of the satisfactions they bring appear to make the activity 'leisure'.

'Self-actualization' is a Maslow word invented to describe self-fulfilment, a personal harmony with oneself and the world. Self-actualization can be regarded as one of the goals of leisure – and of life. Hence, leisure can be a means of meeting personal goals and, in a social context, of creating balanced communities.

So, as one of our building blocks in the debate, can we agree that leisure is potentially good for one and all? Agreed. So why can't a good administrator handle it?

'There are No Ends in Administration, Minister. Just Means.'
('Yes Minister', BBC TV series)

So what is wrong with administration? Nothing. Good administrators are essential to good management. However, administration is a skill applied to given tasks, it is not a beginning-to-end process. Administration, in and of itself, can also be a means of standing in the way of progress and opportunity.

Bureaucracy Saps Human Potential

Dr Lawrence Peter in *The Peter Pyramid* (1986) demonstrates the ways bureaucracies sap human resources: major organizations are constructed upside-down, with the point of the operation all but invisible beneath the bulk of a top-heavy administration. 'The bureaucrat is so busy keeping his job that he has not time to do it!'

Eliminating hierarchy liberates energy and enthusiasm and identifies the good managers. It also exposes weak managers, who, fearful of change, hide behind bureaucracy. As Tom Peters (personal communication) urges: 'Forget hierarchies, bureaucracy and narrowly defined job functions. It's imagination, knowledge and creativity that will drive forward the truly successful companies of the future.'

Administration-only services tend towards:

- following, rather than leading and planning;
- lacking demand assessment, instead of marketing;
- being re-active as distinct from pro-active;
- re-cycling the same old programmes, rather than looking to new ways, expansion, choice, variety and outreach;
- a facility lettings policy, as opposed to developing a balance in programming;
- risk-avoidance, rather than experimentation: 'The centre is there; use it' – a take-it-or-leave-it approach – compared to entrepreneurial flair and enabling;
- quantitative monitoring, ignoring qualitative measuring and evaluating benefits;
- putting emphasis on finding the right answer, rather than on asking the right question;
- efficiency, rather than effectiveness;
- defending the *status quo*, rather than thinking differently about traditional problems.

No Use Being Super-efficient, But Ineffective!

Efficiency, making the best use of resources – running a well-organized, tight and tidy ship – doing things right, is very important. But efficiency alone is like a ship without a sail: it is going nowhere. Effectiveness is

Box 1.1   Case 1.
A centre was built to meet local needs in a deprived area of the north-west of England. At first, the centre was busy, but unpopular because it was being used mainly by commuters. Financial performance was good, but the centre was not doing what it was built for. It was being administered efficiently but towards the wrong goals. Good management turned it round by questioning performance and setting the right goals through improved programming (which improved local perception even if the financial performance was not as good).

Case 2.
A similar story comes from a seaside town. This centre was built for the local population as a response to an horrific murder of two young girls from a local housing estate, but the community was not consulted. Matters were made worse when the council appointed an entertainment manager, who organized flower arranging and ballroom dancing, instead of mums-and-tots sessions and five-a-side football. Only when consultants carried out a review, and experienced community leisure managers took over, did the place gain any acceptance. Lessons to learn are a lack of local consultation at planning and operational stages, showing lack of good leisure management.

concerned with the voyage and sailing to a destination. It is measured by the degree to which an organization meets its aims and objectives. Effectiveness means doing the right things.

Two key elements in management effectiveness are, first, the interaction between the organization and those who use the services – meeting the needs of people – and, second, managers who are involved in the achievement of the organization's goals.

There is One Thing Worse than Change, and that is the *Status Quo*

Administrators don't like change. They like the *status quo*. Normality. In his earlier days, Peter Drucker once said (personal communication):

> The job of management is never to be concerned with restoring or maintaining normality, because normality is the condition of yesterday. The major concern of managers – if they are to make their business effective – must be in the direction of systematically trying to understand the condition of the future, so that they can decide on the changes that can take them from today into tomorrow.

> **Box 1.2** Case 3.
> An example of administrators preferring the *status quo* is well made at
> leisure services in one large UK borough with a predominantly black
> community. 'Positive discrimination' jobs have been created, but the key
> staff are not leisure managers. Structures and systems have been established
> which provide administration and supervision; service is poor. Numerous
> answers are given and excuses made as to why things can't change. The
> community have real fears about private management altering the service
> to a profit-based one. These fears can be overcome by setting the right
> goals and employing experienced community leisure managers. Staff fears,
> however, are that they will be found out and shown to be poor managers.
> Hence, currently, the *status quo* remains.

Managership is Different from Administration

'Management' is a word carrying widely contrasting definitions and
descriptions. Usually, it is concerned with the achievement of results
through the involvement of others: getting things done, with and
through people. It is concerned with performance: economic (in terms
of value for money), operational (in terms of efficiency) and people (in
terms of effectiveness). Good management is concerned with high
performance: quality performance.

But can Leisure be Managed?

If leisure is about human experience, and management is about
organization and control, do we not have a contradiction in terms? If
leisure is a freedom to choose, personal management is of far greater
importance than management by someone else, particularly the
faceless 'someone'. However, in our culture, effective management is
needed to open up opportunity for more people.

Some would say that leisure cannot be organized and managed and
still remain leisure. How can managers guarantee other people's satisfying experiences? They cannot. However, they can shape environments,
provide opportunities, offer choice and manage resources in such a
way that more people can find and enjoy leisure activities which
enhance their lives. The greater variety of choice, the greater the opportunity for more people to find a recreation of their choice.

Managers can therefore create the opportunity and the environment
where leisure can happen; moreover, land, property, money, politics

and policies have to be brought together by good management to provide better opportunity for all.

A second building block in the debate, therefore, is that resources can be better used and greater opportunities can be provided, with good management. There are a number of new ways and styles of management that suit leisure service delivery.

More with Less! And Handle the Pain of Change!

In the UK and in many parts of the world, there are forces affecting the management of leisure services. An inverse relationship exists: there are diminishing resources ('downsizing' in the jargon!) and increasing demand. We are asked to do more, for less. How? We can work longer, work smarter, manage volunteers and establish partnerships. Yet, one of the best ways is by motivating staff and customers.

Rosabeth Moss Kanter, in *When Giants Learn to Dance* (1989), sets out future organizations as 'post-entrepreneurial', empowering individuals as a force for change. New organizations will be leaner, fitter and with fewer management levels. Successful business comes from cooperation inside the organization, and competition outside. Too many organizations are fighting internal battles. Customer service should function within as well as without.

Managers must understand about running organizations.

Successful organizations tend to have:

- Corporate values – understood throughout the organization.
- Shared goals – staff involved in goal setting.
- Matching staff to jobs and job satisfaction – right people in the right job. Too often, good staff are in the wrong job!
- An 'obsession' with customers and their needs – too often we are obsessed with our own.
- Manager flexibility, with a high capacity for adjustment – an ability to handle the pain of change. Every change presents a new opportunity.

Horizontal Rather than Vertical

A relatively new concept is the 'horizontal organization', managing across teams horizontally, rather than vertically.

- Organize around key processes, not tasks – functions become seamless, rather than 'disconnects'.
- Hierarchies are flattened – fragmented tasks are combined or eliminated if they do not add value.

- Teams become the organization's 'building blocks' – self-managed ownership teams.
- Performance is customer-driven not administration-driven – customer satisfaction (not share price) is the hallmark; satisfied customers become loyal, repeat-visit customers.
- Staff are involved and trained.
- Performance is rewarded.

Managers as Team Leaders

Good leadership is concerned with both results and relationships. Leadership is as much to do with the spirit as with science and the mind. Good leaders create a vision, champion a cause and develop strategies. Three broad types of skill are needed: conceptual skills, technical skills and human relationship skills. And the people-skills count for most in leisure service delivery.

Individuals working as a team can achieve much more than any one of them can alone. As self-managing teams become part of an organization, the skills that used to be called 'management skills', have to be learned by each team member.

Blend the Team

Meredith Belbin (1991) identified nine team roles: problem-solver, resourcer, coordinator, shaper, evaluator, team worker, implementer, finisher and specialist. He found the teams that are likely to perform best are the ones that have the best blend of team roles to play off against each other. The team is built up on the strengths we bring to the collective. No individual is perfect, but by putting together and developing different, yet competent, people, you can build the perfect team for the right job.

People, unlike machines, are flexible, and leisure management calls for stepping into other roles when the need arises. Then staff look upon it as 'our job'. When flexibility is needed, the team can stretch. (Bamboo scaffolding around Hong Kong tower blocks bends with hurricanes; the rigid metal poles cannot cope when the pressure is on!)

Work Teams Need Coaching – Administration is About Things

Coaching is about people. Coaching enhances performance at work, cost-effectively – no time is lost off-site. Moreover, passing on your own skills and seeing others achieve is one of the most rewarding aspects of work.

A coach is a person who gets people to play their roles to the best of their ability. Coaching aims to create an environment where people work in self-managed teams that identify and solve problems on their own.

Like sports teams, management teams need coaching. Leisure managers have an abundance of practical situations and opportunities for inculcating fine leadership qualities in their staff.

Staff need to work to their potential. If they do not, they are an expensive liability and they weaken the team. Valued, competent and confident staff lead to a motivated workforce which operates willingly and efficiently. Pulling together is better than pulling apart. When people work as a team, they motivate each other; no one wants to let the side down, so the team is more productive. Staff will feel, think and work like a team and will also gain job enrichment.

Quality Management

The quality of management determines, to a large extent, the type of use and viability of leisure services and facilities. It is a key component, whether facilities are large or small, whether they are run publicly, commercially or privately.

Quality management systems are ways of organizing and involving the whole business: every department, every activity and every person.

Such systems must be firmly tied to a continuous assessment of customer needs. The three basic principles of never-ending improvement are: focusing on the customer, understanding the process and involving the staff and customers. The Japanese word *kaizen* denotes a management style based on a foundation of gradual change, building up a culture of quality awareness and constant learning. The spirit of *kaizen* can trigger dramatic breakthroughs.

So We Need Good Managers. But Who Needs Leisure Managers?

I don't. I have my degree in management.

As Peter Drucker is famous for saying, 'A good manager can manage anything.'

However, management is varied and situational. Rosemary Stewart (1970) argues that, because managers' jobs and situations vary, they have different functions to perform – they need knowledge of the area of work. We need leisure knowledge and an understanding of people in the leisure situation and what motivates them to leisure.

Leisure service is less tangible than the material product. You can buy a tennis racket and keep it, but leisure participation is intangible until you experience it. A shop can sell the racket tomorrow, but if the court space is not sold today, it is lost for ever. Leisure cannot be stored. It is perishable, unpredictable and easily damaged. Customers treated rudely or double-booked can go elsewhere. The leisure 'product', therefore, is fragile and, in many instances, dependent on the staff giving the service.

If quality is synonymous with meeting customer requirements, then the first item on the agenda will be to find out who the potential customers are, what they need and want and, in many cases, what they are prepared to pay for.

Managers, therefore, are concerned with the 'totality' of quality leisure, an all-round concern, not just with separate functions, nor just with efficiency, the hallmark and *raison d'être* of the administrator. Leisure managers need to be practical. They convert philosophies and principles into actions. They set goals. Managers must achieve optimal use of resources, identify markets and create new ones. They must achieve objectives and offer the most attractive services to meet needs and demands of the market.

Good management, then, is largely the result of good managers! They are individuals who have the responsibility for providing leadership of the organization and the ability to move it towards its goals.

We Need to Sell Benefits

Too often, managers think their products are facilities and activities like squash courts and aerobics. However, these are the vehicles for getting to the 'real' product – experiencing satisfaction. We have to sell benefits, helping to make people happier, healthier, fitter, better educated, more skilful. We can sell fun, glamour, excitement and adventure. The potential benefits are abundant.

Management is often appraised in terms of economic efficiency – the bottom line. However, in 'people service' programmes, 'profit' needs to be defined, not just in terms of money, but also in terms of benefits offered.

Charles Handy, in *Inside Organizations* (1990), believes that commercial companies need to reach goals far beyond financial profit levels, because organizations are more than structures and systems.

'It's Not What You Do, it's the Way that You Do it. That's What Gets Results'

Managers, therefore, have substantial influence, not only in what they do, but in the way they do it. They have influence on the objectives and targets, programmes, activities and the results; their style of management can influence dramatically both staff and customers. Their style has to be appropriate to the situation. You need a set of clubs to play the golf course!

Management needs to be flexible in order to be appropriate to different people and groups of people. For example, all customers arrive with a whole range of needs which should be met. The goal of leisure – that of self-actualization and psychological well-being – is often dependent on other more basic needs having been met – such as the need to feel welcomed, to be with friends, to feel at ease, to feel capable of taking part and to be helped to achieve. The right atmosphere and the appropriate encouragement may be all that is needed to overcome a person's anxiety.

Sensitive, appropriate and capable management is, therefore, one of the keys to opening up leisure opportunity for each person. Such an opening door can help people towards achieving their potential.

People Need Goals, or They Go Nowhere

Helen Sharman had a run-of-the-mill job in manufacturing. In 1991, she took off in a Soviet rocket on a mission to dock with a space station. She became the first Briton in space. 'I think we let too many opportunities slip by because they are too much hassle,' she said. 'Once you recognize your goal is achievable, go for it 100%.'

Her story is one of staying focused and determined, being trained and preparing thoroughly. It is also a story of not being afraid of failure, but giving all to succeed, and working effectively as part of a team. Motivation is the key.

Motivation – the Key that Unlocks Human Potential

Motivation is a process whereby the capabilities of people are released.

People are stimulated and influenced to accomplish goals. Motivated staff, for example, have a willingness to invest effort. They:

- Enjoy their job.
- Perform jobs efficiently and hold themselves accountable for outcomes.
- Are consistent in their work.
- Are effective in what they do and add value.
- Become self-motivated and need less direction.
- Accept ambiguity and uncertainty.
- Make their own decisions, instead of: 'Tell us what to do and we'll do it.'

People support what they help create and resist what is forced upon them.

The great advantage of leisure management is that those involved often need very little motivation:

> I don't need to psyche the players up – my job is to calm them down!
> (Bernard Gallacher, Captain, Ryder Cup)

Leisure managers, trainees, sports and arts teachers and coaches, countryside rangers, music directors, librarians, museum curators, play leaders, tourism managers, theme park staff and holiday activity organizers, are usually highly motivated to begin with. This gives leisure leadership a head start over working in the tax office!

Motivated staff are more likely to carry out their work with enthusiasm and efficiency. They rise to challenges, working in groups to support one another; they also put up with upheaval, show resilience and come through change and crisis more quickly than less motivated staff.

People have psychological needs – to live to their full potential. The uppermost needs for respect and meaningful work remain unsatisfied for many people. It is at these levels that leadership can have the greatest impact in motivating staff.

Frederick Herzberg distinguished 'hygiene' factors and 'motivation'. Hygiene factors, like working conditions and benefits, keep staff from being unhappy; motivators drive staff towards higher ideals: they make staff happy – at work!

Leaders need to instil confidence in staff and let them know they are valuable; the team needs them. Kenneth Blanchard's *One Minute Manager* (Blanchard and Johnson, 1983) remarked: 'I try to catch people doing something right.' Motivation builds confidence. Management guru, Charles Handy, reminds us that we are all insecure at heart; we all respond positively to being stroked – psychologically, that is!

> Unfortunately, human beings are not always logical; they think with their feelings as much as their brains.

Motivation and training can bring out the best in people:

> What lies behind us and what lies before us are tiny matters compared to
> what lies within us.
>
> (Oliver Wendell Holmes)

Mentor – a Wise and Trusted Adviser

In Homer's *Odyssey*, Mentor was the friend whom Ulysses (the Greek
King of Ithaca) put in charge of his household when he left on his epic
voyage to Troy. In particular, he was responsible for advising and developing Ulysses' son, Telemachus.

A mentor is an understanding, experienced guide, promoting the
cause and showing the way, a teacher and coach that can make a lasting
impression on an individual's life. Students will know the value of an
inspiring personal tutor.

Mentors provide a helping hand, inspire mutual trust, loyalty and
friendship. The bond between mentor and protégé is an emotional one.
Professions such as law and accountancy include 'apprenticeship'
periods; a time when recent graduates must work with qualified professionals to 'learn the ropes'. In this process, the apprentice absorbs an
approach, a style, a life view, which can shape their future.

Visionary leaders make good mentors because they have principles
and values which stem from inner convictions. These convictions,
enthusiastically projected, influence others positively. They have trodden
the path before. In the words of the psalm, they seek first to understand.
In the shoes of their protégé, they can empathize. The ability comes
from the personal vision that is large and clear enough to be shared.

Benefits for All Through Vision and Action

Successful individuals and organizations appear to have in common a
powerful vision of their future.

> Vision without action is merely a dream. Action without vision just
> passes the time. Vision with action can change the world.
>
> (Joel Barker)

The field of leisure needs visionary leaders – people with principles,
values and inner convictions, right-brain thinkers who are intuitive and
holistic, rather than ordered and sequential. Leaders must understand
human nature.

My hope for leisure providers and managers is that they will not
just concentrate on efficiency, finding more administration to satisfy

less activity, but to aim for effectiveness and put their talents into ideas. The spirit of the world is not changed only through money and facilities, nor by government, but by imagination and ideas. Those ideas need the backing of our enthusiasm, confidence and vision.

The leisure experience described in this chapter stems from intrinsic, rather than extrinsic, rewards: it is person-centred. Society, in turn, will benefit, for people who function at their optimal potential can help society to reach a far better level of collective well-being – meaning for the individual, enrichment for the community.

In a social and community context, leisure can help to give people self-worth and confidence. Resourceful people are those who can overcome obstacles and find preoccupying activities and interests. All people appear to have a quest for personal identity; leisure and recreation management has much to offer in the way of enabling people to develop skills, to discover themselves and reach beyond their immediate grasp.

Children, whose play exudes manifest joy, inquisitiveness, spontaneity and a sense of humour, and adults who embrace the benefits of leisure, are more likely to be resourceful people able to cope better with this complex world.

Some people are in mundane jobs, others have a poor quality of life. Leisure can be a means of improving one's lot in life.

In terms of public money, I believe that priority should be given to the greatest number and those in greatest need. The able and advantaged are better placed to help themselves.

Principles First – Begin with the End in Mind

Administrators carry out instructions. Leader-managers, increasingly, need to influence others to make their own decisions. This is easier if there are no conflicts in your value system: leisure can provide personal, social, economic and environmental benefits. As Stephen Covey (1992), in *The Seven Habits of Highly Effective People*, says: 'Begin with the end in mind.'

My paper has been an attempt to justify three main propositions which I have held for some years, and an opportunity to put forward a fourth idea.

(i) Providers and managers should be concerned with the quality of experience for the individual and not just with the quantity of facilities and income-generating potential;

(ii) Leisure opportunity can lead to satisfying experiences which, in turn, have positive effects on the quality of life of individual people;

(iii) Management policy and performance can be powerful influences on people's participation;
(iv) Leisure management can become a leading profession – but only if values and fulfilling needs underpin the structure.

Enter in the New Profession?

Yesterday, over 2000 years ago, Aristotle asked 'With what activity will we occupy our leisure?' and I add today, 'And how will we best provide and manage its delivery?'

Leisure managers need to be good advocates. We need to tell, sell and profess our profession. Professionalism is traditionally seen as incorporating a body of knowledge, lengthy training, restrictive entry, codes of practice, structure, identity, status. 'Real' professionals do not have to rely on structure, but inner strength, insight (inner sight), confidence, competence and calm assurance; none the less, leisure management should assert itself as a leading, different, 21st century profession.

People are losing faith in the primary professions – the law, medicine and even the church – and the secondary ones like accountancy and politics. In leisure management, we have the products which are important to the quality of life of people and the values and knowledge for an emerging profession.

There is Nothing Nore Practical than a Good Theory!

A leisure philosophy which embraces the objectives of personal self-fulfilment, self-knowledge, self-esteem, happiness, skill, and is fun in the doing, has got the most positive selling points of any profession. If, through education, training and development, we can inculcate values and good attitudes, and motivate leisure professionals and practitioners, then leisure management can emerge as a leading profession in the early 21st century.

Many erudite papers on aspects of management in the leisure field, across the world, appear to support my view that we have the foundation stones. And remember, there is nothing more practical than a good theory – if you put it into practice!

There is a Chinese proverb: 'To be for one day entirely at leisure, is to be for one day an immortal.'

May you have many days of immortality.

Acknowledgements

I value the critiques of colleagues Gwynne Griffiths, Jim Lynch and Colin Tilley.

References

Belbin, M., cited in Hemingway, J. (1991) *Building the Perfect Team*. Video Arts, London.

Blanchard, K. and Johnson, S. (1983) *The One Minute Manager*. Willow Books, London.

Covey, S. (1992) *The Seven Habits of Highly Effective People*. Simon & Schuster, London.

Handy, C. (1990) *Inside Organizations*. BBC Books, London, and BBC TV Series 'Walk and Talk', 1990.

Kanter, R.M. (1989) *When Giants Learn to Dance*. Simon & Schuster, London.

Peter, L.J. (1986) *The Peter Pyramid*. Allen & Unwin, London.

Stewart, R. (1970) *Managers and Their Jobs*. Pan Piper, London.

2

The Accessibility of Australian Aboriginal People to Sport and Recreation

Heather MacGowan

Director Regional and Aboriginal Services, Ministry of Sport and Recreation, Western Australian Government, PO Box 66, Wembley, Western Australia 6014, Australia

Background

Throughout history, people have imposed one culture upon another for a variety of reasons, and in all instances this action has resulted in a breakdown of the original culture. It has often over time been replaced with a hybrid culture that is neither one nor the other.

Accompanying this cultural breakdown is a certain degree of social upheaval which often results in the people of the original or replaced culture becoming extremely socially dislocated. This situation has been well documented in Australia through reports on Aboriginal people and their needs (Aboriginal Affairs Planning Authority, 1991; House of Representatives, 1992; Daube, 1994).

This social dislocation also leads to a redefining, although unintentional, of social and cultural values and norms. Traditional values all change: the values of the family, social groupings, social well-being, education, the land, language, music, creative expression and, of interest in this chapter, sport and recreation.

There have been many changes in sport and recreation for Aboriginal people in Australia over the last 200 years and we are gradually coming to terms with what that means in a contemporary society.

In order to understand the current situation, it is necessary to comprehend some of the history of Australian Aboriginal people in sport and recreation and the impact this has had upon them as a nation.

© CAB INTERNATIONAL 1998. *Leisure Management: Issues and Applications*
(eds M.F. Collins and I.S. Cooper)

Traditional Activities

Traditionally, Aboriginal people do not differentiate between sport and recreation and there have been a number of reports written presenting a view of what sport and recreation is to Aboriginal people, in both the traditional and contemporary context (Atkinson, 1991; Ministry of Sport and Recreation, 1993; Greatorex, 1994).

Throughout history, Aboriginal people have seen sport and recreation, or what we in contemporary society might refer to as sport and recreation, as part of everyday living – not as an independent segment of life to be pursued during one's 'leisure time'. As such, in the traditional context, sport and recreation do not exist, and activities that might in a contemporary sense be likened to sport and recreation were important for social reasons and the development of skills and traditional activities (Atkinson, 1991; Ministry of Sport and Recreation, 1993; Greatorex, 1994). Children played games and learnt to hit, throw, strike, run, jump, climb, fish, swim, wrestle – all skills that to Aboriginal people were essential for hunting, food gathering and survival. These activities were a part of the traditional day, and when at times there were competitions they were of a friendly nature, including the involvement of families and all age groups. Such occasions also included corroborees, storytelling and fire-making (Australian Sports Commission, 1987a). Today, these festival-like occasions provide an opportunity for a mixing of the traditional and contemporary sporting and cultural activities (Ah Chee, 1994) and have become a vital component in Aboriginal socialization (Atkinson, 1991).

In a more traditional context, it is interesting to note that Aboriginal people had a number of games that resembled several contemporary sports. The Noongar people of the south-west of Western Australia played a game, a bit like field hockey, which on occasions was incorporated into more recreational and social activities (Hayward, 1994). The Tiwi people of the Northern Territory played a form of hand-ball by hitting a seed between two people and using their hands as the hitting implement. In north-eastern Australia, a similar game was played, hitting the seed with a flattened piece of wood (Australian Sports Commission, 1987a). A form of football was also played in the Northern Territory by the Djingili people who selected two teams based upon their kinship. A ball the size of a tennis ball was used and the objective was to keep the ball off the ground, using only the feet (Australian Sports Commission, 1987a).

Knowledge of these traditional games has remained limited over the years and it is only in the last decade that they have been more formally documented. In placing sport and recreation for Aboriginal people in perspective, it is important that we develop an understanding of these traditional activities and the potential impact they may have had on contemporary activities.

Contemporary Sport and Recreation

Aboriginal people have always demonstrated a great deal of 'natural talent' for some of the more contemporary sport and recreation activities, such as running, football, netball, basketball, martial arts and field hockey (Australian Sports Commission, 1987a).

In the later part of the 19th century, many Aboriginal people were very successful in pedestrianism, a form of athletics. In 1886, Charlie Samuels ran the equivalent of 100 yards in 9.1 seconds; with no training, no synthetic track and no modern footwear. At that time in history, the world record for 100 metres was 9.93 seconds or the equivalent of 9.17 seconds for 100 yards (Australian Sports Commission, 1987a). In many instances these 'peds', as they were called, had managers who made a profit from 'managing' their affairs and there was little that they could do about this, as Aboriginal people had no rights as citizens at that time (Australian Sports Commission, 1987a; Aboriginal Affairs Planning Authority, 1993).

The first Australian cricket team to tour England was an Aboriginal team in 1868. They played 47 matches with 14 wins, 14 losses and 19 draws (Australian Sports Commission, 1987a).

In 1913, Jerry Jerome became the first Aboriginal to win the Australian middleweight boxing title. Many other Aboriginal people have followed his example (Australian Sports Commission, 1987b).

Australian football is an extremely popular sport with Aboriginal people and one in which they have significant achievements. Aboriginal people made their impact on this sport from the early part of this century and they have continued to feature in the top professional teams throughout the nation. Although the development of Australian football is often attributed to two cricketers who, last century, wanted an 'off-season' activity, many Aboriginal people can relate to a traditional football very similar to the contemporary game.

Aboriginal people have also achieved in soccer, rugby league, rugby union (Australian Sports Commission, 1987a), horse racing, golf, volleyball, cycling and basketball (Australian Sports Commission, 1987b).

Aboriginal women should also not be overlooked in all of these more traditional, male-dominated sports and their achievements. Women have performed well and many would be more familiar with people such as Yvonne Cawley (Goolagong) (tennis) (Australian Sports

Commission, 1987b) and Kathy Freeman (athletics). Over the years, they have been supported by women such as May Chalker (golf), Marcia Ella (netball) (Australian Sports Commission, 1987), and currently Nova Peris in the Australian women's field hockey team – a certainty for gold in the 1996 Olympics.

In 1995, the National Coach of the Year for Aboriginal people was Patsy Elarde, who coaches basketball and has taken on the role of the head coach at the Australian Capital Territory Academy of Sport (Michelle Wells, personal communication, 1996).

As Aboriginal people had no rights of citizenship in Australia until 1967 (Aboriginal Affairs Planning Authority, 1991; Chaney, 1995), if they received payment for their performances prior to this date, as many did, it often went to their 'managers'. This meant that others gained financially from their achievements and they had no recourse (Aboriginal Affairs Planning Authority, 1991; Chaney, 1995). This form of management clearly reflected the social status of Aboriginal people during the last century and up until the 1960s (Australian Sports Commission, 1987b).

Fortunately, in Australia today there is a strong recognition of the need to foster and nurture Aboriginal culture and to view it as an essential element of Australian culture. There is a greater respect for Aboriginal people, their values and beliefs, and how they view the country in which we live.

As with many indigenous groups, Aboriginal people have an extremely strong affinity with the land and their respective family relationships which are based upon language groups and the dreamtime. In this context, sport and recreation take on a different social and cultural perspective which directly impacts upon the types of services and infrastructures that need to be developed today, and the manner in which these services are presented. As non-Aboriginal people, it is important that we listen, watch and learn from Aboriginal people; that we work with them, side by side and at times following behind so that we are not overshadowing the process of self-management and empowerment.

There is no doubt that Aboriginal people today still see sport and recreation as an important component of their lives and as a multi-faceted strategy, providing them with opportunities to learn, to achieve and to fulfil lifetime dreams. It is all-inclusive of everyday skills, culture, dancing, storytelling, family gatherings and social opportunities.

It is through sport and recreation that Aboriginal people develop skills; gain pride in themselves and their culture; develop fitness, well-being and an improved self-esteem; and increase their employability (Atkinson, 1991; Ministry of Sport and Recreation, 1993; Greatorex, 1994; Hayward, 1994).

It must also be recognized that there is no universal definition of sport and recreation for Aboriginal people (Atkinson, 1991). It may vary from one group to another, but there is consensus that it is not a static element (Atkinson, 1991; Greatorex, 1994).

The family unit also remains extremely important and gains strength through family involvement (Ah Chee, 1994; Greatorex, 1994). This is reinforced through the participation of families in festivals and carnivals.

Sport and recreation also play a strong social role in assisting to break down racial barriers, where Aboriginal people are often perceived as being able to perform better than non-Aboriginal people (Greatorex, 1994). Through this success they have gained the respect and admiration of the wider community (Ah Chee, 1994).

Sport and recreation are also seen as means by which culture is supported and maintained, or in some cases, revived (Ah Chee, 1994).

As it is not possible to divide sport and recreation into separate boxes, the nature of the activity is influenced by the community setting and the spirit and attitude of those participating. It is possible in some instances, however, to replace recreation with culture which in turn is driven by the community, and hence will be more culturally appropriate. Carnivals, for example, may be viewed as modern day corroborees (Ah Chee, 1994).

Another example of the lack of a need to separate sport and recreation as concepts, is reflected in the name of a regional Aboriginal sport and recreation group in the north-west of Western Australia, *Garnduwa Amboorny Wirnan*. The words mean a meeting of the 'mob' or a group of people, with the emphasis on the meeting of people, not the sport and recreation function. There is also a focus upon people meeting from both ends of the region, from the east and west and talking through issues related to sport and recreation.

In addition, numerous government reviews of Aboriginal affairs have identified sport and recreation as a preventative strategy to social issues, such as alcoholism, lack of self-esteem, truancy, vandalism and deaths in custody (Aboriginal Affairs Planning Authority, 1991; Atkinson, 1991; House of Representatives, 1992; Daube, 1994). It is in this context that the Ministry of Sport and Recreation has embarked upon the Aboriginal sport and recreation programme and has established a set of operational principles.

Operational Principles

These operational principles underlie all the Ministry of Sport and Recreation Aboriginal sport and recreation programmes and have, over the years, supported the development of a number of successful strategies.

It is essential in any Aboriginal programme, then, that (Atkinson, 1991; Chaney, 1995):

- Aboriginal people be involved from the beginning of a project.
- Ideas be supported as they come from the community, rather than imposing ideas that others might believe are appropriate or may address a need.
- Community ownership develop, as a result of community involvement.
- Cultural appropriateness be maintained and developed.
- Self-management be encompassed, promoted and actively supported.
- Appropriate training be provided so that Aboriginal people are empowered with the necessary skills and knowledge.
- There is support for an infrastructure that in turn supports the individual working in the field.

Issues

In addition, there are still a number of issues that need to be acknowledged and that present a challenge to those working in the industry. These must be worked through in order for Aboriginal people to become empowered to manage their own sport and recreation and to have equal access to resources and services.

These issues include:

1. Access to mainstream services, such as local government facilities and programmes, State sporting-association services, courses, funding, talent identification and development, and competition (Atkinson, 1991; Daube, 1994).
2. Training that is adequate and appropriate for Aboriginal people so that they have the skills and knowledge to develop and implement culturally relevant sport and recreation programmes (Atkinson, 1991). This is part of empowering Aboriginal people to manage their affairs and is supported by a nationally accredited Community Recreation Officer course. Stage two of this course is now being developed and we have had preliminary discussions regarding the development of a culturally appropriate associate diploma in recreation.
3. The need to foster family involvement and to create an atmosphere which supports and encourages family involvement (Atkinson, 1991). Without the family support, much involvement becomes individual and there is little relationship to the family infrastructure.
4. The cost of accessing activities and venues, which is often prohibitive.

This might include the cost of uniforms and footwear, transport, registration fees, venue entrance and equipment.

5. Mentor support, which is also crucial for the very talented individuals who make it through to a State team or squad and are required to be away from home and family for training and competition. The removal of Aboriginal people from their family and a familiar environment is critical and often not adequately managed. In most instances, this means that they are moving from a smaller rural community to a larger more urban environment or maybe the city (Ministry of Sport and Recreation, 1993).

When this occurs, Aboriginal people need support in the form of a mentor with whom they can share concerns and seek guidance when needed. The environmental and cultural changes are significant and bring with them family and peer pressures, lifestyle changes, changes in employment and/or education and financial implications not encountered before (Atkinson, 1991).

6. Aboriginal women also requiring a great deal of affirmative action as they are often overlooked. Strategies need to be developed to recognize cultural norms, and facilities developed that accommodate these (Atkinson, 1991). There have been instances where this issue has been acknowledged and strategies implemented, such as a women's basketball carnival, softball carnivals, swimming pools designed so that Aboriginal women can come and sit in the water in their dresses and read stories to the children or supervise the younger ones.

7. Young people, in particular young men, who are another target group. Many young Aboriginal men in both rural and urban settings are unemployed. This results in its own set of social challenges which the community needs to address. Often it is possible for sport, such as a regular football or basketball competition, to provide a positive experience for them and to support the development of positive self-esteem (Atkinson, 1991).

8. Isolation: in the Kimberley Region of Western Australia there are 96 isolated communities, and similar types of communities exist throughout the state. The size of the communities varies from several hundred to maybe a thousand and these numbers will vary according to the weather. During the drier months of the year the community population will increase, and when it is wetter it will decrease. Population shifts may also be associated with cultural activities and law-making.

This isolation makes it more difficult to service communities than in a larger urban setting or the metropolitan area.

9. The possibility for the young men to learn to umpire and coach so that they are skilled to work with the younger children. There is also the potential involvement in many national sport leadership programmes aimed at teenagers and young adults.

On the face of it, these issues may appear no different to those presented for many communities throughout the world. The difference is that the manner in which they are managed needs to be culturally relevant for Aboriginal people. There is no quick fix or well established recipe for a positive outcome. The outcomes need to be developed by the Aboriginal people with the necessary and appropriate support of other agencies.

In this instance, the Ministry of Sport and Recreation in Western Australia has over a number of years, supported a variety of strategies in response to the issues listed above. Some of these have been successful while others have not. In either instance, we try to learn from our experiences to ensure that we are better prepared and more informed in the next instance.

Effective Strategies

The successful strategies to date have included:

1. The establishment of regional Aboriginal sport and recreation groups such as *Garnduwa Amboorny Wirnan* and *Marle Yaragan*.

2. Working through regional Aboriginal groups such as the two listed above and the Geraldton Sporting and Aboriginal Corporation.

3. Community festivals such as the Looma festival, developed and managed by *Garnduwa Amboorny Wirnan*. Such festivals provide an opportunity for people to visit, share stories, participate, and learn new skills of event management, officiating, coaching and administration. There is also strong support from community and family groups and people will travel hundreds, if not thousands, of kilometres, to participate.

4. The establishment of the State peak body, the Aboriginal Development Foundation for Sport and Recreation (WA).

5. The development and implementation of a Community Recreation Officer course which is now being delivered by several Technical and Further Education Colleges throughout the state. This course now has national accreditation and will provide Aboriginal people with formal and appropriate professional education in sport and recreation.

6. Support for the Community Development and Employment Programme (CDEP) to employ Aboriginal people in sport and recreation. This has been extremely successful in many isolated communities where unemployment is high and there are few alternatives for sport and recreation development. The CDEP is a form of unemployment benefit and people are encouraged to work for the benefit.

7. The support of trainees working in sport and recreation and funded through Federal Government programmes. The Ministry acts as a host and mentor for the young people and supports their training and work experience.

8. The development and implementation of activities and programmes aimed at meeting the specific needs of Aboriginal people, such as Streetsport and Community Games. In the Streetsport programme a trailer of equipment is transported to the local neighbourhood and young people are encouraged to participate in a variety of activities and to take up the role of coach or official. This provides opportunities for them to remain in their neighbourhood, closer to home and family.

9, Youth leadership programmes including initiatives such as Sports-fun, and Challenge and Pathways in Sport, where participants undergo coaching and officiating training. Upon the completion of the programme the young people have a national accreditation in the selected sport.

10. Keyways, a successful neighbourhood three-on-three programme where a basketball keyway is established in a neighbourhood. Often the local government or service club will provide the materials and construct the facility which is then available to the young people to use as they choose. The consequence is that young people remain in their neighbourhood.

11. Access to mainstream funding programmes, which has been successful. Aboriginal groups now access these resources and the Ministry has assisted these groups to prepare their submissions. The Ministry also provides advice to the funding agencies, if required, in support of their willingness to recognize the needs of Aboriginal people.

12. The appointment of staff to work within regions or in the local area. This has provided a state-wide network at the 'grass roots level', where Aboriginal people can be supported while at the same time helping to strengthen their network through more contemporary channels of the sport and recreation industry.

13. A cross-cultural programme, developed and presented to all Ministry staff, as well many others working in sport and recreation. The programme is a 3- to 4-hour session aimed at raising the awareness of non-Aboriginals to the issues facing Aboriginal people. The programme also provides an historical perspective to the treatment of Aboriginal people in Australia and relates this to the contemporary situation we face today.

14. The development of a music project as part of a community recreation initiative. The young men formed their bands and played contemporary music, much of which they composed with no formal training in music or composition. The result was the cutting of several cassettes and compact discs which were made available for sale. This was a success from a commercial perspective as well reflecting cultural ideas and values.

15. Week-long in-service training courses, developed to provide increased opportunities for Aboriginal people to learn fundamental skills in sport and recreation leadership and management. More recently, a programme specifically targeting Aboriginal women was conducted. During these courses, lectures in coaching, administration, marketing and promotion, injury prevention and officiating are included. The women's course included sessions on women's health.

16. A role model programme, developed and being implemented in conjunction with several agencies, such as the State football (Australian) association, Aboriginal sporting and health promotion groups and State government agencies. In this programme, Aboriginal role models who have been extremely successful in contemporary sport visit young people in remand centres, schools, communities and community groups. The essence of the programme is to demonstrate to young Aboriginal people, although in many instances non-Aboriginal children are involved, that they can achieve if they wish to and are prepared to set objectives and work to meet them.

These are a few of the strategies that have been successfully developed and implemented throughout Western Australia. In all instances where there has been success, Aboriginal people have been involved from the very early stages of development and the programme has responded to their cultural needs. These programmes have been self-generating and supported by Aboriginal people; this is essential (Atkinson, 1991).

Those strategies that have been less successful strongly reflect a lack of involvement of Aboriginal people in the planning and implementation stages. This results in a lack of ownership, lack of understanding of the concept and rationale behind the strategy, lack of commitment, and a lack of resources allocated to the ongoing function. There is little interest in continuing an activity if it is perceived as not belonging to the community (Atkinson, 1991).

At the end of the day, it is the outcome that is important. Aboriginal people need to be supported in the development of what they view as being appropriate strategies to support the development of sport and recreation for them. There are many instances where things will dovetail and feed into contemporary infrastructures and programmes. On the other hand, there will be just as many instances where cultural expectations and styles will need to be respected and accommodated.

References

Aboriginal Affairs Planning Authority (1991) *Royal Commission into Aboriginal Deaths in Custody: a Summary.* Government of Western Australia, Perth.

Aboriginal Affairs Planning Authority (1993) *Brief Chronology of Aboriginal Affairs in Western Australia.* Government of Western Australia, Perth.

Ah Chee, P. (1994) Differences between sport and recreation. *National Aboriginal Conference on Sport and Recreation.* Ministry of Sport and Recreation, Government of Western Australia, Perth.

Atkinson, J. (1991) *Recreation in the Aboriginal Community.* Australian Government Publishing Service, Canberra.

Australian Sports Commission (1987a) *AUSSIE SPORT: Aboriginals and Torres Strait Islanders*, 1–10. ASC, Canberra.

Australian Sports Commission (1987b) *AUSSIE SPORT: 20th Century*, 33. ASC, Canberra.

Chaney, F. (1995) Aboriginal survival across incompatible domains. *Canberra Bulletin of Public Administration*, 78. Canberra.

Daube, M. (1994) *Report of the Task Force on Aboriginal Social Justice.* Government of Western Australia, Perth.

Greatorex, L. (1994) Welcoming speech. *Proceedings of the National Aboriginal Sport and Recreation Conference.* Ministry of Sport and Recreation, Western Australian Government, Perth.

Hayward, E. (1994) An historical perspective on Aboriginal sport and recreation – and some pointers for the future. *Proceedings of the National Aboriginal Conference.* Ministry of Sport and Recreation, Western Australian Government, Perth.

House of Representatives Standing Committee on Aboriginal and Torres Strait Islander Affairs (1992) *Mainly Urban. Report of the Inquiry into the Needs of Urban Dwelling Aboriginal and Torres Strait Islander People.* Government Printer, Canberra.

Ministry of Sport and Recreation (1993) Sport and recreation defined the Aboriginal way: what is Aboriginal sport and recreation? *Proceedings of the Aboriginal Sport and Recreation State Conference.* Government of Western Australia, Perth.

3

Leisure and Recreation and the 'Sport for All' Policy in Developing Countries: a Critical Examination

Claude Cousineau

Department of Leisure Studies, University of Ottawa, 550 Cumberland, Ottawa, K1N 6N5, Canada

Introduction

At the 1996 World Leisure and Recreation Congress in Cardiff, Wales, the British government's opposition Sport Minister (The Rt Hon. Tom Pendry, MP) gave the opening address. Presumably in an attempt to inspire the delegates, he presented his party's position with regard to sport. He rejoiced at the growth of the sports 'industry' and reaffirmed his party's determination to promote the 'important' sports in his country. This was not an isolated discourse, but similar to many others in which politicians around the world extol the monetary benefits of sport and make arbitrary value judgements as to which sports are worth supporting. There was polite applause from the delegates but not a standing ovation. They were concerned with leisure for all and he was focusing on revenues and selected sports for some.

Much energy has been devoted to the promotion of sports over the past decades; certain sports more than others. While some promoters were motivated by the economic or political benefits of sport, others saw it as a worthwhile activity in which everyone should engage. 'Sport for All' became the rallying cry and the foundation of many government policies and programmes. But the question remains: Is 'sport' really 'for all'?

The proponents of Sport for All will argue that 'sport' is not limited to those competitive activities governed by rules but that it also incorporates spontaneous and non-structured physical activities in which people choose to engage during their free time. These activities take place either in the city environment or out-of-doors and they are chosen for fitness purposes or for other intrinsic benefits.

While such a broad view of sport is promoted, the general public associates 'sports' with competition, skills, schedules and rules. It views sport as a 'game' where scores are kept to determine a winner and a loser. The same perception is also reflected in many countries' sports policies. The dichotomy with these two views on the meaning of 'sport' leads to confusion as to its significance and relevancy.

The purpose of this chapter is to take a critical look at the Sport for All movement. It challenges conventional wisdom and posits that perhaps Sport for All policies, especially in developing countries, are limiting the development of leisure and recreation opportunities 'for all'.

It is important to acknowledge the fact that this author is not a sport expert but one who has encountered the predominance of, and the enthusiasm for, the Sport for All philosophy while examining the development of leisure and recreation in developing countries, especially in Asia, and who has recognized that sport occupied a much more important place than recreation in public policies and foreign aid programmes (Cousineau, 1995). Sport will therefore be examined in the perspective of the use of leisure time and in the context of 'grassroots' community recreation. The reader will also note the author's biases, not to mention limitations, as references are made to his Canadian experience with policies for the promotion of more active lifestyles.

A World Phenomenon

Since its origin in the mid-1960s, the concept of Sport for All has grown into an important world phenomenon (Palm, 1991). Efforts to increase participation in sports and other physical activities have been made in the past by governments, physical education professionals, sports organizations and the fitness community, but this was seen mainly in industrialized countries.

Sport for All acquired its legitimacy as a distinct movement when the Council of Europe adopted it as one of its goals for the development of European societies in 1966. This was the turning point that led to the adoption of the Sport for All Charter by the European Ministers responsible for sport, in 1975, and many other initiatives (De Knop and Oja, 1996). By the 1990s, the movement had spread beyond the European community to more than 100 countries in which Sport for All had been adopted as a government policy or was being promoted by voluntary organizations (Trim and Fitness International Sport for All Association, 1995). Often better known by its marketing slogans, Sport

Table 3.1. Other names for Sport for All.

Name	Country
Life Be In It	Australia
Be Active – Be Alive	Ireland
Moving A Nation	New Zealand
Moving Together	Malaysia
Active Living	Canada
Activate America	United States

for All comes under different names in different countries (see Table 3.1), thus adding to the confusion.

The international organizations that have been instrumental in promoting Sport for All include the International Council of Sport Science and Physical Education, the International Council for Health, Physical Education and Recreation, the Trim and Fitness International Sport For All Association, the International Sport for All Federation, the International Association of National Sport Organizations, the International Workers Sport Committee, the Fédération Internationale du Sport pour Tous, and others (Skirstad, 1991). The International Olympic Committee joined the ranks in the mid-1980s.

To date, over a dozen international conferences have been held by various organizations under the theme of Sport for All. Regional conferences with the same theme have also taken place in Eastern Europe and in Asia. One of the most recent took place in São Paulo, Brazil, in 1996.

The movement's progress is also substantially documented. For example, the Canadian Sport Discus CD-ROM includes over 600 references to Sport for All, mostly in the English language. However, a cursory review of this material reveals that while the merits of Sport for All, as a movement, are sufficiently described, empirical evidence in support of its claims remains weak. Nevertheless, Sport for All continues to be a significant social force influencing recreation policies and the nature of the recreation service delivery system in numerous countries.

The Leadership Behind Sport for All

The Sport for All movement finds its voice through several stakeholders that have become involved since its origins (see Table 3.2). On the one hand, we find public agencies such as government ministries responsible for sports and/or health, who, in some countries, play a key governing role. These ministries act as promoter, funding agency and programme organizer. On the other hand, singular sports associations, often funded by their respective governments, are also attempting to

Table 3.2.   The stakeholders in Sport for All.

Public and para-public agencies	Fields of studies and professions
Ministries of youth and sports	Sports medicine
National sports organizations	Physical education
National Olympic committees	Leisure and recreation

promote their particular sport 'for all'. As well, there are several Olympic committees in different countries that now champion the cause of Sport for All.

Parallel to the leadership roles exercised by public and voluntary organizations in this area, there is increasing participation of academics and professionals in the fields of physical education, sports medicine, and leisure and recreation. These fields of studies and professions contribute to the development of Sport for All by training professionals, conducting research and, occasionally, by advocating and even delivering programmes. We can also recognize the involvement of these professionals through their affiliation and participation in national or international organizations devoted entirely or in part to the promotion of Sport for All.

It should be noted that the field of leisure and recreation has not been in the forefront of the Sport for All movement. Sport for All was often considered to be someone else's 'show'. Perhaps it is because the recreation profession felt that it has always been involved in 'recreation for all' and saw sport as only one of the sectors in the field of recreation. Recreation professionals view other non-sport forms of recreation activities as being of equal importance as a means of individual and community development. The recreation field recognizes the importance of physical activities in the lives of everyone and the benefits of sports participation for some, but it does not limit itself to sport in the delivery of leisure opportunities and services.

As is the case with many other human endeavours, the stakeholders in Sport for All sometimes overlap in the actions they take and in the ways they compete with each other for a better position within their respective nations and on the international scene. However, in recent years, with the push for the improvement of health, more common grounds and partnerships have been forged between governments, voluntary organizations and academic institutions.

Sport for All: the Rationale

The major aims of the Sport for All ideology are, firstly, to democratize sport participation and, secondly, to improve the health of citizens.

Having denounced the attention devoted to élite sport as excessive, the proponents of Sports for All have declared 'access to sport' as a basic right, and demanded that the limited resources allocated to people who are not inclined towards or interested in high-performance sport be increased. It recognizes the legitimacy of high-performance sport, of course, but its mission is to ensure that every citizen has an equal opportunity to engage in a chosen sport, regardless of age or skill level.

The democratization of sport is a noble cause but also a tall order to fill. Although Sport for All acts as a counter-balance to élite sport, in a sense it is contributing to it since mass participation in sport is often promoted as a way of producing a large pool of participants from which a few champions may emerge. In certain developing as well as industrialized countries, the implementation of a Sport for All policy would seem to be merely a strategy to produce national champions for international sport competitions.

The scientific evidence showing that regular participation in sports and other physical activities prevents disease, enhances health and increases productivity is also cited as a *raison d'être* of Sport for All. With the advent of industrialization, much of the population was freed from manual labour, from having to walk to go anywhere, and from the manual work associated with home care. This decrease in physical activity leads to an increase in disease and a greater reliance on healthcare systems. The escalating cost of healthcare provision is used to justify the push for preventive measures, including the promotion of all types of physical activity. In controlled societies, the idea of Sport for All is well received since greater participation leads to healthier citizens, who can be more productive for the benefit of the nation.

Aside from lower health costs and increased productivity, another economic benefit is derived. With greater numbers engaging in sports and other recreational activities, there is increased consumption of sporting and recreational goods and services resulting in job creation and tax revenues. In some regions, sport and recreation have become a major industry. Consequently, promoting and facilitating greater participation in sports is simply good business. Multinational corporations selling their sport products around the world are probably the greatest beneficiaries of increased participation in sport.

From a socio-cultural perspective, Sport for All advocates claim that there is an enhanced quality of life for those who engage in sports. The enjoyment of better health and the perceived kinetic and social pleasure derived from freely participating undoubtedly add to the overall well-being of the participants. Sports participation is also known to contribute to the social development of individuals, helping to create friendships and fostering a better understanding between peoples from different origins and milieux. Sports, particularly sports indigenous to a region, can serve as a means of preserving cultural identity and traditions.

These socio-economic benefits are usually cited in government policy documents where the Sport for All model has been adopted. In some countries, governments have developed realistic strategies to meet these goals and reap the benefits of Sport for All. In others, these policies only make for good reading and serve as a smokescreen for concealing inaction. Overall, it appears that resources available for sport and recreation continue to be disproportionately allocated to developing a few élite athletes.

Sport for All Action Menu

Sport for All is essentially a philosophy, a message to motivate citizens to engage in sport and other physical activities. It is also a message to policy-makers inciting them to use their positions to advance the cause and provide the necessary opportunities for participation. As with anything purportedly 'good' for people, the Sport for All movement needs tangible actions to give it momentum and ensure its visibility. It needed programmes to showcase its growth. In the 30 years of Sport for All's existence, interventions have been noted in four major areas: national mass media campaigns, national mass sport events, leadership development activities and achievement awards programmes.

Several countries have succeeded in mobilizing the necessary resources from public funds and corporate sponsorship to launch national media campaigns through television, radio and the print media. These campaigns have focused on 'selling' the ideology that participating in sport and other physical activities is 'good for you' and 'good for all'. These efforts are attempts to convince individuals and groups of the importance and benefits of regular participation in sports and other physical activities. By using a social marketing approach, the campaigns target various segments of the population, such as children and youth, women, older adults, the disabled and lower-income groups, with messages adapted to each group.

Some of these national campaigns have achieved a degree of success, if not in increasing participation at least in raising awareness. In certain countries, the campaigns have also served as propaganda tools for governments who link sport participation with other causes such as national unity, spiritual development or cultural identity. However, when sponsored by large multinational sports-equipment corporations the success of such campaigns is measured more in terms of product awareness and increased sales than the rate of participation.

Elsewhere, some government-sponsored campaigns are less centred on creating awareness but are more interested in presenting a generic prescription of exercises judged to be good for all citizens. An interesting example of this can be observed in Indonesia where health officials developed a 10-minute exercise video incorporating indigenous dance movements. The intent is for all of its 200 million residents to perform these same exercises daily. The irony is that, in Indonesia, video cassette players are owned by less than 5% of the population.

As well as media campaigns, several countries have organized annual 1-day 'mass sport events', also known as Sport for All events. Surrounded by a festival-like atmosphere, in one or more of the larger cities, a long distance walk or run is organized for anyone who wishes to join in and where participation is emphasized rather than winning. Thousands of people, young and old, are invited to come and join in the 'fun' of being active. Streets are closed to traffic for the occasion and the whole community is involved in staging the event.

National mass sport events have now grown into international events, due substantially to the efforts of the Trim and Fitness International Sport for All Association. In 1994, 74 cities in 35 countries around the world participated in a special rivalry called the International Challenge Day. They strove to register the largest number of participants engaged in 15 minutes of physical activity on a specific day. Residents of each city were asked to register their 15-minute participation, be it gardening, playing ball, or any other physical activity. The results were then channelled to an international Sport for All organization which announced the winning city.

Another Sport for All event that is also gaining popularity is the Olympic-Day Run which has enjoyed worldwide support from Coca-Cola and the World Federation of Sporting Goods Industry (Echard, 1994). Once again it was a mass-participation event, in this case organized by the local National Olympic Committee. The World Walking Day is a typical example where, for instance in Rio de Janeiro, 250,000 people turn out to participate (Da Costa, 1995).

Obviously, a certain expertise is required to manage these campaigns and mass-participation events. That is why a number of leadership development activities revolving around the Sport for All theme have taken place. Numerous local, regional and national conferences and workshops have been held by Sport for All organizations and organizations with similar goals. Universities and governments have also played a role in leadership development. Exchanges of expertise between countries and at international conferences have also contributed to the popularization of Sport for All. Together, these efforts to develop leadership have resulted in a number of papers in which the body of knowledge about Sport for All is presented.

Sport for All has also become a commodity in foreign-aid programmes to developing countries. Under the heading of human resource development, selected countries in Europe and North America have provided assistance to developing countries in areas related to Sport for All. Canada, for example, conducted several workshops related to health, physical education and recreation in South-east Asia with the involvement of local governments and national associations. This was accomplished through partnerships with the Canadian International Development Agency; the Canadian Association of Health, Physical Education, Recreation and Dance; and academics from various Canadian universities.

These combined efforts have contributed to raising an element of righteousness with regard to physical activity as well as to the strengthening of Sport for All as a social institution, if not as a culture unto itself. While there seems to be evidence that these efforts have created an awareness of the message and the messenger, it remains to be seen to what extent they have actually increased participation, improved the health of citizens or contributed to the democratization of sport.

Sport for All and the Sport Pyramid

A popular concept in the sport world is the pyramid model, with mass participation at the base representing a large number of people engaged in sport activities. This first tier feeds the next level where serious sports competition is practised, and from which a few champions emerge and move to the top of the pyramid as a country's best representatives at international games. Sport for All fits nicely within this feeder system, especially in countries with an umbrella national sports policy that includes a stated goal of 'producing' more gold-medal athletes. The American John Mosher said it well when he wrote that Sport For All is like a 'garden in which Olympic competitors and champions grow' (Mosher, 1991:161).

This is a well-accepted model, particularly in underdeveloped countries that feel a need to be represented at international games, most likely to satisfy national pride. Virtually all countries, for that matter, strive to some extent to have a core of élite athletes as a means of expressing national identity and pride. It is like having a national anthem, a flag or a national park. Having national athletic heroes is seen as a symbol of strength, maturity and perhaps even superiority.

While élite sports programmes at the top of the pyramid benefit from having a large pool of grassroots participants at the bottom, the reverse is not necessarily true. If the *raison d'être* of Sport for All is to be the entry level point on a continuum towards élite sport, there is a risk that its governance will be shaped to accommodate the needs and requirements of that élite sport. In the high-performance sport context, Sport for All is often confined, despite all the rhetoric, to selected competitive sports, to sports governed by rules and schedules requiring sophisticated and expensive facilities and equipment, to the acquisition of skill, to the need for trained coaches and to team participation. Here, sport is seldom viewed as spontaneous, autonomous or simple. Moreover, attention is directed largely towards youth, more precisely male youth. The only activities likely to be promoted and to receive support from government and corporate sponsorship are those 'important' sports, the sports found at international games.

Sport for All that is linked to élite sport becomes 'Sport for All Those Who Fit the Mould'. It effectively serves well those who have the predisposition to enjoy competitive sport, those who have the potential for excellence, and those with strong young bodies, especially young male bodies. As well as being male dominated, the sport pyramid is essentially an elimination process as one advances in age; older people are rarely at the top. Nevertheless, it provides gratification for those few who succeed in climbing up the ladder.

On the other hand, élite sport is often considered to be an important element for promoting mass participation. Its proponents maintain that élite sport, such as the Olympic Games, motivate more people to engage in sport and physical activities. People are said to be inspired by the achievement of the athletes and motivated to follow in their footsteps (Arnaudon, 1995). In fact, research describing what motivates people to engage in any kind of leisure activity indicates that it is seldom to imitate a champion. While some may well emulate their sport hero, the fact remains that some top athletes and their entourage do not always provide inspiring role models. The instances of doping, corruption, cheating and exorbitant monetary demands associated with élite sport are far from positive images.

In spite of these limitations, élite sport has its place in any society and élite sport programmes deserve some support. The benefits to the national spirit and glory of the country, as well as the contribution to its economy and political pride, well justify the efforts to maintain such programmes.

However, it is important to recognize that competitive sports have never been, nor will they ever be, 'for all'. They will be for a very few. If Sport for All is to reach the masses, it must be equally attentive to non-competitive and unstructured physical activities. If it wishes to remain true to its ideology, it must concentrate its efforts on creating equal opportunities for engaging in physical activities for people of all ages, all levels of skill and, crucially, both sexes.

The Olympic Connection

The International Olympic Committee (IOC) is considered the ultimate force in international élite sport. Since its beginnings, it has promulgated the virtues of sports competition worldwide. Despite its supreme role in sport, it was only in 1985, some 25 years after the birth of the Sport for All movement, that the IOC felt the need to create a Sport For All Commission within its ranks (Troger, 1991).

The Commission was established to create greater links between 'mass sport' and élite sport (International Olympic Committee, undated). More precisely, the Commission wanted to encourage, assist, and coordinate mass sport events in conjunction with local National Olympic Committees (NOCs) but without interfering with the work of other world organizations such as the Trim and Fitness International Sport for All Association. This required delicate political manoeuvring in the sport arena. In the view of the President of the International Olympic Committee, Mr Samaranch, Sport for All is the greatest challenge facing the Olympic Movement (Echard, 1994).

Every year, the IOC provides financial assistance to about 15 countries for staging Sport for All events, on the basis of three events per continent. In 1987, the first Olympic Day Run was organized by 45 National Olympic Committees. Today, more than 150 NOCs organize a 5- or 10-km run. These events are held each year, on 23 June, to commemorate Olympic Day, the day that the IOC was founded in 1894.

The IOC Sport for All Commission also plays a role in promoting 'heritage sports' by reviving forgotten sports or other physical activities indigenous to a particular culture. The Commission encourages the staging of activities once considered work but which have since been replaced by modern technology. With the development of a set of rules, these activities are easily turned into a sporting competition without any attempt at authenticity. Such is the case with the blowpipe competitions held every year in South-east Asia, where approximately a dozen countries are represented by a national team. Dressed in modern gym suits, the athletes blow their darts at a fixed televised target. A points system determines the winners who are subsequently honoured at a trophy ceremony. This sport event is an attempt to symbolize the past, but little is displayed and explained about the heritage dimension of this ancestral activity.

Another aim of the Commission is to transmit the values of the Olympic Movement to developing countries (Troger, 1991). Working with the local sports organizations, the Commission encourages the practice of Sport for All as part of the Olympic system. It approaches a form of cultural imperialism inasmuch as something that has been judged to be good by someone, somewhere, should therefore be implemented everywhere, whether it has anything to do with local collective needs, local culture or regional geography. The focus becomes more the development of sport through people rather than the development of people through sport.

In fact, some critics find it rather strange and suspicious that the IOC, an organization devoted to high-performance sports, would choose to be involved in sport for the general public. Others, on the other hand, find it commendable that the IOC has extended its mandate to include the participation of ordinary, everyday citizens (De Knop and Oja, 1996). Is it a return to its Aristotelian roots of amateurism? Is it an attempt to purge some of the malaise predominant in the modern Olympic movement? Or is it simply an effective marketing strategy on the part of the IOC?

The Olympics are surrounded in their own mystique and many have become cynical of this enormous business enterprise. Chang (1991) sees Sport for All as a cure for the Olympics. The 'success' of the Sport for All component of the Olympic system is not only measured by the number of athletes it produces but also by the increased number of sport fans as well increased television viewing ratings. This sustains the Olympic system since corporate sponsors enjoy increased consumption of their products advertised at the Games.

It has become difficult for the Olympic movement to maintain its relevance in an era when new recreation activities are constantly being created and older ones evolve. For the sake of tradition, the Olympics persist in maintaining certain sports that have no mass appeal. Many never even make the list of activities in which people engage in their leisure time. No one for example, except for the few aspiring to élite competition, engages in javelin throwing, an activity from an early era of hunting and wars. Bobsledding, an activity reserved for those rare winter communities equipped with a bobsled run, is an other example of disconnection with the life of most people. The Olympics may have the merit of preserving the past but, at the same time, they are far from representing the preferences of the masses with respect to sports activities.

Also, the IOC Sport for All discourse promotes the Olympic ideal, described as an attempt to educate youth in the virtues of fair play, effort, discipline and the pursuit of excellence. A very noble cause indeed, but not what ordinary people aspire to when it comes to enjoying a physical activity in their limited leisure time.

In spite of this, the promotion of Sport for All under the philosophy and governance of NOCs is probably better than nothing, especially in communities where there are no other institutions with the mandate, leadership and capability of providing a wide range of recreational sport services. The Olympic name at least lends a certain credibility for politicians and government officials and can act as a catalyst for the launching of community-based sport and recreation services adapted to the local needs of all citizens, and not merely the promotion of a few Olympic sports.

Sport for All and the Canadian Experience

Many countries have adopted the blueprint of the Sport for All ideology but some have been decidedly hesitant. Canada is one of those who bought into the general concept but not the specific wording. Since the 1970s, the Canadian government has actively supported the idea of marketing campaigns encouraging Canadians to become more physically active. Through the social marketing strategies developed by ParticipAction, a non-profit organization funded by the Canadian government and private sponsors, Canada became an innovator in the use of the media in physical activity promotion. It became the envy of many other countries which have since adopted the Canadian approach.

Canada also endorsed the idea of mass events such as the International Challenge Day and various awards systems for participation and achievement in physical activities. However, with diminishing public funding and the realization of the limited effectiveness of these approaches, both programmes have now been phased out.

A diversity of leisure opportunities already existed for Canadians and the word 'sport' was too limited a concept in their culture to expect the mass to engage in it. After all, sport is simply another element competing for people's precious leisure time. This is not to say that there is not an avid interest in sport; in fact, substantial numbers of Canadians regularly engage in competitive sport and fitness activities. Their number represents about 20% of the youth and adult population and this figure has remained constant over the years, despite the media efforts, the mass participation events and the awards programmes (Jackson, 1994).

The message 'for all' sent by the Europeans, at that time, did not have the same impact in Canada as it had in other countries. In the 1970s, Canada was already embarked in a programme for the democratization of leisure opportunities, including sports. Democratization of leisure and recreation was accomplished through decentralizing service provision. Municipal governments, along with local volunteer organizations, were officially granted the key responsibilities in the delivery of recreation for all. Sport, in this context, was included as one of the recreation sectors to be provided. 'Serious' élite sport competitions were the domain of higher government levels along with provincial and national sports-governing bodies.

Table 3.3. Comparison of two health promotion models: 'Sport for All' and 'Active Living'.

Sport for All	Active Living
Sports	Physical activity
Scheduled events	Daily lifestyle
Sports facilities	Anywhere
Sport as exercise	Activities as recreation
National initiative	Community-driven
A goal	A process
Persuasion	Empowerment

The message to Canadians regarding improving their health and quality of life had to be more inclusive than simply sport and exercise. It had to be broad enough to encompass the notion of all 'physical activity'. The media blitz sent by ParticipAction would not say 'play sports and exercise' but rather 'be more active' everywhere, at play, at work or at home. The institutionalization of the concept later evolved into the notion of 'Active Living' and, as such, provided a wider umbrella under which many organizations directly or indirectly involved in promoting health could find a niche.

Active Living differs from Sport for All in several areas as a health promotion model (see Table 3.3). From the perspective of Active Living, sport is extended to include the notion of physical activities such as gardening, walking up the stairs as opposed to using the elevator, or cycling to school or work, which are given equal importance to sports or exercises. Active Living does not emphasize scheduled events but rather a daily lifestyle which incorporates physical activities not always depending on complex sports and fitness facilities. An example of this is the increasing popularity of walking clubs where older adults use indoor shopping malls for their walks. In this sense, physical activities are promoted not as a prescription of exercise but rather as a form of recreation.

Sport for All is goal oriented and uses persuasion through national initiatives as its main approach, while Active Living favours a community-driven approach, a community process of empowerment (Edwards, 1995). Active Living is an ongoing process. It is a perpetual search by each community to find the best way to activate itself and become a healthy community (Levy and Levy, 1996). In other words, it is the community as well as the individual that fills its own prescription for a more active life, physically and otherwise.

Sport and Recreation in Developing Countries

In developing countries the quality of life is often associated with the effects of poverty, unsanitary conditions, pollution, unemployment, illiteracy, malnutrition, crime, corruption and human rights abuses, to name but a few. In comparison to these difficult conditions, the implementation of public sport and recreation services is often and understandably considered a low priority, if not a luxury.

In such economically challenged countries where government resources are scarce, sport and recreation facilities for the masses are inadequate, and sometimes non-existent. Financial constraints, the absence of trained leaders and a lack of public and voluntary institutions result in poor planning and very limited diversity of sport and recreation opportunities. Often, what is offered does not correspond to the needs of the local communities. Consequently, the rate of citizen participation in sport and recreation activities is noticeably lower than the rate recorded in more developed countries (Palm, 1991).

Paradoxically, governments in poorer countries seem able to find the resources to support an élite sports programme and send national teams to compete in a variety of sports at the Olympics or other international games. It is not uncommon, for example, to find former Russian coaches and Canadian sport psychologists hired by the government of a poorer country to train a talented group of young and mostly male athletes. Large symbolic sports stadiums, often found in the capitals of such countries, are built for the occasional national and international sport competitions. These facilities are generally unsuited for the needs of the local community and are rarely open to the public. The public can only use them as spectators during major events. They nevertheless provide entertainment and a platform to show with pride what the country can produce (Tripps, 1991).

The focus of sport becomes directly related to the reputation of the country. There seems to be a strong desire for poorer countries to acquire status and prestige by winning medals at international sport competitions. The pursuit of gold medals and the construction of monumental stadiums are perhaps efforts to demonstrate some sign of progress and parity with the rest of the world. Sport, in this context, is used as a public relations exercise.

In an attempt to imitate European nations, several developing countries have willingly endorsed the Sport for All concept and made it the frontispiece of their national sport policy, while maintaining élite sport as their ultimate aim. A Sport for All policy is justifiable, at least on paper, as it has the potential to provide a base from which more talented individuals can be discovered and nurtured to represent the best of the country. Such a policy, however, fails to address the needs of most members of local communities. Rather, it is centralized at the national level and sometimes presented as a national recreation policy. The development of élite sport appears more important than the development of the masses of people through sport and other recreation activities. In such instances, 'All for Sport' might be a more appropriate title.

Corporate sponsorship is another force that favours élite sports over citizen participation in sports and other recreation activity. Developing countries, as elsewhere, are seeking funds from corporate sponsors for their sport programmes and events, but these sponsors are only interested in highly visible sport competitions, especially those with large mass spectator or TV appeal where the products can be advertised. Nevertheless, poorer countries have a great deal of difficulty in attracting private sponsorship to finance Sport for All activities as well as an élite sport programme, except from the alcohol and tobacco industries which are enthusiastically willing to provide funds in return for the advertisement of their products. This temptation places these countries in a difficult dilemma as they would like to maintain the discourse that sport improves health but while knowing of mounting evidence that these products, at least tobacco, have harmful effects on health (Kidane, 1996).

Universities in developing countries, where academics have developed programmes of studies in fitness, sports administration and sports medicine, also focused on élite sports. While these fields may have contributed to the advancement of sport in their respective developing countries, universities, with very few exceptions, have not yet implemented programmes of study in the wider field of leisure and recreation (D'Amours, 1991). The concern for the needs of ordinary citizens not only to play sports, but to engage in a variety of activities, regardless of age, sex or talent, is rarely examined in developing countries.

Ironically, such disproportionate emphasis on élite sport is often supported by foreign aid received from more developed countries that, indirectly, reinforces the dominance of élite sports to the detriment of ordinary citizens who have little opportunity for recreation. This puts into question foreign aid that benefits national government agendas and a few talented athletes rather than the development of individuals and communities. Recreation development projects aiming at ordinary citizens have not been a priority for donor countries, probably because these projects are not as visible and glamorous as those for élite sport.

Apart from economic constraints and the dominance of élite sports, there are other barriers to the development of recreation for all in developing countries. Religion and traditions can also dictate what is acceptable and who can participate in certain sports and recreation activities. Concepts like Sport for All sometimes infringe on certain mores and beliefs. This is true for women in certain cultures who do not have the same opportunities as their male counterparts.

Climate is another factor that influences the development of leisure and recreation in developing countries. Many of the world's poorer countries are located near the equator in a tropical environment. While this may prove advantageous for certain sport and recreation activities, the fact remains that high temperatures, humidity and long rainy seasons can be a major deterrent to participation in a good number of outdoor activities. The 12 hours of daylight and 12 hours of darkness experienced year-round in equatorial countries also influence the leisure patterns of the inhabitants. For instance, outdoor activities scheduled in the evening are restricted to facilities equipped with extensive and expensive lighting systems.

In the light of the above concerns, countries who are in a position to provide aid to developing countries should carefully examine the type of assistance they provide in the area of sports and recreation. Donor countries need to determine the fundamental objectives of their contribution. Who will be the real beneficiaries? Will the aid provided address humanitarian needs, or promote the glory of the government in power?

Providing Assistance to Developing Countries in the Area of Sport and Recreation

Foreign aid policies and practices, in the area of sport and recreation or in any other field, are often the reflection of the traditional attitudes of donor countries towards aid. Some donor countries once were colonial powers while others limited their international interventions to trade. Regardless of the type of relationships donor countries have had with underdeveloped countries, humanitarian assistance has always meant different things over time. Today, we find lingering attitudes that shape the form of assistance provided to those who seek it (Tripps, 1991).

Firstly, there is the notion that development is a linear process. Such a notion views development as a process by which every nation must go through the same sequential stages until they reach the level attained by more developed countries.

Secondly, there is a paternalistic attitude sometimes exhibited by donor countries. The majority of donor countries in the Western world hold the belief that change in itself is good, that people want and should experience change. For many years, Western countries, especially those with a colonial past, felt that they had a moral obligation, if not a religious duty, to transform people of other countries to their own image.

What was good for the Western world had to be good for others. History abounds with examples not only of religious, cultural and economic impositions but also with the importation and implementation of sports and recreation views and activities alien to many cultures.

Thirdly, foreign aid programmes are often prompted by an economic or political agenda. Donor countries hope that, if aid is provided to a poorer country, that country might in turn acquire prosperity and power and thus become a good trade partner or political ally. Foreign aid is sometimes offered with the understanding that certain products be purchased from the donor country or that the recipient support specific causes important to the donor country. Foreign aid then ceases to be charity and becomes an investment.

These traditional attitudes and practices may affect assistance programmes in the area of sport and recreation. Caution must be exercised. Assistance offered to developing countries in the area of sport and recreation cannot merely consist of transplanting what is practised in the donor country to the country receiving the assistance.

Some basic questions should be addressed, both by the donor country and those receiving aid, before programmes are implemented. Programme plans should clearly outline what needs the programmes are attempting to meet. It should establish the desired outcomes and set up ways to measure them. Time frames should be set up and included in the plan as well as decisions made about where the intervention will take place. And last but not least, it should be clearly established who the beneficiaries of the programmes will be. Above all, answers to these questions and many others have to pass the true tests of compassion, equity and democracy.

Scott and Ball (1991), officials with the Canadian government, formulated five principles which should govern aid initiatives in developing countries, in the area of Sport for All:

1. Development is about change, change being a process and not a string of independent projects.
2. Western notions and approaches to change are not always appropriate for application in developing countries.
3. The diversity of developing nations precludes any single solution or stock formula.
4. Cooperative aid initiatives are not designed 'for' recipient nations, but 'with' recipient nations.
5. Quality aid initiatives build partnerships, initially interdependent but clearly focused on long-term independence and sustainable success on the part of the recipient nations.

Further planning and negotiation would then lead to the implementation of a programme that would include one or more of the following areas: human resource development, institution building, information resources, facilities and equipment, and financial aid. While there are some exceptions, like in the case of the 'Jeux de la francophonie', direct monetary assistance is rarely supplied in the area of sport and recreation. Donor countries prefer helping in the area of leadership development by providing expertise to conduct training sessions or to advise on policy matters. Hosting the leaders of underdeveloped countries in the donor countries and providing student scholarships have also been favoured approaches.

Overall, donor countries need to review their policies regarding their assistance programmes for developing countries in the area of sports. In addition, international organizations dedicated to promoting sports, physical activities and recreation also need to work together in a common purpose when attempting to assist developing countries.

In a final analysis, one of the most perplexing questions to answer when helping other countries to develop their sport and recreation service capability is: what happened after the assistance programme was completed? Was it worth it? Was the legacy left by the donor country sufficiently strong for the receiving country to have acquired enough autonomy to continue the actions?

Suggested Strategies for the Development of Recreation in Developing Countries

Based on the preceding discussion, certain conclusions can be drawn. Without diminishing its merits, let us first recognize that Sport for All it is not a substitute for a nation's comprehensive public recreation policy. Satisfying the recreational needs of communities requires a wider perspective than simply sports activities. It must favour an approach that is based on local needs and wishes, a process that is client-centred as opposed to product-centred.

Secondly, the approaches used by the Sport for All community to motivate participation in sport and physical activities are often ineffective (Beran and Semotiuk, 1991). There is no evidence that élite sports events stimulate greater participation. If anything, they favour a spectator culture on which they depend. There is equally no supporting evidence that mass-media campaigns increase participation. At best, they increase awareness. Neither is there evidence that mass sports events, such as a 'day run for all', lead participants to continue to engage in more sport activities beyond the 1-day effort of the specific event, nor is there evidence that they inspire others to participate. The intentions of the Sport for All proponents are commendable, but when their efforts are claimed as successes the movement risks losing its credibility.

If Sport for All is to remain true to its ideology of serving the masses, it needs to dissociate itself from the culture of the beginner–élite continuum of the sport pyramid. The policies and programmes that Sport for All has engendered in different parts of the world need not be influenced or guided by the requirements of the élite sports industry. If Sport for All is important enough, it should stand on its own merit and cease to define itself as a point on a continuum, as a base to produce athletes, or even less as a counter-balance to élite sport.

For Sport for All to fulfil its mission of health and democracy and for it to become a viable vehicle for recreation development in developing countries, it needs to broaden its scope. The terms 'sports' and even 'physical activities' are far too limiting. Perhaps the term 'recreation', which encompasses sports and all other forms of activities, might be more suitable, as it embraces a more holistic approach to health promotion and fits a much wider base of the population.

This outlook brings the attention to leisure and leisure time as the foundation for understanding the obstacles people face and the choices that they need to make in order to use leisure as an empowerment tool for individual and community growth. It leads to a call of Recreation for All and the provision of leisure services with a bottom-up strategy. Along with other areas of community development, this strategy would support people in their search for opportunities to develop suitable forms of leisure spaces and activities, made for the people and by the people. These choices would not be limited to sports. A more inclusive approach to activity, one that embraces all forms of leisure pursuits, could provide the building blocks for a better quality of life for all and bring hope for a better future.

References

Arnaudon, S. (1995) Australian South Pacific 2000 Sports Programme: a regional approach to Sport for All. *Proceedings of the 14th TAFISA International Conference.* TAFISA and Israel Sport for All Association, Netanya, Israel.

Beran, J.A. and Semotiuk, D. (1991) Sport for All: facts and fantasy in the United States and Canada. In: Standeven, J. *et al.* (eds) *Sport for All in the 90s.* Meyer and Meyer Verlag, Aachen, Germany.

Chang, J.-H. (1991) *The Asian Concept of Sport for All and its Impact on the Olympic Movement.* Ancient Olympia – Report of the Thirty-first Session. International Olympic Academy.

Cousineau, C. (1995) Leisure and recreation in Malaysia: an interpretive overview. *World Leisure and Recreation* 37(4) 5–22.

D'Amours, M. (1991) *International Directory of Academic Institutions in Leisure, Recreation and Related Fields,* 2nd edn. Presses de l'Université du Québec and the World Leisure and Recreation Association, Montreal, Canada.

Da Costa, L.P. (1995) In search of the right mix in marketing and promotion of Sport for All. *Proceedings of the 14th TAFISA International Conference.* TAFISA and Israel Sport for All Association, Netanya, Israel.

De Knop, P. and Oja, P. (1996) Sport for All. In: *Current Issues of Sport Sciences.* International Council of Sport Sciences and Physical Education, Sport Science Studies 8. Verlag Karl Hofmann, Schorndorf, Germany.

Echard (1994) Sport For All. *Olympic Review* no. 319. International Olympic Committee, Lausanne.

Edwards, P. (1995) *Collective Action: the Community-driven Approach to Active Living.* Active Living Canada, Ottawa, Canada.

International Olympic Committee (undated) *Sport for All and the International Olympic Committee.* International Olympic Committee, Lausanne, Switzerland.

Jackson, J.J. (1994) Communication and Sport for All in historical perspective. *International Journal of Physical Education* 31(2), 29–33.

Kidane, F. (1996) Government: the main sponsor in developing countries. *Olympic Message* July–September. Lausanne, Switzerland.

Levy, J. and Levy, M. (1996) Active Living Canada in the 21st century: the healthy communities model. Paper presented at the World Leisure and Recreation Association Congress, Cardiff, Wales, UK. WLRA Secretariat, Lithbridge, Canada.

Mosher, J. (1991) *Sport for All and the Olympic Philosophy.* Ancient Olympia – Report of the Thirty-first Session. International Olympic Academy.

Palm, J. (1991) *Sport for All: Approaches from Utopia to Reality.* International Council of Sport Sciences and Physical Education, Sport Science Studies 5. Verlag Karl Hofmann, Schorndorf, Germany.

Scott, J.M. and Ball, J.R. (1991) Analysis of current initiatives and a process for effective intervention. In: Oja, P. and Telama, R. (eds) *Sport for All.* Elsevier Science Publishing, Oxford, UK.

Skirstad, B. (1991) Sport for All in international organizations. In: Oja and Telama (eds) *Sport for All.* Elsevier Science Publishing, Oxford, UK.

Trim and Fitness International Sport for All Association (1995) *TAFISA Newsletter 8/95.* TAFISA, Bordeaux, France.

Tripps, D.G. (1991) Paradigm lost: crises in the development of Sport for All. In: Landry *et al. Sport . . . the Third Millennium.* Les Presses de l'Université Laval, Ste-Foy, Québec, Canada.

Troger, W. (1991) *Sport for All: Aims and Expected Influence of the Olympic Movement.* Ancient Olympia – Report of the Thirty-first Session. International Olympic Academy.

4

Leisure Lifestyles in a Developing Country: Reasons for Non-participation

Antônio Carlos Bramante

College of Physical Education, State University of Campinas, Rua Alemanha, 522, 18045–150 Sorocaba, São Paulo, Brazil

Introduction

The components that identify contemporary Brazilian society are characterized by marked regional differences, a political process still settling down and establishing a democratic option, a very young population with marked social gradients, a rapid urbanizing process, an increase in the tertiary economy, a search for work opportunities for everybody in a period of increasing unemployment, and a resulting fight for fairer laws on employment. These factors define a unique frame of reference compared with other developing countries, relative to the access of their peoples to consumer goods and to services. These trends constantly call into question what is referred to as recreation and leisure, taken as an individual ludic experience, freedom-orientated, seeking a better social organization in relation to the priorities of a country like Brazil.

Notwithstanding the facts that build the profile of Brazilian society and theoretical discussions about a priority for recreation and leisure in this developing country, reality shows a growing popular search for experiences that, rightly or wrongly, are referred to as recreation and leisure. At an institutional/public level, the increase in the offers of spaces, equipment and programmes in this sector is clear.

There is empirical evidence that public administrations, at all levels, tend to give priorities to building up physical resources for recreation, without taking into account the need for a deeper study of the demand for these services by the people. It can be also noted that these community resources are not always properly used, in quality or quantity.

The notions of need and demand for recreation and leisure services held by the public authorities may be measured. According to Godbey (1980), they can be understood through:

1. The quantity of existing physical resources and services in proportion to the people who are to benefit from them;
2. Distribution of these physical resources and services in direct relation to indicators of priority for leisure services;
3. Activities in which people are more heavily interested and engaged; and
4. Parameters measuring the participation of the people.

However, it appears evident that the most common idea of need or demand for leisure is the one indicated by 'expressed need', that is, when the person indicates what he wants, or what must be done, by his behaviour. In this way, the rendering of public services in the field of recreation and leisure tends to be evaluated by the presence, frequency and use of existing resources.

Howard and Crompton (1984) have mentioned that, although the justification for the maintenance and the development of new recreation facilities may be based on quantitative data, this approach has proved inadequate. The data do not reflect reality, lacking any equation with the satisfaction of the participants and the changes over time or for certain segments of the population.

The assertion 'the more participants, the better' should be reconsidered in view of local conditions, where variables such as ecological balance, safety, health and aesthetic conditions must be observed. In spite of these facts, attendance is still the indicator used to evaluate whether a certain place is successful for the practice of recreation. For this reason there is a constant search for ways to increase the attendance of participants in public recreation programmes.

Specialized literature shows numerous studies that point out the various barriers to participation (Mueller *et al.*, 1962; Banges and Mahler, 1970; University of Wisconsin, 1974; McLean and Hermanson, 1974; Grubb, 1975; Hatry *et al.*, 1977; HCRS,1977), but few authors have examined people's level of knowledge about the services available to them.

Investigating the problems of non-participation, Godbey (1984) effected two studies in cities of the north-eastern USA. After presenting a model, he reached the conclusion in both studies that people lacked knowledge about their resources and public services in the field of recreation and leisure, and that this was the main reason for non-participation. In terms of costs/benefits, he argued also that to fight this lack of knowledge is a more effective way to increase participation than to alter the existing programming for those who know what is happening, but still do not take part in the activities.

With reference to Brazil, other hypotheses should be tested, besides misinformation and lack of knowledge. One is the total lack of urban planning in most Brazilian municipalities, disregarding the need to allocate proper spaces for leisure as a necessity. This results from the high cost of expropriating city land, leaving only institutional spaces set aside by law from being built on, or those surplus areas that remain after establishing other higher priority urban resources.

Another hypothesized cause of the non-utilization of physical resources for recreation and leisure activities is the limited involvement of the population in decisions about their establishment. Some studies have demonstrated the political character of most work done in this field, that is related to inauguration days and to feasts, confirming the lack of a more rational plan. With this, the people who, in the opinion of some public administrators and of the political élite, are 'receiving' a benefit, are in fact receiving a 'white elephant', installed through squandering important sums from the public budget. A clear example of this is the establishment of 'Urban Social Centres' during the government of General Geisel, done without trying to involve the community in either the founding or operating processes.

Finally, non-participation may also result from the lack of a specific programme that takes care of people's interests. Again, as a question of a political nature and due to the infancy of planning, the scattered existing resources are allocated, almost exclusively, for building facilities, leaving little for investment in human resources that would make viable use of the spaces developed. Other elements that inhibit participation are poor maintenance of the installations and damage to equipment. The participation of the community in the planning, execution and evaluation of facilities and programmes should be part of a structural focus, taking into consideration the socio-political moments that Brazil has gone through and that it still follows in its search for real citizenship.

This means that it is necessary to study more deeply the variables that determine non-participation of people in recreation and leisure activities, to better orientate the public sector in allocating its resources.

Objectives

The aim of this study was to examine reasons for the non-participation of people at certain urban leisure resources in the city of Sorocaba, São Paulo State (SP), which is 90 km south of the city of São Paulo; it has approximately 500,000 inhabitants, and is one of the most important centres for production and services in the state.

This city has been chosen because it has stood out in the field of public recreation and leisure in the national scene, due to concrete policies since 1972 in these services. After 10 years' experience in community recreation, the local municipality has created a specific division to support this type of service, through a technical group formed by various professionals.

Research Development

In the second semester of 1988 a research group was formed in Sorocaba that met once a month to discuss previously selected texts about recreation and leisure. This group was formed by local professionals who worked with the municipality, and by students of the Physical Education Faculty of the ACM (YMCA) of Sorocaba. Besides keeping the group up-to-date in this field of study, another aim of these meetings was to select a relevant research theme to complement its work. So, as one result of these meetings, the idea for this research was formed.

In the phase of data collection, through documentary research, the Municipal Administration supplied complete information on relevant legislation, especially regarding setting up an administrative infrastructure to take care of recreation and leisure.

Hitherto, the Municipal Administration of Sorocaba (PMS – Prefeitura Municipal de Sorocaba) acted only occasionally in this service area, with such initiatives as the Central Commission of Sports and the Municipal Service for Sports. It was only in 1982, with a reorganization of the Municipal Administration, that the Division for Leisure and Recreation was created, with two advisory groups (Community Recreation and Leisure Parks). This made official the practical work done since 1977 by a small group of professionals responsible for the Leisure Programme of the Municipality (Plano Setorial de Educaçâo, 1977).

The Organic Law of Sorocaba, published in April 1990, gave special privileges to recreation and leisure in various places, referring to the establishment of specific community councils, to sport incentives, to educational projects based on the environment, to a competence to provide parks and gardens, to the historic heritage, to the use of urban land and, in a special separate chapter, to tourism.

Through a preliminary analysis, the various organs of the PMS acted, directly or indirectly, in the field of recreation and leisure. This obliged us to programme a series of interviews, to ask for documentation on the various sectors in sports, leisure, tourism, culture, municipal parks, social promotion, planning, and use of urban land. On this occasion, an analysis was made of the existing programmes, schedules of events, projects, reports, human resources involved, and space and equipment used. The specialized bibliography indicates that a fundamental piece of information needed to formulate a leisure policy in the municipality is to check how much time is available to the people, as well as the supply of space/equipment and the existence of an animation system; these points form a 'tripod' that sustains a leisure policy (Requixa, 1980). Once again it was verified that the public sector often made efforts in duplicate and lacked coordination in applying resources.

The first task was to define a concept for the term: 'urban resources for leisure of the Municipality of Sorocaba' (Recursos Urbanos de Lazer, Prefeitura Municipal de Sorocaba – RUL/PMS). The specialized bibliography consulted (Requixa, 1977a,b; Platajen, 1978; Camargo, 1979; Yurgel, 1983; and Vaz, 1988, amongst others) allowed us to define primary parameters for choosing fieldwork locations: the RUL/PMS should be within the urban perimeter of the town, and should be equipped to meet at least one of the cultural interests of leisure (Dumazedier, 1980). As secondary considerations, they should have at least one municipal civil servant assigned to the place; there should be budgeted funds for leisure; they should have had a programme directed by the PMS in the last 12 months; and the facilities should have been in use for at least a year.

Consequently, 11 locations were chosen: six Sport Centres, two Centres for Community Living, two Centres for Social Integration and one Public Square. In this way, geographic location, the size of the place, and the various cultural interests in leisure were taken into account.

The next step was to define how to sample at each selected location:

1. On a large-scale map, three circles were drawn around each site, at distances of 100, 300 and 500 metres (A, B and C bands).
2. In each band, three streets were selected.
3. In each selected street, a sample of five dwellings, of different sizes and types, were selected.

A total of 455 dwellings were selected for the study.

At this stage, a new study group was organized under the direction of the professor teaching recreation at the Physical Education College of the ACM (YMCA) of Sorocaba. Some 25 undergraduate students were trained to improve their knowledge of research, in drawing the sample and learning how to undertake semi-structured interviews.

The data collection instrument was enlarged, beyond its original purpose of diagnosing the reasons for non-participation, to cover:

1. The opinion of the resident families about the public facilities and programmes for recreation and leisure:
- degree of knowledge/information;
- desire for better information;
- reasons making participation difficult;
- sources of information about public provision; and
- vacation habits.

2. Knowledge of personal habits of each member of the family in recreation and leisure:
- time spent at work;
- recreation and leisure opportunities at the workplace;
- time available during the week for recreation and leisure;
- recreational activities carried out in the last 30 days;
- preferences in the field of culture; and
- their understanding of the recreation and leisure activities.

3. Demographic data, including:
- marital status;
- gender;
- age;
- level of education;
- type of work;
- monthly income;
- length of residence at present location;
- presence of people with special needs in the household; and
- space for volunteering personal ideas.

Following Dillman's suggestions (1978), to prevent possible constraints in giving personal data, these were placed at the end of the questionnaire.

Before collecting data in the field, a preliminary reconnaissance of each location was made, covering:

- location;
- size;
- existing equipment and materials (quantity and quality);
- calendar of activities (high impact and ancillary occasional events);
- human resources, and their jobs/roles; and
- average attendances observed in mornings, afternoons and evenings on weekdays, Saturdays and Sundays.

A week in advance of the interviewer's visit, a letter explaining the aims of the research and seeking cooperation was delivered to each family and, during the training phase of this Support Group, pilot data collections were made.

4.1(a). Age of the Sorocaba sample.

Years	%
7–11	12.0
12–15	12.2
16–19	9.8
20–35	29.1
36–45	17.2
46–55	11.4
56–65	5.4
Over 65	2.9
Total	100.0

4.1(b). Education of the Sorocaba sample.

	%
Illiterate	5.1
Primary School, incomplete	49.0
Primary School, completed	17.6
Secondary School, incomplete	11.0
Secondary School, completed	9.2
Complementary School, incomplete	2.5
Complementary School, completed	5.6
Total	100.0

4.1(c). Monthly family income $US of the Sorocaba sample.

	%
Up to 199	27.3
200–499	37.8
500–999	23.3
1000–1499	6.3
1500–1999	1.6
More than 2000	3.7
Total	100.0

4.1(d). Field of employment of the Sorocaba sample.

	%
Agriculture	1.2
Banks	2.7
Teaching	5.0
Self-employed	15.7
Trade	19.8
Services	19.8
Industry	35.8
Total	100.0

Results of the Research

Profile of the sample

Of the group, 50.2% were men and 49.8% were women; 51.2% were married, 45.9% were single and 2.8% legally separated.

Tables 4.1a–d show the distribution by age, level of education, family income and type of work. It will be seen that this is a very young population (63% under 35 years) of which fewer than half completed primary school; three-fifths earned less than $US500 a year; and a third were employed in industry.

Following the growing attention given to people with special needs by public policies at all levels, a survey of this group was included in the research, even though at that time PMS had no specific programme for these clients. Confirming results of other studies of this type, it was found that 9.9% of households who took part in this study declared that they had someone in the family with special needs: a fact which makes it necessary for leisure services planners to give special attention to this group.

Finally, due to our interest in knowing the degree of mobility of the sample, the length of current residence was checked. It was found that two-thirds of the families had been living at that location for more than 5 years and 18.5% for more than 20 years, indicating a high level of neighbourhood stability.

Participation in leisure experiences

The opinions of the families interviewed about the public recreation and leisure spaces and activities revealed meaningful data for evaluating participation, and besides covering the 11 research locations this question included nine other major facilities which drew people from the whole town.

In the 11 neighbourhood locations, the crucial problem in non-use was the great lack of information: 45% declared that they had never heard mention of those facilities. The average of visiting/participation was low at 20%, and so was potential demand at 9%; only 4% knew of these facilities and rejected using them. So, before changing the programme schedule in these places to attract more users, they must be made better known.

The level of ignorance about the major facilities was lower, remaining under 10%. In this group the Municipal Zoological Garden Quinzinho de Barros stands out, with only 4% of the people claiming not to know about it.

For people to get know these spaces better, an administration which involved greater community participation can only increase the potential demand, which was still too low (only 9% declared that one or more members of the family would like to visit the local site or take part in activities there, but they were unable to). More importantly, it would contribute to the fuller use of these public spaces. It was also suggested to expand the services offered in the Sport Centres, transforming them into 'Community Leisure Centres'.

In the second question, 13 public recreational and leisure activities were listed, so that the interviewees could indicate how much they knew about them, and if they wished to know them better. More than 50% of the people recognized the Festival de Pipas (kites festival), Semana do Tropeiro (animal drivers' week), Manhã/Tarde de Lazer (morning/afternoon of leisure) and Expo-Verde (green exhibition). Special mention should be made of Feira da Barganha (bartering fair), Férias

Quentes (hot vacations) and Festa Junina (June feast) that were recognized by respectively 72%, 79% and 79% of the interviewed group. Such activities as Escolinha de Esporte (the little school for sports), Tranzoo (trans-zoo), Festival de Brincadeiras Tradicionais (traditional games festival), Festival de Teatro Tropeiro (animal drivers' theatre festival) and Cursos de Ecologia por Correspondência (correspondence courses in ecology) were recognized by less than 30% of the group.

These figures confirm the importance of the regularity of a specific event when one wants to establish an attitude. It can be merely coincidental, but the events with the highest repercussion in the community (in terms of knowledge) have been systematically operated at the same time of year for more than 15 years.

When checking the population's information with reference to recreational spaces and public leisure activities, it was found that more than half the interviewees (51%) already had some information, but not as much as they would have liked; 22% said that they had little or no information. These figures confirm the need for Sorocaba's leisure service to improve its communication with residents.

One of the most important elements of this research was to diagnose the reasons other than knowledge that made participation in public recreational and leisure spaces/events difficult.

Through bibliographic research and pilot interviews, 15 factors were listed and respondents could add others. The three most important factors uncovered were 'lack of time' (21%), 'lack of money' (13%) and 'I do not know the place or the programme that is carried out there very well' (10%). With reference to the 'lack of time', this study only confirmed a great number of others. Taking into account the principle that 'time available is a question of preference and of priorities', this reason starts to lose some strength. On the side of suppliers of recreational and leisure services, it must be remembered that when a policy in this sector is formulated, elements outside the simple offering of activities must be encompassed (Marcellino, 1990), and questions of space and of time should be reconsidered (Requixa, 1980).

It is important to point out that, in more than a quarter of the reasons alleged (26%), the direct intervention of the leisure service could result in wider access for people. This percentage includes matters such as 'operating schedule' (4%), 'crowded location' (4%), 'lack of maintenance of the space' (3%), 'the available activities are not interesting' (2%), 'the location for the activities is dangerous' (3%), besides the 'lack of information on location and on programmes' (10%) mentioned before. Two other items also indicated lack of adequate planning in the choice of the localities as responsible for 15% of the reasons for non-participation: 'poor location' (6%) and 'lack of transportation' (9%).

As the lack of information is a major feature in this research, it was important to find out how the people interviewed had got their information about the public recreational and leisure events: 26% through the two city daily papers, another 26% through radios (17% FM and 9% AM) and 31% through posters, publicity strips and leaflets (15%, 9% and 7% respectively). It is important to include, as in almost every awareness study, the importance of the reason 'through friends', mentioned by 16% of respondents.

To conclude this section of the research, two concrete means that could make access to public leisure experiences easier were taken into consideration: vacation habits and participation through a socio-recreational club. For holidays, it was found that nearly half of those interviewed (46%) had gone on holidays in the last 2 years and, of this number, those who went travelling (60%) were more numerous than those who stayed at home. The variety of socio-recreational clubs listed by 38% of the interviewed people was surprising; they said that they were associated to 41 different entities. The *Associação Cristã de Moços* (YMCA) had the greatest affiliation (12%), followed by SESI/Sorocaba (11%) and *Clube União Recreativo* (10%).

In a cross-comparison of the figures for 'club members' and 'socio-economic class', we observed that there were no members in these clubs from the lowest socio-economic class. This confirms the necessity for the public sector to maintain and widen the spaces/equipment for recreation and leisure for the more needy parts of the population, with programmes conducted by local professionals.

Lifestyle and leisure

The lack of systematic information defining the leisure habits of the Brazilian people is evident. Generally, the existing data result from studies covering specific groups (for instance, employees of a certain firm, members of a socio-recreational club, people who visit a certain leisure space, etc.). We were not able to find any literature for a city the size of Sorocaba. For this research, questionnaires took into account up to five members in each family, aged above 7, and the information was recorded by adults (18 years and over).

The figures showed that more than one-third of the family heads work longer hours than the maximum limit established by law: 34.3% work more than 44 hours a week and, of these, one-third work more than 60 hours a week. Although on a smaller scale, similar results were found for 'housewives': 23.4% work more than 44 hours a week, and of these 42% work more than 60 hours a week. Another important figure was that 23.4% of the people investigated have a paid job at weekends.

This confirms that a leisure policy needs to deal with questions

Table 4.2.   Free time for the Sorocaba residents.

No. of hours	Men (%)	Women (%)	Dependants (%)
Up to 10	54.4	53.6	20.0
11–15	9.7	13.0	6.4
16–20	6.7	7.0	5.7
21–25	2.3	2.8	4.1
26 or more	5.6	5.1	6.8
No answer	21.3	18.5	57.0
Total	100.0	100.0	100.0

related to work, although Brazilians are now living at the peak of the most serious unemployment ever seen in their history, apart from the alarming number of so-called 'semi-employees' (under-employed). All this ignores those who significantly extend their 'overtime hours' in order to gain a living wage. This context reinforces the thesis that the 'leisure society' that had been projected in the 1960s and 1970s for the end of the century was deceptive and is now more than doubtful (Bramante, 1992b). The same situation is found to a lesser but noticeable extent in the USA, Japan, The Netherlands, the UK and other parts of Europe (see Gratton, 1996).

Trying to minimize this 'life of work', a growing number of firms are offering recreational activities for their employees, either through an appropriate personnel policy, or through encouraging initiatives by their employees, who often create their own workplace recreational associations. In this research, it was found that 7.9% of the people interviewed declared that they had opportunities for recreation and leisure at their workplace. It is interesting to observe the contrasting figures for men and women: 17.4% and 6.5% respectively, indicating that a prejudice still exists regarding the access of women to leisure experiences compared to men, of about three to one. Thus Brazil is following a path trodden by many countries (see Kruger and Riordan, 1996).

If the time available for leisure is reduced by a protracted work schedule, how did our sample of residents perceive their engagement in recreational and leisure activities in terms of hours a week?

Table 4.2 gives an overall picture of the time available for the 'men of the house', the 'housewives' and the 'dependants'. Despite the number of 'no answers' for the group called 'dependants', it is interesting to observe the homogeneity of the patterns for the three groups. Notice that more than half of the family heads had fewer than 10 hours a week for their leisure.

Just as the perceptions of leisure time are important for identifying alternatives for a municipal policy, so to operationalize this one needs to know about people's activity choices; for this, we prepared a list of activities covering widely different interests and gave respondents the chance to make additions to it, and we were also interested in discovering any meaningful differences between the three groups mentioned above.

Although, when we speak of leisure activities, one of the first ideas that comes to mind is sport or some other physical activity, we found that sample declared that, in the previous 30 days, they had carried out 'less-energetic' leisure activities; for men their three top preferences were 'watching television/video', 'doing home repair work' and 'listening to music'; for women the sequence was 'watching television/video', 'cooking' and 'listening to music'. The percentage for 'watching television/video' stands out: 59.4% for men and 66.8% for women. These figures are consistent with that for the dependants group, 55.1% of whom declared to be filling part of their free time with TV/video. In this way, the study showed that the leisure activities that were most in demand by the population as a whole are directly connected with home-life (Bramante, 1992b).

The figures found for sports showed that these constituted 22% of all leisure activities, with special emphasis on soccer (24% of the sample had played soccer in the previous 30 days) and walking (12.6%). These percentages were lower for housewives; only 9.4% said that they had taken part in one of the 12 listed sports in the previous month.

These figures deserve a more careful analysis when compared with those referring to aspirations, that is, those interests in leisure that people indicate as desired/preferred. Marcellino (1990) studied the difference between 'wanting' and 'doing'. Bramante (1992a) also made this contrast, comparing six studies carried out in different segments of the population and in highly different situations, finding that there is a 'distance' between the expressed desire ('the things that I like most to do in my leisure time') and reality ('the things that I actually do'), and emphasizes the need for leisure planners to go deeper into this question, to narrow the distance between them.

The sequence of priorities given by the people under study, relative to their cultural interests in leisure (Dumazedier, 1980), was:

1. Physical sports interests.
2. Tourism interests.
3. Social interests.
4. Artistic interests.
5. Manual interests.
6. Intellectual interests.

The contrast is evident between the desire, expressed as mainly active occupations and open air activities (sports, tourism, social), and the reality, with leisure activities making the home an entertainment centre as well as the place where one lives ('watching TV/video', 'listening to music', 'cooking', 'doing home repair work', 'reading', etc.).

To conclude this second part of the study, an open question was put, asking what concept the person had of recreation and leisure. This was done because the Brazilian literature in this sector has very few studies interpreting these ideas (Neto Franceschi, 1993), and so ideas generally are taken from research work done in other countries or result from a process of theorizing carried out by national authors (including Requixa, 1977a; Gaelzer, 1979; Marcellino, 1987; Bramante 1992b).

A certain homogeneity was observed in the concepts expressed by the interviewees about the meaning of leisure. The key word for 18% was 'amusement', independent of gender or position in the family; the term 'rest' came second, mainly amongst the family heads (11%). Although more than 100 words/phrases were mentioned to describe the concept of leisure, it is worthwhile stressing the coincidence with the studies of Dumazedier (1980) when he proposed three stages/functions of leisure, forming the '3Ds' (in Portuguese): rest (*Descanso*), amusement (*Divertimento*), development (*Desenvolvimento*). Although only mentioned by a very small proportion, some people understand leisure as being development.

The results made it clear that Sorocaba's leisure service needs to carry out better maintenance of its facilities, to obtain a better utilization of its leisure equipment. Another important factor was a certain lack of attention to the activities offered in these locations that, according to some, 'are not directed to, or at least planned and prepared for, the people of the district'.

With the perspective of a better use of these spaces, some segments of the sample felt that they had been disadvantaged; for instance, workmen who suffered restrictions due to the operating schedules of these places, and old-aged people and women who see a virtual lack of activities planned especially for them. Various proposals were made relative to the safety of these places: according to many of the persons interviewed, this factor is not treated seriously enough, discouraging a great number of potential users.

Concluding the suggestions, we noticed many times that some basic needs, such as means of transportation, provision of schools and nurseries, among others, were given priority without taking consideration for the pertinence of leisure as a basic need of the population.

Conclusion

Some of the hypotheses formulated when this study was started were confirmed by the data collected. It was confirmed that, in the city of

Sorocaba, the geographic distribution of public leisure opportunities is out of balance, with great residential and commercial developments recently installed in the city lacking any type of leisure space. These problems are felt especially in the northern parts of the city. An imbalance also exists with reference to the cultural interests of people's leisure time, with a prevalence of facilities for physical sports over the others.

The under-utilization of public leisure facilities was also observed, especially on working days. During weekends, although the level of use is higher, it is not yet significant with reference to effective participation of the local people. In most cases, these events are brought to the locals without consideration for the identity of that community as a whole (for instance: games of the local soccer championship 'scheduled' in Sports Centres).

Municipal policy for this sector is non-existent, and when one tries to correlate proposals that could form a beginning for planned action, results are obviously fragmented and discontinuous. In the case of the Municipality of Sorocaba, in the period of this study, this has been made worse by the fact that five municipal secretaries have successively occupied the position of coordinator of the leisure services. It is important, then, to obtain from each community an answer to the key question: what is the role of leisure activities in a municipality in a developing country? What is the mission of public sector in this case? What is the articulation desired between the community's own expressions and the programmes organized by the public-sector managers?

Although one would expect that, due to the small scale of the public leisure facilities in the city, the people near these places would participate more, the figures are not very meaningful, mainly due to people's great lack of information about what takes place in these spaces. The explanation that can be inferred for this situation is the lack of attention by the public managers to information and marketing. This is a lesson learned long and hard in previous decades in Europe and North America.

Generally, these facilities are built with a minimum of participation by the community that is supposed to use them. Due either to pressure by unrepresentative small groups or to decisions by the municipal administration based on party politics, the population cannot practically intervene in these places. In Brazil, it is still an unusual administrative practice to establish a strong liaison of community participation in implementing community services. Nor do the providers undertake surveys that would inform them of the wishes and motives of the community, making this break wider. It is still quite common for these public leisure facilities to have a single 'menu' of activities. There is no dialogue between the technical team and the population, aimed to make the services meet the wishes of the people.

In the period this research was conducted, for instance, the construction of new sports centres was interrupted. This decision could have been justified if the under-utilization of the existing equipment was taken into account, and the available resources were invested in a basic 'tripod' to increase both in quantity and in quality the participation of the people in the facilities, namely:

- Improving the maintenance of the existing sites.
- Opening a dialogue with the people, and responding to the needs and wishes to provide them with better service.
- Obtaining human resources for developing such programmes.

What was observed was a perverse combination: unfortunately very little has been done with reference to these items, and not even the physical network of local facilities was expanded! Considering these facts, our initial opinion on the 'question of not beginning new buildings' in order to use existing resources better for maintenance and animation of the existing spaces, must be re-examined. Although the absence of one thing does not guarantee the presence of the other, we are reformulating our concepts regarding the construction of new facilities, because, at least one of the three dimensions of the policy for leisure then may be attended to (time – space – animation). Once the equipment has been installed, the community and the technical group have to see that the services rendered have the necessary quality.

Finally, the binomial relationship of political willingness–technical competence should be given due attention when formulating public leisure policies, requiring for this end sympathetic administrative systems to expedite the desired changes regarding improving participation and identifying the leisure lifestyles the people desire.

References

Banges, H.P. and Mahler, S. (1970) User of local parks. *Journal of the American Institute of Planners* 36(5), 330–334.

Bramante, A. (1992a) *O Desporto e a Cultura do Tempo Livre*. Conferência no III Congresso de Educação Física dos Países de Língua Portuguesa, Recife.

Bramante, A. (1992b) Recreação e lazer: o futuro em nossas mãos. In: Moreira, W. *Educação Física e Esportes, Perspectativas para o Século XXI*. Papirus Editora, Campinas.

Camargo, L.O. (1979) Recreação pública. *Cadernos de Lazer* 4, 29–36.

Dillman, D.A. (1978) *Mail and Telephone Surveys*. John Wiley and Sons, New York.

Dumazedier, J. (1980) *Valores e Conteúdos Culturais do Lazer*. SESC, São Paulo.

Gaelzer, L. (1979) *Lazer, Benção ou Maldição*. Editora Sulina, Porto Alegre.

Godbey, G. (1980) Categories of recreation need. In: Gold, S.M. (ed.) *Recreation Planning and Design*. McGraw-Hill, New York, pp. 194–195.

Godbey, G. (1984) Non-use of public leisure services: a model. _Journal of Leisure Research_ 16(1), 1–12.

Gratton, C. (ed.) (1996) _Work Leisure and the Quality of Life: a Global Perspective._ Leisure Industries Research Centre, Sheffield.

Grubb, E.A. (1975) Assembly line boredom and individual differences in recreation participation. _Journal of Leisure Research_ 7(4), 256–259.

Hatry, H.P. _et al._ (1977) _How Effective are Your Community Services?_ The Urban Institute, Washington DC.

HCRS (Heritage Conservation and Recreation Service) (1977) _Nationwide Outdoor Recreation Survey._ United States Department of Interior, Washington DC.

Howard, D.R. and Crompton, J.L. (1984) Who are the consumers of Public Park and Recreation Services? An analysis of the users and non-users of three municipal leisure service organizations. _Journal of Park and Recreation Administration_ 2(3), 33–48.

Kruger, A. and Riordan, J. (1996) _The Story of Worker Sport._ Human Kinetics, Champaign, Illinois.

Marcellino, N.C. (1987) _Lazer e Educação._ Papirus Editora, Campinas.

Marcellino, N.C. (1990) Subsídios para uma política de lazer – o papel da administração municipal. _Revista Brasileira de Ciências do Esporte_ 11(3), 206–209.

McLean, C. and Hermanson, D. (1974) _Leisure Services: The Measurement of Programme Performance._ Urban Observatory of Metropolitan Nashville University Centres, Nashville, Tennessee.

Mueller, E., Gulrin, G. and Wood, M. (1962) _Participation in Outdoor Recreation: Factors Affecting Demand Among American Adults._ Outdoor Recreation Resources Review Commission Study Report 20. Governmental Printing Office, Washington DC.

Neto Franceschi, M. (1993) _Lazer: Opção Pessoal._ Departamento de Edução Fisica, Esporte e Recreação, Brasilia.

Plano Setorial da Educação (1977) _Sorocaba, São Paulo: Secretaria da Educação e Saúde._ Prefeitura Municipal de Sorocaba.

Platajen, T. (1978) Urbanização e Lazer. _Cadernos de Lazer_ 3.

Requixa, R. (1977a) _O Lazer no Brasil._ Editora Brasiliense, São Paulo.

Requixa, R. (1977b) O lazer na grande cidade e os espaços urbanizados. _Cadernos de Lazer_ 1.

Requixa, R. (1980) _Sugestões de Diretrizes para uma Política Nacional de Lazer._ SESC, São Paulo.

University of Wisconsin (1974) _Characteristics and Recreational Participation Patterns of Low Income, Inner-city Residents._ College of Agricultural and Life Sciences Research Division, Madison, Wisconsin.

Vaz, L.G. (1988) _Sugestões para Uso de Espaço Aberto Urbano no Planejamento de Ambientes para o Lazer: Propostas para São Luís do Maranhão._ Monografia, São Luís.

Yurgel, M. (1983) _Urbanismo e Lazer._ Livraria Nobel S.A., São Paulo.

Access to Museums as Leisure Providers: Still a Long Way to Go

5

Frans Schouten

National Institute for Tourism and Transport Studies, Department of Tourism and Leisure, PO Box 3931, 4800 DX Breda,The Netherlands

Introduction

Destinations have always been one of the focus points of the tourism industry. There is, however, an increasing interest in the mix of elements that makes the destination worthwhile to visit: the attractions. Within the attractions there is an growing awareness of the importance of cultural attractions. Of the cultural attractions, the most significant for generating a flow of visitors seems to be heritage attractions. This contribution focuses on heritage sites and museums and their response to the increasing demand for their resources for tourism and leisure.

In the 1970s there has been an enormous increase in the attendance figures of museums, so there does not seem to be much of a problem. But a closer look at the statistics shows us that the number of visits has been growing, not so much the numbers of visitors. In other words, the frequent users come more frequently, but new audiences are hardly reached.

It is not my intention to bother with too many statistics, but I will quote a few figures, just to illustrate the growth in both heritage resources and the use of these resources. From 1945 until 1975 the number of museums in The Netherlands doubled to 355, while in the subsequent two decades the number has almost tripled again to over 1000.

The same trend can be seen elsewhere in Europe: Germany counted 1539 museums in 1971 and 2314 museums in 1987. In Switzerland in the same period the growth rate was 50% (De Haan, 1995). In the UK a new museum is opened approximately every 20 days. Attendance figures have also gone up dramatically: in The Netherlands in 1946 a little more than 2 million visits were made to museums (22 per 100 inhabitants); in 1992 this was up to more than 22 million (149 per 100 inhabitants). The growth of the number of visits is greater than the growth of museums: in 1960 the average visits per museum was 15,000 and in 1990 this average had gone up to 32,000 (De Haan, 1995). From a survey amongst the Dutch we know that in the same period visiting museums has gone up, with 34% visiting a museum within a period of 12 months. However, participation amongst people with only a basic education has gone down in the same period by 6%. The same can be said of the frequency of visits: it has gone down for the 12- to 19-year-olds: from 2.3 visits a year in 1979, to 1.9 visits a year in 1991. It has gone up for the 65 years and older age group: from 2 visits (1979) to 2.5 (1991). In general, the frequency of visits to museums has gone down between 1979 and 1991 for family groups, is stable for couples without children and has gone up from 2.5 to almost 3 for people living alone (De Haan, 1995). The conclusion is evident: the heavy users visit the heritage resources more frequently and museums are losing their appeal for the young and the less educated. For many groups of people, museums are still regarded as 'not for our kind of people'.

Do Museums Really Care for their Visitors?

There are several reasons why museums and sites are still regarded as élitist institutions, somewhat remote from everyday life. In the first place, is the world as represented by museums not the world as perceived by the general public? It is a world structured by scientific laws, by taxonomy, and by a division in periods which are not at all common ground for the layperson. Museum professionals tend to forget that what is obvious for them is not clear to everyone else. Once, Sir Pope-Hennessy – former director of the British Museum – made a provocative comment on curators: 'Their defect is that they know their collections much too well. They simply cannot see them from outside' (ROM, 1976:87). Often curators – who spend their lifetimes reading books – consider words and letters to be the only medium for transferring an idea. But the age of TV has brought into being a generation for whom reading is a secondary means of collecting information. Their learning is primarily focused on visual impact and they are used to receiving very well-staged images. For those used to looking at large amounts of TV, videos and films, the staging in museums is not only poor, but often increasingly incomprehensible (Schouten, 1993).

The communication in museums is furthermore rather conventional: everyone is presumed to start from the same point, and to undergo the same knowledge-enhancing experience at the same pace. Thus the visitor plays the passive role and the museum the active role. Access to museums is highly structured, predetermined and controlled by the staff so as to be 'correct', 'understandable' and 'educational'. This is connected to the conviction that visitors come to learn something in the museum.

Although visitors also stubbornly continue to see exhibitions as places where they can learn something, they rarely do so (Miles, 1986). Their behaviour in the galleries is more akin to window-shopping on a Saturday afternoon than to the intelligent acquisition of new knowledge. A much neglected fact in this respect is that one of the most important reasons for visiting museums is the opportunity for social interaction. Visitors hardly ever come alone: they present themselves in small groups as a family, a group of friends, etc. Visiting the displays is a means of interacting with each other (McManus, 1987).

Finally, the well-known distinction between work and leisure tends to obscure a rather important psychological distinction; namely, the distinction between activities that are performed under conditions of stress, and activities that are performed under conditions of no stress (Miles *et al.*, 1982). Our customers are visiting us in their free time and the very essence of a leisure-time activity is a non-stress environment. Roughly speaking, a stressful situation is any situation that people consider – not necessarily correctly – as threatening. The explicit learning environment is such a threatening environment. It puts you in the situation of the one who does not know; it often makes you feel stupid. Learning is done by people who are curious, who wonder about the world around them, and not by people who might be intimidated by our so-called educational displays. A lot of the communication in inter-pretation centres and museums is not inviting, but simply pedantic.

Gradually this attitude is changing, but there is still a gap between the way most heritage professionals see their core product and their visitors, and the way their customers evaluate the services provided. In terms of quality management, the critical quality features for visitors do not match with the actual product delivered. In most cases, the public's assessment of the heritage attraction is not based upon the scientific cor-rectness of the core product, but on how effective the site or exhibition is in raising curiosity, appealing to fantasy, and in providing a challenge. That is as well as: how clean are the toilets, how easy is it to park the car, what choice of items is there in the shop, and what is the quality of the catering?

The UNIQUE-experience

The cornerstone of any policy on visitor care in museum- and heritage-management is, first of all, pleasure; it contains what I would like to call the UNIQUE-experience, which stands for:

- Uncommon: visitors are looking for the extraordinary, an experience or an insight they have not yet encountered;
- Novelty: visitors want to see or do something that rouses their curiosity, something to make them wonder about the world around them or its past;
- Informative: visitors want to be informed about the processes of the objects on display, and more about the world behind the objects than the objects themselves;
- Quality: visitors want quality of services, good facilities, shops that provide items worth buying – not necessarily just expensive catalogues – and proper catering;
- Understanding: visitors are not so much looking for learned knowledge, but to understand the phenomena;
- Emotions: visitors want to be emotionally involved and touched by the items on display.

If the visit is not such a unique experience, we will continue to be faced with a very common phenomenon in museums: museum fatigue. One of the first research projects on museums was Melton's 1933 investigation in which he discovered, or rather first described, this well-known feeling. This sensation – that you have a cotton-wool head, leaden legs and painful feet – is an experience with which we are all familiar. Museum fatigue leads to a specific behaviour amongst museum visitors: the longer they stay in a museum, the faster they move towards the exit; and the greater the time visitors spend in the galleries, the less attention they pay to the displays (Schouten, 1987).

In developing visitor attractions a good concept is of vital importance. Canadian Heritage starts any site development, whether cultural or natural, with the questions: 'What is the spirit of the place?' and 'How do we get that across?' Such statements may sound vague, but it is nevertheless the prime function of an attraction to communicate these questions. Attractions can only be successful if they lift something out of the ordinary. This is true to the extent that if this is not done by the developers or the managers of the attraction, the visitors will give their interpretation, invent their own stories, or dream their own dreams. Visiting a castle and standing behind the battlements, imagining yourself as one of the defenders against a cruel enemy, might be considered day-dreaming. I would call it interpretation by active imagination. Glastonbury is not just a nice historical town, it is a place of pilgrimage; whether or not this is related to historical facts is irrelevant, for reality is shaped by convictions and conventions, not by facts. Any place needs a myth around which its magic can be spun. In many attractions we see the use of archetypical figures as leading elements in the storyline. In some places the stories are there to be picked up. In other places they have to be created, whether the archetypes are King Arthur, dragons, Robin Hood, the hero and the villain, cowboys and Indians, eternal romantic figures like Romeo and Juliet, or whatever you can lay your hands on. It can be put into a formula:

$$VA = Dm3$$

Where visitor attraction (VA) consists of (=) a dream (D) made out of myth, magic and mystery (m3).

Of course this is only part of the story; an attraction can take its inspiration from the legends of more or less historical times, from mythical times, from fairy tales, novels or from TV series. This is, however, not in itself a recipe for success, as Celtworld in Ireland has shown us. There is more to it than using a good idea and technological tricks. It also involves a good story to tell, commitment to the subject, linking it with the world of the visitors, determination to communicate, involving the emotions, the human touch, all to create the possibility of visitors identifying with the subject.

Research in the USA has showed that the popularity of video games depends on three criteria (C. Screven, personal communication):

1. Does it provide a challenge?
2. Does it raise curiosity?
3. Does it give you something to discover?

If these three criteria – and the lessons of the commercial heritage industry – were to be applied seriously in the world of museums and heritage sites, it would make them nicer places to be. Such an approach would enable them to reach their goals more thoroughly, for popular science is preferred above popular belief.

References

De Haan, J. (1995) *Het Gedeelde Erfgoed, een Tussentijds Rapport*. SCP, Rijswijk.
McManus, P. (1987) Communication With and Between Visitors to a Science Museum. PhD thesis, University of London.
Miles, R. (1986) Museum audiences. *Museum Management and Curatorship* 5, 73–88.

Miles, R. *et al.* (1982) *The Design of Educational Exhibits.* Allen & Unwin, London.

ROM (1976) *Communication with the Museum Visitor.* Royal Ontario Museum, Toronto.

Schouten, F. (1987) Psychology and exhibit design. *Museum Management and Curatorship* 6, 259–262.

Schouten, F. (1993) The future of museums. *Museum Management and Curatorship* 12, 381–386.

Schouten, F. (1995) Improving visitor care in heritage attractions. *Tourism Management* 16, 259–291.

6

Access for All? Paradigm Shift in Government Support for the Provision of Countryside Recreation in England and Wales

Neil Ravenscroft

School of Management Studies for the Service Sector, University of Surrey, Guildford GU2 5XH, UK

Introduction

The question of access to the countryside of England and Wales for the pursuit of informal recreation activities such as rambling and walking has, since the mid-19th century, never moved far from the political agenda. Not only does the countryside enjoy a unique cultural signifi-cance (see, for example, Shoard, 1980; Pye-Smith and Hall, 1987; or Archbishops' Commission on Rural Areas, 1990), but walking in it is one of the most popular forms of active recreation in Britain. Indeed, about 80% of the population venture into the countryside at least once a year (Countryside Commission, 1991b) while nearly half the population are considered by the Sports Council to be frequent walkers (McInnes, 1993).

Notwithstanding the popularity of walking and rambling, provision for recreational access to the countryside is highly complex, involving both the use of facilities and the exercising of a variety of classes of right. It therefore involves not only the public sector, but also the private–commercial and the private not-for-profit sectors of the economy (see Curry, 1994). At the core of the provision are legal rights of passage over approximately 140,000 km of public paths and bridleways, where responsibility for maintenance lies with local highways authorities. In addition, the public sector also provides open access areas, in the form of country parks and picnic sites. However, much informal recreation takes place on privately owned land over which there is no long-term legal 'right' to recreation. Rather, access is granted via a variety of means, including local by-law rights over some land owned by public agencies such as the Forestry Commission and not-for-profit charities such as the National Trust; access agreements negotiated by the local planning authority over a small amount of private land (mainly in National Parks); and 'unlawful' access over other land, whether public or private.

Regardless of any rights rhetoric, however, none of these latter conditional or contractual arrangements provides more than a short-term licence. This emphasizes the essential 'gift' nature of much recreational access, resulting in the public enjoyment of the country-side being dependent upon 'a fragile combination of rights and the tolerance of landowners' (Bonyhady, 1987:18). Nowhere is this more the case than with the category of 'unlawful', or *de facto*, access. For, while a narrow view might have been taken over the creation of legal rights, both Parliament and the courts have sought consistently to maintain the public's *de facto* 'rights'. This has been achieved by both refusing to criminalize simple trespass and by awarding minimal damages in cases which have come to court. Thus, rather than being a residual 'loophole' in provision, such access has been as much a part of government access policy as legal rights of way or other provisions. However, as Bonyhady points out:

> *De facto* rights are . . . inherently a partial and unreliable substitute for public rights of access . . . The problem is that these 'rights' are no more than a result of Parliament and the courts denying landowners an effective remedy for trivial wrongs.
>
> (Bonyhady, 1987:16)

As a result, the legal construction of countryside recreation is much more closely associated with a 'civilizing' mission than it is with the narrower legal definition of rights of access. By constructing those demanding greater rights of access as 'alien other' (what the landed are not), the inherent power relations effectively direct the debate away from equality before the law towards expropriation and personal liberty: the private expropriation of property and the personal liberty of the landed. Any claim for increased public access to private land is therefore constructed by landowners as an encroachment on their libertarian freedom, only to be secured under a 'voluntary' arrangement of public recognition and compensation for their loss.

What emerges is a judicial/administrative partnership, comprising the state and landowners, seemingly (and somewhat curiously) seeking to protect certain 'rights' of non-landowners. Rather than being of a formally juridical construction, however, this partnership is rooted in custom and incorporates non-landowners as well. Equally, rather than the protection of non-landowner rights *per se*, this partnership is based on the synchronous legitimatory needs of landowners and the state.

Thus landowners rely upon the sanction of the state to maintain their status (Harrison, 1987), while the state itself demands support from the landowners to maintain its strength and stability (Shivji, 1989). Rather than being incidental, the role of the third party, the landless, is arguably the most significant of the three. In assuming the effective alter-ego of the landed, the landless attract both 'protection' from the state, and paternal sensibility and responsibility from landowners (Thompson, 1993).

The foundation of this public/private partnership is, therefore, based upon the regulation of competing claims over the ownership and use of rural land. This is coupled with an outward show of bene-volence, in terms of the protection of certain access 'rights', which attempts to conceal the continuing expropriation and élitism of land-ownership. Rather than recreational access representing an example of neo-classical market failure, therefore, the situation is more accurately represented as an enduring site of class struggle and stratification (Whatmore *et al.*, 1990).

This struggle has traditionally been one-sided, reflecting the nexus between private property and the state. As a consequence, the public/private partnership in England and Wales has been firmly located within the mercantile discourse of profitability and power. Indeed, since the Agriculture Act 1947 the partnership has assumed a corpora-tist nature, involving directly the landowning and farming community in the generation and implementation of rural policy (see Cox *et al.*, 1988). However, a number of factors have recently coincided to cause a reassessment of the situation.

In particular, there has been growing support for the extension of the corporatist partnership to include non-farming and non-landowning interests, particularly with a view to incorporating environmental interests more fully in the policy community. Throughout the 1990s this has led to the progressive introduction of a number of 'agri-environment' incentive schemes for farmers, based on encouraging them to replace their current farming systems with 'traditional' methods which are more sensitive to the environment (Whitehead, 1994).

Associated with the wider environmental interests has been a renewed focus on informal recreation and access to private land, includ-ing calls for a general 'right to roam' over open, uncultivated country (Blunden and Curry, 1990). While this has consistently been resisted by farmers and landowners (see Country Landowners' Association, 1991, for example), the idea of 'regularizing' *de facto* access arrangements through payments linked to the agri-environmental incentive schemes has been received with apparent enthusiasm (Curry, 1994). While it has been argued by the farming and landowning lobby that the enthusiasm is based on the recognition that informal access can be accommodated on commercial farms without state coercion (Bosanquet, 1995), it is apparent that it is more probably associated with the evident retention of the 'permissive corporatism' which has underpinned agricultural policy since 1947 (Whitby and Lowe, 1994).

Access Payment Schemes

The early 1980s review of the European Common Agricultural Policy (CAP), which led to a reduction in food support prices and the introduction of levies and quotas, focused attention on helping those same farmers to replace agricultural income with money from other sources (Ravenscroft, 1992). Recreation was seen as a primary source of new income for farmers, with the UK Government's Farm Diversification Grant Scheme and a number of Department of the Environment planning circulars encouraging the development of non-agricultural enterprises on farms (see Byrne and Ravenscroft, 1989).

Apart from the introduction of set-aside (grant-aided fallowing of arable land) in the first CAP reform, the first major designation of land was under the Environmentally Sensitive Area (ESA) scheme, introduced by the Ministry of Agriculture, Fisheries and Food (MAFF) in the Agriculture Act 1986. Under this scheme those farming in certain identified areas were offered grant aid to manage their land in an environmentally sensitive manner, thus providing a model of non-production financial support for farmers. To this was added the Countryside Premium Scheme, an additional financial incentive for allowing public access to privately owned set-aside land in the eastern counties of England. This was followed, in 1991, by the introduction of the Countryside Stewardship Scheme (CSS), sponsored not by the agricultural sector, but by the Countryside Commission, the government's advisor on landscape conservation and countryside recreation. The aims for developing the CSS were:

> . . . to demonstrate that conservation and public enjoyment of the countryside can be combined with commercial land management through a national system of incentives. The long-term objective is to develop a basis for a comprehensive scheme to achieve environmental and recreational benefits as an integral part of agricultural support.
>
> (Countryside Commission, 1991a:1)

These various initiatives have recently been reorganized, in response to the latest reform of the CAP, into five environmental schemes, four of which provide for improved access to the countryside. These are:

- A new Countryside Access scheme for set-aside land, based on the previous Countryside Premium scheme, but not now limited to the eastern counties of England (Ministry of Agriculture, Fisheries and Food, 1993b, 1993d and 1993e).

- A new option for public access to land in the ESA scheme (Ministry of Agriculture, Fisheries and Food, 1993c).
- The Countryside Stewardship Scheme, to be taken over from the Countryside Commission (Ministry of Agriculture, Fisheries and Food, 1993a, and Department of the Environment and Ministry of Agriculture, Fisheries and Food, 1995).
- A new Farm Woodland Premium Scheme (Ministry of Agriculture, Fisheries and Food, 1993a).

In addition to the primary purposes of conservation and tree planting, the secondary intention for all the payment schemes is to provide new opportunities for walking and other forms of quiet recreation in areas already subject to grant aid for environmental management and improvement (Ministry of Agriculture, Fisheries and Food, 1993c). The extra grant paid to participating farmers and landowners is supposed to cover the additional costs incurred in making the land available for access, including signposting and publicity. The criteria for selecting suitable sites are designed to ensure that the new opportunities will enhance existing access, either by linking rights of way, providing new circular routes close to urban areas or providing access to previously inaccessible features such as vantage points.

At the core of the new system, therefore, is a two-tier designation of farmland, under which the most environmentally significant areas are accorded ESA status and financial support, while the wider country-side has no formal status, but can gain financial support through the CSS. Designation of ESAs has been an evolving process since 1987, with 22 designated in England by 1994 (Whitehead, 1994). As Whitby and Lowe (1994) have discovered, farmer reception to these designations has been favourable, with nearly 90% of the area targeted in the first round of ESA designation, in 1987, being entered into management schemes. While this level of success has not been achieved in the more recent designations, it is clear that farmers, in general, have responded favourably to the opportunities offered in ESAs:

> The ESA programme, with its direct and tangible commitment to con-servationist farming, marks a significant departure for agricultural policy in the UK. For the first time farmers are being paid by MAFF to 'produce' countryside, and they seem to be responding to the challenge as keenly as they once did to past encouragements to produce more milk or barley.
>
> (Whitby and Lowe, 1994:18)

Although much smaller in scope at present, the CSS has similarly been well received by the farming community since its introduction in 1991 with, by the end of 1994, nearly 5000 agreements covering about

100,000 ha of land (Davies, 1995). Rather than the essentially passive restraint characterizing ESA agreements, however, CSS agreements have focused on the delivery or improvement of specified 'products', usually in the form of habitats. This has led supporters, such as Bishop and Phillips (1993), to favour the CSS incentive scheme over the ESA version, on the grounds that it conforms to the rigours of market allocation, in that the purchaser is under no obligation to purchase and any payment made is for the 'product' rather than simply the process:

> Under schemes such as Countryside Stewardship . . . a market is being created in environment and related recreation services, with incentives offered to farmers who manage their land according to certain prescriptions. The schemes allow farmers to identify relevant environmental services and goods which they can provide and the opportunity to market these and promote their role as custodians and managers of the countryside. Unlike ESAs or compensation arrangements under the Wildlife and Countryside Act 1981, the rules of the market operate.
>
> (Bishop and Phillips, 1993:335)

The number of agreements containing provision for public access, at somewhere between one-third and one-fifth of all CSS agreements (Countryside Commission, 1994b; Bosanquet, 1995) is put forward as evidence that market allocation is operating, on the supposed basis that only these agreements were considered suitable for additional access payments. However, there is no evidence to indicate that this disparity has been caused by the 'consumer choice' championed by Bishop and Phillips (1993), with substantial numbers of farmer or landowner applicants being denied the access payments. Rather, evidence from the Ramblers' Association (1993a; 1994) indicates the opposite, that even amongst those sites which have gained access payments, not all are suitable for their purpose. This hardly suggests that the 'rules of the market' are in evidence, let alone in operation.

Paradigm Shift in Government Support

It is at this point that clear evidence emerges about the nature of the paradigm shift in government support for access. For while it may be a legitimate aspect of government policy to support recreational access to private land as a means of supplementing public facilities, any notion that this is being achieved through a market mechanism is a fallacy. Even the identity of one of the most basic elements of the market, the buyer, is uncertain. The imperative of the policy is that the government, acting on behalf of its citizenry, is the buyer, thereby securing new access opportunities for everyone to enjoy *at no direct user charge*. Yet there is no direct evidence that the citizenry have actually demanded these additional opportunities *per se*, while Clark *et al.* (1994) found a strong public antipathy to paying farmers for access to their land.

In addition to concerns about the identity of the buyer, it is also clear that, in many cases, the extent of the product being purchased may be equally uncertain. Since access has to be in addition to what is already available, no plans or representations of the access sites are readily available at the start of the schemes. As a consequence, agreements have been reached with, and payments made to, farmers prior to the public having any knowledge of where they could walk (Ramblers' Association, 1993a). Subsequently, site plans have been produced, although they are not widely available to the ordinary public. Any wider circulation of information about the sites, especially by adding them to Ordnance Survey maps, has been resisted, as explained by Anthony Bosanquet, Chair of the Country Landowners' Association Agriculture and Rural Economy Committee, when giving evidence to the House of Commons Environment Committee inquiry into the environmental impact of leisure activities:

> The risk about putting [*access sites*] on maps . . . is that in a voluntary scheme, as under Countryside Stewardship, the areas subject to access agreements may change in the future. Access marked on an Ordnance Survey map may no longer be available in ten years' time . . . but someone walking there could still produce the map and say, 'Here it is, it's marked down'; that cannot take any account of the fact that circumstances change, so that there is a risk there.
>
> (Bosanquet, 1995)

As a result, few access payment sites have received much use since the schemes started, with one site in the north of England having about 200 visitors in each of its first 2 years (Ravenscroft *et al.,* 1995). This is confirmed by the Ramblers' Association (1993a, 1994), which found that many potential users were unable to find the sites, while others were culturally 'unable' to use them, when faced with inadequate information about their rights and opportunities.

Although hailed as a major advancement in promulgating public access as a legitimate objective of agricultural policy (Reynolds, 1992), these new access payment schemes really do little more than confirm the continuation of traditional values: the asymmetric position of public subsidy for the maintenance of the libertarian freedom of farmers and landowners. Indeed, rather than being focused on the extension of access rights, it is clearly evident that the government's action amounts to a reaffirmation of the authority of property power. In addition, this authority has now provided a legal means of diverting public funds into the income and capital worth of landowners and some farmers (Ravenscroft *et al.*, 1995). There has been no discussion of citizen's rights nor, apparently, any consideration of what the public might reasonably have expected, in addition to cheap food, from its vast investment in farming businesses and, ultimately, the land. Instead, the very expressions of demand for improved access by organizations such as the Ramblers' Association (1993b) have been interpreted against them, through the effective privatization of their erstwhile 'public' rights.

Rather than rights, therefore, the public has gained little more than short-term contractual obligations. The first of these is to pay farmers and landowners in recognition of their generosity in temporarily foregoing some of their traditional freedom. The second obligation is to make use of the new opportunities in order to establish the legitimacy of their access claims. Finally, the third obligation is to ensure that the public use of this private land is 'responsible', thereby rebutting farmers' fears of vandalism.

Paradoxically therefore, rather than strengthening public access, these contractual arrangements or 'partnerships' effectively undermine it. Even the Countryside Commission (1994a) recognizes that the 'short-termism' implicit in these initiatives could diminish access opportunities in the longer term. More pervasively, however, access 'rights' are further undermined by granting the legal, and thus the moral, high ground to farmers and landowners. This high ground is itself now being reinforced further through the criminalization of trespass contained in the Criminal Justice and Public Order Act 1994. Although ostensibly designed to streamline the eviction from private property of squatters, 'new age' travellers and other 'undesirables', the legislation will, as Fairlie (1994) suggests, apply to any 'assembly' of trespassers failing to comply with police requests to vacate property to which they do not have a legal right of access.

Rather than signifying the acceptance of public rights in the countryside as a legitimate aim of public policy, therefore, the dualism of purchased access 'rights' to pre-determined areas combined with potentially punitive consequences for those who stray from them, is more redolent of a return to the property-dominated class schisms of the past. In common with the short-lived Access to Mountains Act 1937 and, to a lesser extent, the National Parks and Access to the Countryside Act 1949, public access to the countryside has been appropriated by public policy and packaged as an enhanced citizen 'right', while actually reaffirming the hegemonic power of property and its owners at the expense of the wider citizenry.

Conclusion

What is apparent in the analysis of the issues associated with access to the countryside is that the construction of the 'problem', and hence the solution, is very much determined by the nature of the parties to the 'partnership'. The dominant construction, cited by a wide range of interests in the debate, is concerned with values; that differences can be explained by reference to relative values, as expressed by Glyptis:

> The whole access issue has to do with values accorded to areas by those who do not own them, and to do with the values and attitudes of the parties involved towards each other, be it the planner's, landowner's or farmer's attitude to the activity, the views of competing users, such as conservationists and recreationists, or the views of one set of recreational users about another.
>
> (Glyptis, 1992:7)

However, the discourse on values is far from neutral. It may suit certain groups or classes to construct the relative positions in terms of values, but the relativity is more associated with the force of legitimation, the power to substantiate value claims, than it is with values *per se*. It is clear that the dominant values associated with access to the countryside have little to do with notions of society, equity, need or citizen rights and everything to do with property, underwritten by the power of a legal system in which the market is assumed (Bergeron 1993). Rather than a situation in which both owners and non-owners of land can promote their values through the exercise of legally enforceable rights, therefore, the issue of access demonstrates the degree to which the public has become responsible for the maintenance of the property rights of individuals. This is the predominant position even in situations where citizen rights do exist. For example, in the case of landowner responsibilities with respect to public rights of way, the lengthy attempt by the Countryside Commission to improve the condition and accessibility of public rights of way has yielded only marginal benefits for the public (see Joint Centre for Land Development Studies, 1985).

Any representation of the access 'problem' as one of rights is ultimately an obfuscation of what is more fundamentally a means of alienation and control. This is based on deceptive notions of civil or social rights promulgated by the dominant ideological forces associated with property. This dominance has achieved the acquiescence of the 'landless' in the hypocrisy that access claims have been materially substantiated, when in reality all that has happened has been a redistribution of resources within the dominant group to ensure the maintenance of property-based power (see Hargreaves, 1992).

Even this level of power-based discrimination misses the full significance of the 'access debate'. The deception goes much deeper than mere resource allocation, into the very validity of property itself. This is particularly so in attempting constantly to overcome the disparity between the message of property-based capitalism and the reality for most people (see Fudge and Glasbeek, 1992). As such, the benevolent and 'voluntary' extension of access has been more about coercion and control than it has about the rights of people, as Hay suggests in his essay on eighteenth-century England:

> Benevolence . . . was not a simple positive act: it contained within it the ever-present threat of malice. In economic relations a landlord keeping his rents low was benevolent because he could, with impunity, raise them . . . Benevolence, all patronage, was given meaning by its contingency. It was the obverse of coercion, terror's conspiracy of silence.
>
> (Hay, 1975:62)

Rather than 'freedom to roam' or some similar evocation, therefore, what the recent access initiatives have promoted is the reinvention of a sanitized countryside in which recreation is allowed, or actually encouraged, and in which people's respect for the countryside is developed. This is a corollary of the situation in the 1960s and 1970s where relatively insignificant areas of English and Welsh countryside were designated as country parks; 'sacrificed' to the visitor as a diversion from more 'important' or valuable pieces of land, in both landscape and tenurial terms. Now the diversion is not from other land, but from wider and more deeply philosophical issues about the relationship between public policy and private property.

By effectively separating the politics of the access debate from the economic implications of its outcome, many issues remain unanswered, not least the popularity of the schemes, the distribution and longevity of any rights created and the degree to which the staged irrelevance of the schemes has deflected claims for wider freedom to roam. What has become patently clear, however, is that the annexation by the market of access 'rights', together with the draconian criminalization of trespass, is yet another stage in the reconstruction of civil society away from fixed social divisions and class relations.

As such, it is clear that whatever may have been achieved in the social democratic era since World War II, it was not the reconstruction of the state away from its roots in the protection of the 'naturalness' of property. Indeed, just as surely as the state/property alliance of the eighteenth century ensured its authority through the threat of the death penalty for trivial crimes against property (Hay, 1975), the state has continued to sanction the dominance of property through the provisions of the Criminal Justice and Public Order Act 1994. The current state of the 'access debate' emphasizes, therefore, the continuing hegemony of the state/property partnership, with its increasing cultural regression to the wealth-related and propertied élitism of eighteenth-century England:

> ... wealth does not exist outside a social context, theft is given definition only within a set of social relations, and the connections between property, power and authority are close and crucial. The criminal law was critically important in maintaining bonds of obedience and deference, in legitimizing the *status quo*, in constantly recreating the structure of authority which arose from property and in turn protected its interests.
>
> (Hay, 1975:25)

The paradigm shift in late twentieth-century England is, thus, not so much public versus private, as it is legitimation versus criminalization. Regardless of the empirical construction and regulation of public rights over private land, it is clear that the current and future 'citizen' project is not so much about property itself as it is about the binary division between the ruling élite and the remainder of the population.

Postscript

This paper was written prior to the General Election of 1 May 1997, when a new Labour administration was returned to office with a manifesto commitment to legalize a general freedom to roam over open country. Although Parliamentary time has yet to be designated for this purpose, it is understood that an enquiry into the form which this might take is currently being conducted by the Ministry of Agriculture, Fisheries and Food.

References

Archbishops' Commission on Rural Areas (1990) *Faith in the Countryside.* Churchman Publishing Ltd, Worthing, W. Sussex.

Bergeron, J.H. (1993) From property to contract: political economy and the transformation of value in English common law. *Social and Legal Studies* 2, 5–23.

Bishop, K.D. and Phillips, A.A.C. (1993) Seven steps to market – the development of the market-led approach to countryside conservation and recreation. *Journal of Rural Studies* 9, 315–338.

Blunden, J. and Curry, N. (1990) *A People's Charter?* HMSO, London.

Bonyhady, T. (1987) *The Law of the Countryside. The Rights of the Public.* Professional Books, Abingdon.

Bosanquet, A. (1995) Minutes of evidence to the House of Commons Environment Committee, *The Environmental Impact of Leisure Activities, Volume II, Minutes of Evidence.* House of Commons Papers 246–II, HMSO, London, paragraph 869.

Byrne, P. and Ravenscroft, N. (1989) *The Land Report. Diversification and Alternative Land Uses for the Landowner and Farmer.* Humberts, Chartered Surveyors, London.

Clark, G., Darrall, J., Grove-White, R., MacNaughten, P. and Urry, J. (1994) *Leisure Landscapes. Leisure, Culture and the English Countryside: Challenges and Conflicts.* Centre for the Study of Environmental Change, Lancaster University.

Country Landowners' Association (1991) *Recreation and Access in the Countryside: a Better Way Forward.* Country Landowners' Association, London.

Countryside Commission (1991a) *Countryside Stewardship: an Outline.* Publication CCP 346. Countryside Commission, Cheltenham.

Countryside Commission (1991b). *Visitors to the Countryside.* Publication CCP 341. Countryside Commission, Cheltenham.

Countryside Commission (1994a) *Access Payment Schemes.* Publication CCP 443. Countryside Commission, Cheltenham.

Countryside Commission (1994b) *Annual Report, 1993–1994.* Publication CCP 456. Countryside Commission, Cheltenham.

Cox, G., Lowe, P. and Winter, M. (1988) Private rights and public responsibilities: the prospects for agricultural and environmental controls. *Journal of Rural Studies* 4, 323–337.

Curry, N.R. (1994) *Countryside Recreation, Access and Land Use Planning.* E. & F.N. Spon, London..

Davies, G.H. (1995) Pay-off for conservation. *Countryside* 76, 4–5.

Department of the Environment and Ministry of Agriculture, Fisheries and Food (1995) *Rural England: a Nation Committed to a Living Countryside.* Cm 3016, HMSO, London.

Fairlie, S. (1994) On the march. *The Guardian,* section 2, 21.1.94, 14–15.

Fudge, J. and Glasbeek, H. (1992) The politics of rights: a politics with little class. *Social and Legal Studies* 1(1), 45–70.

Glyptis, S. (1992) Setting the scene. In: Bishop, K. (ed.) *Off the Beaten Track: Access to Open Land in the UK.* Proceedings of the 1992 Countryside Recreation Conference. Countryside Recreation Network, Cardiff, pp. 4–18.

Hargreaves, J. (1992) Revisiting the hegemony thesis. In: Sugden, J. and Knox, C. (eds) *Leisure in the 1990s: Rolling Back the Welfare State.* Leisure Studies Association Publication No. 46. LSA Publications, Eastbourne, pp. 263–280.

Harrison, M.L. (1987) Property rights, philosophies and the justification of planning control. In: Harrison, M.L. and Mordey, R. (eds) *Planning Control: Philosophies, Prospects and Practice.* Croom Helm Ltd, Beckenham, Kent, pp. 32–58.

Hay, D. (1975) Property, authority and the criminal law. In: Hay, D., Linebaugh, P., Rule, J.G., Thompson, E.P. and Winslow, C. (eds) *Albion's Fatal Tree. Crime and Society in Eighteenth-century England.* Allen Lane, London, pp. 17–63.

Joint Centre for Land Development Studies (1985) *Ploughing Footpaths and Bridleways.* Publication CCP 190. Countryside Commission, Cheltenham.

McInnes, H. (1993) *Trends in Sports Participation.* Sports Council Facilities Factfile 2; Planning and Provision for Sport. Sports Council, London.

Ministry of Agriculture, Fisheries and Food (1993a) *Agriculture and England's Environment.* Ministry of Agriculture, Fisheries and Food, London.

Ministry of Agriculture, Fisheries and Food (1993b) *Agriculture and England's Environment.* News Release 266/93. Ministry of Agriculture, Fisheries and Food, London.

Ministry of Agriculture, Fisheries and Food (1993c) *Agriculture and England's Environment. Provision of New Public Access in ESAs: a Consultation Document.* Ministry of Agriculture, Fisheries and Food, London.

Ministry of Agriculture, Fisheries and Food (1993d) *Agriculture and England's Environment. Set-aside Management: a Consultation Document.* Ministry of Agriculture, Fisheries and Food, London.

Ministry of Agriculture, Fisheries and Food (1993e) *CAP Reform: Proposed Countryside Access Scheme.* Leaflet AR 15. Ministry of Agriculture, Fisheries and Food, London.

Pye-Smith, C. and Hall, C. (eds) (1987) *The Countryside We Want: a Manifesto for the Year 2000.* Green Books, Bideford, Devon.

Ramblers' Association (1993a) *Countryside Stewardship Scheme – Survey by the Ramblers' Association of Public Access Sites.* Ramblers' Association, London.

Ramblers' Association (1993b) *Harmony in the Hills.* Ramblers' Association, London.

Ramblers' Association (1994) *Countryside Stewardship Scheme Public Access Sites. Survey Report on Access Provisions at Second-year Public Access Sites.* Ramblers' Association, London.

Ravenscroft, N. (1992) *Recreation Planning and Development.* The Macmillan Press Ltd, Basingstoke.

Ravenscroft, N., Prag, P.A.B., Gibbard, R. and Markwell, S.S. (1995) *The Financial Implications to Landowners and Farmers of the Countryside Stewardship Scheme.* Research Series 95/1. Centre for Environment and Land Tenure Studies, The University of Reading.

Reynolds, F. (1992) Lowland countryside. In: Bishop, K. (ed.) *Off the Beaten Track: Access to Open Land in the UK.* Proceedings of the 1992 Countryside Recreation Conference. Countryside Recreation Network, Cardiff, pp. 33–37.

Shivji, I.G. (1989) *The Concept of Human Rights in Africa.* Codesria Book Series, London.

Shoard, M. (1980) *The Theft of the Countryside.* Maurice Temple Smith Ltd, London.

Thompson, E.P. (1993) *Customs in Common.* Penguin Books Ltd., Harmondsworth.

Whatmore, S., Munton, R. and Marsden, T. (1990) The rural restructuring process: emerging divisions of agricultural property rights. *Regional Studies* 24(3), 235–245.

Whitby, M. and Lowe, P. (1994) The political and economic roots of environ-
      mental policy in agriculture. In: Whitby, M. (ed.) *Incentives for Country-
      side Management. The Case of Environmentally Sensitive Areas.* CAB
      International, Wallingford, Oxon, pp. 1–24.
Whitehead, I.R.G. (1994) *The Agri-environmental Package 1994.* Rural Practice
      Division, Royal Institution of Chartered Surveyors, London.

7

Recreation Pressures on the Countryside: Real Concerns or Crises of the Imagination?

Roger Sidaway

Research and Policy Consultant, 4 Church Hill Place, Edinburgh EH10 4BD, UK

Introduction

Concerns about recreation pressures on the countryside have been with us since the 1960s, arguably since the middle of the last century. But has the basis of these concerns been well founded for the issue has varied from Dower's (1965) 'fourth wave' of recreational growth to more recent concerns about endangered wildlife? What really has changed in the last 20 to 30 years? Have demands increased, is there clear evidence of damage and disturbance or is it that people perceive unwelcome change and hanker after the past?

This chapter recognizes the changes in perception of the problem – from initial concerns about damage to vegetation, then disturbance to birds and most recently widespread incremental cultural change. It raises the issue: if the focus of concern has changed, have the problems recognized and the solutions adopted by managers really altered, or have we merely come full circle? This chapter also recognizes that sport in the countryside challenges established notions of what is appropriate in the countryside. Young people with new equipment and bright clothes disturb the tranquillity of minds seeking to get away from it all. Do we have the right information and management techniques to cope with these challenges?

© CAB INTERNATIONAL 1998. *Leisure Management: Issues and Applications*
(eds M.F. Collins and I.S. Cooper)

Real Concerns and Imagined Pressures

Concern about visitor numbers and the resulting pressures on the countryside formed part of the terms of reference of the inquiry conducted
by the House of Commons Environment Committee which investigated
the Environmental Impact of Leisure in 1995. The Committee's terms of
reference were to assess:

- to what degree large numbers of visitors, and the pursuit of certain
  leisure activities, cause harm to the countryside and wildlife;
- how conflicts of interest between conservation, agriculture, public
  access and local economic development should be addressed;
- whether current planning controls and guidance notes form an
  adequate safeguard against excessive or inappropriate leisure
  development in environmentally sensitive areas; and
- options for the development of more sustainable forms of leisure and
  tourism.

(House of Commons Environment Committee, 1995)

Members of the Committee might have expected that the topic under
investigation was not entirely new but were probably surprised to find
that, even in official inquiries, it had such a long history. In the event,
they quoted from a series of earlier reports:

> With regard to the question of open spaces, under the present circum-
> stances of this country, increase of population, spread of cities and manu-
> factures, and so on, is it not annually becoming a vital question for the
> consideration of Parliament? If England goes on progressing in wealth
> and population, the probability is that in 50 years hence, it will be very
> much more important to the nation than it is now; and the same remark
> holds good with regard to all open spaces; the number of people who visit
> the New Forest is rapidly increasing, and I feel certain that the increase
> will continue.
>
> (Debate on Report of the Select Committee on the New Forest, 1875)

> It is unthinkable that this pleasant land should be allowed to be
> irreparably defaced. None the less, rapid progress in recent years in
> urbanization, the natural ambition of the town worker to have a house in
> the country or at the seaside, the break-up of large estates for building
> development, the extension of traffic facilities, the development of
> industrial undertakings on rural sites, and the eruption, in places of
> beauty, of ill-designed houses and shanties all constitute a real menace to
> the preservation of its natural beauty.
>
> (National Park Committee, 1929)

> The greatest threat to the essential character of the area lies in the
> increased day visitor traffic that may be expected over the next decade.
> Sheer weight of numbers will inevitably change the tourist 'product' (that

is the combination of natural resources such as scenery and transport, accommodation and other services) and raise the question of evolving techniques to manage and direct traffic within the Park.

(Peak Park Planning Board, 1965)

Such concerns had been a major theme of the Countryside in 1970 conference and featured prominently in the House of Lords Select Committee Report on Sport and Leisure (the Cobham Report) in 1973. Indeed, paragraphs of the Cobham Report have a very familiar ring in their description of the apparent problem:

The Peak Park, for instance, with about 10 million visitors a year is in danger of being overused. In Cannock Chase the crowding has begun to produce soil erosion. Climbers on Snowdonia have to queue while waiting their turn at certain rock faces, and some crags, sand dune systems and footpaths are under great ecological pressure. Even in Scotland the countryside is beginning to come under pressure in places.

(House of Lords, 1973: paragraph 221)

This view bore a striking similarity to the evidence the Environment Committee received from the Dartmoor National Park Committee:

. . . predictions for the future use of the countryside are frightening in terms of numbers, and even more so when the changing nature of recreation is taken into account . . . the impact of all this is increased enormously by the fact that the pressures are no longer seasonal . . . The future of the rural environment and the future of many of those who use it are at risk unless action is taken now.

(Dartmoor National Park Committee, 1995)

The underlying assumption of the Environment Committee's inquiry was that leisure activities have grown and will continue to grow rapidly and that such growth is unwelcome as it results in pressure on the countryside and threats to the survival of wildlife, that certain activities are inappropriate in a countryside setting, and that the natural resources have reached the limits of their capacity. Not only are these frequently recurring themes in countryside literature but the interpretation of the same evidence can vary according to the perspective of the writer. For example, in two perspectives from the same period – Robert Arvill (the pen name of Bob Boote, the Director General of the Nature Conservancy) perceives a problem where Adrian Phillips (then Assistant Director of the Countryside Commission) sees an opportunity:

In England and Wales all the National Parks suffer increasing onslaughts. The Friends of the Lake District Park have referred to the traffic there as the 'potential destroyer of the Lake District'. In the Peak Park there are many measures in operation to meet the vast recreational and tourist pressures from nearby cities, notably a corps of voluntary wardens . . . The Snowdonia Park and the Gower Area of Outstanding Natural Beauty

also report great pressures. And the south-west of England, with its two
parks and its beautiful coastline, has the greatest summer influx of all.
(Arvill, 1969:89)

Recreation, while it certainly poses problems, is first and foremost an
opportunity to be welcomed. It is an opportunity for two reasons: first,
because through contact with the countryside the townsman can draw
refreshment, literally to be re-created; and secondly, because recreation provides one of the best means available to us to get over to the four-fifths of
the population who live in towns the urgency of conserving the countryside.
(Phillips, 1970:130)

The Growth and Distribution of Leisure Trips to the Countryside

Departmental evidence to the Environment Committee on recreational
growth summarized the current situation:

> 59. Although the overall total of leisure trips to the countryside has not
> grown as rapidly as forecast twenty years ago, the nature of countryside
> recreation is changing. A greater diversity of pursuits reflect increasing
> interest in active recreation, whilst changes in mobility and travel
> patterns are altering the distribution and thereby the impact of leisure
> activity. A constant, however, is the high value put upon the quality of
> the countryside and its importance in attracting visitors.
> (Department of Environment, Ministry of Agriculture,
> Fisheries and Food, and Department of Transport, 1995)

Clearly the Committee had not anticipated such evidence when it stated
that:

> 12. We noted with some surprise that there was little conclusive evidence
> that the number of visitors to the countryside has increased significantly
> in recent years.
> 19 . . . [although] changes have occurred in the types of activity in which
> people engage and the pattern of use throughout the year.
> (House of Commons Environment Committee, 1995)

Yet this assessment of countryside pressure is consistent with earlier
attempts to grapple with the problem:

> The crowded countryside is a relative concept at best. Even in areas of
> evident pressure, the actual numbers involved are relatively small.
> (Patmore, 1972:96)

The Committee recognize that in general the pressure on the countryside
is not as serious as the foregoing paragraph suggests. Out of season, mid-
week or in bad weather the countryside is not overflowing with visitors.
There are still large tracts of lonely and unspoiled land. The conflicts and

crowding occur at peak times in the summer, i.e., at weekends and Bank holidays and in given places such as access roads and footpaths, beauty spots, summits and water edges.

(House of Lords, 1973: paragraph 222)

Five years later a sceptical review also concluded that concern about rapid and inevitable recreational growth was not warranted; that the then current thinking overemphasized problems like carrying capacity; and that most of the problems concerning recreation pressure in National Park Plans were as much to do with local social issues as with ecological problems (Sidaway and O'Connor, 1978). This later point reflects a more specific concern about endangered wildlife which superseded the more general fears about recreational growth.

Recreational Impacts in Perspective

Over recent years a broad consensus appears to have developed over the seriousness of *biological* impacts of recreational activities in the countryside. This is reflected in evidence to the Environment Committee. For example, Department of Environment *et al.* evidence stated that:

63 . . . DOE has assessed recreational impacts alongside other pressures, in lowland heath, calcareous grassland, uplands, river landscapes and coasts. Recreation is generally seen as less important than other factors such as land management, pollution and development (although some development may be linked to leisure activity).

(Department of Environment, Ministry of Agriculture, Fisheries and Food, and Department of Transport, 1995)

While English Nature summarized the current situation in the following way:

Leisure-related impacts should be assessed in the context of other activities which have an impact on the countryside or coast. Leisure activities do not in themselves represent the greatest threat to nature conservation.

Direct impacts on nature conservation include disturbance, trampling and erosion but these are often localized or short-term in duration and can be managed. Impacts from associated development often represent a greater threat.

Potential benefits can accrue through improved awareness and understanding of nature conservation and the diversion of visitor income into managing and enhancing the natural resource.

(English Nature, 1995)

Although local problems may be manageable the basic information for management is surprisingly weak. Relatively few British research studies specifically examine the relationship between a recreational activity and a habitat or species. Although there has been a continuing interest in recreational impacts over the last 20 years, the number of studies on damage to vegetation has declined whilst that on disturbance to birds has remained roughly constant (Sidaway, 1994). As damage to vegetation is usually visible and evident, managers can take a pragmatic approach to categorizing impacts, and the primary contribution of research is likely to be towards developing and applying more efficient management techniques and not towards demonstrating the existence of the problem (Bayfield and Aitken, 1992). The potentially damaging impact of recreational disturbance on breeding or migratory bird populations is more problematic. Although there has been a steady stream of research reviews on disturbance to birds over the last 5 years, most of them have addressed the question of whether recreational impacts are harmful in a general way and very few have covered how those impacts can be managed (Sidaway, 1994).

The recreation manager, who needs to know when impacts matter and whether it is possible to mitigate a harmful impact by taking appropriate action, is none the wiser. Perhaps more surprisingly, many management initiatives have been taken but few have been systematically evaluated so that good practice develops on an *ad hoc* basis, if at all. So that both in relation to policy and practice, there is a constant danger of re-inventing the wheel.

Lack of specific information on biological impacts may contribute to local conflicts (Sidaway, 1996), but if in the main these effects are localized and manageable, why is there continuing concern, or could it be that biological impacts are not the real issue?

Biological and Cultural Change

Most research and reviews of research for government agencies, such as the Countryside Commission, the Sports Council or Scottish Natural Heritage, have concentrated on the biological impacts of specific activities or in particular habitats (e.g. Sidaway, 1988; Anderson and Radford, 1990; Sidaway, 1994). Evidence to the Environment Committee inquiry took a broader view and this is summarized in Table 7.1, which compares the impacts covered in one of the most recent research reviews (Sidaway, 1994) and the evidence of DOE *et al.* (1995) and the Council for the Protection of Rural England (CPRE, 1995). In contrast to the research review, the DOE presented a somewhat broader definition of environmental effects which included effects on local communities, whilst CPRE concentrated on landscape and aesthetic issues, virtually ignoring any potential effects on wildlife, and this was made even clearer in the Council's written evidence.

Table 7.1. Potential recreational impacts.

Biological effects[a]	Environmental effects[b]	Physical impacts[c]
Damage to vegetation and soils	Wear and tear – vegetation loss and fires	Physical wear and tear on landscape and buildings (cumulative effects in most popular areas)
Incremental effects Disturbance to fauna Removal of wildlife Habitat loss from development	Disturbance to wildlife and local communities	
	Inappropriate development	Physical damage, disturbance and intrusion from sports such as power-boating, mountain-biking and motor sports
Recreational traffic Pollution Noise Wave formation and turbidity from fast-moving boats	Overcrowding Traffic – noise, emission and nuisance in local communities	
		Development of inappropriate infrastructure (e.g. golf courses, holiday villages)
Habitat creation and improvement		
		Recreational traffic

[a]Sidaway, 1994; [b]DOE *et al.*, 1995; [c]CPRE, 1995.

4. The countryside is an increasingly important leisure resource. Yet there are growing environmental conflicts associated with a range of leisure activities and related developments in rural areas. CPRE believes the cumulative, long-term implications of these pressures are ill-understood and the policies developed by the relevant public agencies are failing effectively to tackle the resulting conflicts. The quality and beauty of the countryside and its overall value for recreational purposes is, as a result, being constantly eroded. Significant improvements are required in the way conflicts between leisure and the environment are addressed if the environmental quality, character and peace of the countryside is to be safeguarded for the benefit of future generations. We do not share the view of the principal public agencies involved that the conflict between leisure and the environment can be resolved solely through visitor management and existing land use planning mechanisms.

(CPRE, 1995)

CPRE's concerns appear to stem from a perception of a broader perception of conflict and change instigated by what it sees as a range of new and inappropriate activities and their associated commercial developments. CPRE considers that the scale and rate of change brings into question the competence of the countryside agencies and the appropriateness of their management solutions. In so far as CPRE proposes a solution to the problems, it lies in the greater control and restriction of activities by policy instruments or by legislation, such as the unsuccessful attempt to restrict recreation in the national parks of England and Wales to 'quiet enjoyment'. This stance illustrates Harrison's detailed analysis in 1991 of the predominance of the 'countryside aesthetic' – an informal alliance of landowning, environmental interests with rural local authorities which oppose the advance of active recreation in favour of the quiet enjoyment of pastoral landscapes. Indeed, she predicted the new challenge that would arise from a combination of new sports and the commercial interests of landowners prepared to diversify from agriculture (Harrison, 1991).

Changing and Conflicting Values

Working on more intuitive grounds, the Environment Committee, having earlier noted the cultural values invested in the rural landscape and given examples of the disparity of views, highlighted the significance of 'cultural conflicts'.

> 32. We note that according to the balance of evidence we received, compared to other activities, leisure and tourism do not cause significant widespread ecological damage to the countryside. However, there is no need for complacency. We believe that there are important issues to address, involving transport, rural culture, and leisure management, as well as local conflicts in specific areas.
> 33. We also note that the cultural conflicts are just as real as, and sometimes more important than, the physical problems – indeed they are often the root cause of the various tensions and dissatisfactions that are redefined as threats to the environment.
>
> (House of Commons Environment Committee, 1995)

This suggests that, in the debate about changes taking place in the countryside, the currently dominant values will determine which changes are acceptable, irrespective of the merits of the case.

Seen from this perspective, rural conflict is neither new nor surprising as the countryside embodies so many competing images and aspirations. The debate focuses on change but the nature of change is almost immaterial. Perceptions of change depend on value judgements and on anecdote rather than scientifically gathered information. Indeed, the lack of information becomes a virtual advantage to the players as it allows the debate to range over a shifting agenda of uncertainty where assertions can go unchallenged. The temptation to generalize from the specific case is not resisted – for example, congested conditions at peak pressure points are alleged to typify the countryside at large – and this temptation is supported by the inherent difficulties of measuring complex biological and social processes to demonstrate change. Few problems are new – nature, noise and traffic recur frequently – but the perceptions of their significance changes from time to time.

Resolving the Conflicts

The Environment Committee recognized some of the limitations of the land-use planning system in dealing with countryside conflict and commended an approach of local management through partnerships. The approach was based on 'careful, and often prolonged, consultations which had successfully identified local problems'. But the Committee also noted the considerable variation in the level of cooperation between different organizations and the degree of variation in the acceptance of plans by the local community. One method of dealing with this problem, which the Committee supported, was the consensus-building approach which establishes the common ground between interest groups. The Committee considered 'that consultation in local management schemes should begin at an early stage to overcome some of the cultural conflicts which overshadow any evidence of the environmental impacts of leisure'. (House of Commons Environment Committee, 1995:xlvi). It cited the successful approach to negotiation initiated by the Lake District National Park Authority in relation to provision of routes for mountain bikes and off-road vehicles (in marked contrast to the Authority's approach to managing water sports on Windermere on which the Committee felt unable to comment as the case was *sub judice*).

Local conflicts are certainly more amenable to successful negotiation than national debates about prevailing values, particularly where these are orientated towards political lobbying for legislation. This is not to suggest that all disputes should be resolved locally, but merely to differentiate between two levels of decision-making which are often interrelated. Political activity in a democratic society provides an effective, necessary and legitimate form of conflict resolution, particularly at the national level. However, site-based conflicts, which are potentially resolvable locally, can become enmeshed in national disputes when they form set-piece skirmishes in a longer war of attrition. They may set national precedents or prejudice the action of national players and this factor at the very least adds another level of complexity to any attempt at negotiation, if they are negotiable at all.

Conclusions

The sense of *déjà-vu*, that we are barely getting to grips with the problems that were identified at least 20 years ago, stems from a continuing struggle between competing values rather than just a failure to solve local problems. The diagnosis of 'cultural conflict' suggests a continuing process of adversarial debate which operates on at least two levels. At a local level, some recreation interests are denied access yet often active negotiation and cooperation proceeds, despite the national debate. At national level, a degree of conflict appears to be inevitable as new activities are promoted and new concepts such as sustainability are brokered. Meanwhile, existing interests battle to maintain their dominant position.

Recreational impacts may cause problems, particularly when a failure to invest in the research that will clarify the extent of the problem is matched by an inability to evaluate systematically the many management initiatives that amount to no more than constant improvisation. But the changes affecting wildlife may be relatively easy to manage compared to the problems of how to get people to tolerate each other's use of the countryside and mitigate their own demands. In which case, CPRE may well be right to contend that cultural change lies beyond any conventional process of management.

References

Anderson, P. and Radford, P. (1990) *A Review of the Effects of Recreation on Woodland Soils, Vegetation and Fauna.* (English Nature Contract No. F2-19-10), Penny Anderson Associates, Chinley.

Arvill, R. (1969) *Man and Environment.* Penguin Books, Harmondsworth.

Bayfield, N.G. and Aitken, R. (1992) *Managing the Impacts of Recreation on Vegetation and Soils: A Review of Techniques.* Institute of Terrestrial Ecology, Banchory.

Council for the Protection of Rural England (1995) Written evidence to the House of Commons Environment Committee inquiry into the Environmental Impact of Leisure Activities.

Dartmoor National Park Committee (1995) Written evidence to the House of Commons Environment Committee inquiry into the Environmental Impact of Leisure Activities.

Department of Environment, Ministry of Agriculture, Fisheries and Food, and Department of Transport (1995) Written evidence to the House of Commons Environment Committee inquiry into the Environmental Impact of Leisure Activities.

Dower, M. (1965) Fourth Wave, the challenge of leisure, a Civic Trust Survey. *The Architect's Journal,* 20 January 1965, 123–190.

English Nature (1995) Written evidence to the House of Commons Environment Committee inquiry into the Environmental Impact of Leisure Activities.

Harrison, C. (1991) *Countryside Recreation in a Changing Society*. TMS Partnership, London.

House of Commons Environment Committee (1995a) *Session 1994–5 Fourth Report: the Environmental Impact of Leisure Activities* volume 1, report, together with the Proceedings of the Committee relating to the committee. HMSO, London.

House of Commons Environment Committee (1995b) *Session 1994–5 Fourth Report: the Environmental Impact of Leisure Activities*, Vol. II, *Minutes of Evidence*. HMSO, London.

House of Commons Environment Committee (1995c) *Session 1994–5 Fourth Report: the Environmental Impact of Leisure Activities* Vol. III, *Appendices*. HMSO, London.

House of Lords (1973) *Second Report of the Select Committee on Sport and Leisure* (the Cobham Report). HMSO, London.

National Park Committee (1929) reported in House of Commons Environment Committee (1995).

Patmore, A. (1972) *Land and Leisure*. Penguin Books, Harmondsworth.

Peak Park Planning Board (1965) *Thirteenth Report of the Peak Park Planning Board* (Year ending 31 March 1965). PPPB, Bakewell.

Phillips, A. (1970) In: *Proceedings of the Third Conference, October 1970, The Countryside in 1970*. Council for Nature, Nature Conservancy, Royal Society of Arts, London, p. 130.

Sidaway, R. (1988) *Sport, Recreation and Nature Conservation*. Study 32. Sports Council, London.

Sidaway, R. (1994) *Recreation and the Natural Heritage: a Research Review*. Scottish Natural Heritage, Edinburgh.

Sidaway, R. (1996) Outdoor Recreation and Nature Conservation: Conflicts and their Resolution, Unpublished PhD. thesis, Edinburgh University.

Sidaway, R. and O'Connor, F.B. (1978) Recreation Pressures on the Countryside. *Countryside for All? A Review of the Use People Make of the Countryside for Recreation*. Proceedings of the Countryside Recreation Research Advisory Group Conference 1978. Countryside Commission, Cheltenham. 124–151.

Sport, Culture and Urban Regimes: the Case of Bilbao

8

Ian P. Henry and Juan Luis Paramio Salcines

Department of Physical Education, Sports Science and Recreation Management, Loughborough University, Loughborough, Leicestershire LE11 3TU, UK

Introduction

The focus of this chapter is on the roles of sport, leisure and culture in the restructuring of the city. It is part of a wider, ongoing, research programme in the development of sport and leisure policy in western Europe. The chapter represents work in progress and what is reported here are selected features of the analysis of the role of leisure, culture and sport in regeneration strategies in Bilbao.

Although this chapter deals specifically with the case of Bilbao, a number of preliminary observations are worth emphasizing, which go some way towards explaining the significance of urban sport, leisure and cultural policy in restructuring processes.

The first observation relates to the declining significance of the nation-state as a policy actor (or indeed as defining the unit of social analysis). Such a decline is clearly evident in the economic field (the failure for example of Britain and Spain to defend the value of their currencies), in the cultural field (the transnational nature of broadcasting and its control) and in the social and employment field (witness the perceived need for the 'social chapter' in the Treaty of European Union). This decline in policy influence of the nation-state has been accompanied by an increased significance in the roles of both transnational bodies and sub-national bodies, and, in particular, in the significance of cities.

The second observation is that there is a general recognition of the need for policy solutions to restructuring problems to involve more than simply governmental or public sector responses to the problem. The notion of governance (rather than government) involves partnerships between public, private and voluntary sector actors and organizations. Problems of urban *government* have been retitled but also reconceptualized as problems of urban *governance* (Galès, 1995).

The third point to emphasize is that cities in developed economies which have experienced problems of deindustrialization and social restructuring have twin policy priorities. On the one hand, policies of economic development are seeking to generate and protect new or desired forms of economic activity. On the other hand, policies concerned with social integration or social insertion are aimed at countering the social problems of a 'two-tier society', in which there are potential problems of social instability stemming from the economic and social exclusion of the unemployed, under-employed and economically vulnerable members of an urban society. Sport is seen as having a significant role to play in both the economic and social policy areas. In economic terms, sport may generate direct economic opportunities, but also sport as a tool for re-imaging the city or the neighbourhood has a major symbolic function in providing an environment into which investment can be attracted. At the social level, sports policies for disadvantaged youth, for ethnic minority populations or for deprived areas are seen as one means of combating social exclusion.

The final point relates to sport as a cultural phenomenon of growing significance for policy. The economic restructuring experienced by developed economies has been accompanied by a fragmentation of class cultures, and in particular a shrinking in significance of collective working-class cultural identities. Sport has been characterized in a number of national contexts as subject to processes of individualization, commercialization and mediatization (Defrance and Pociello, 1993; Rojek, 1995). With collective identities subject to restructuring forces, the symbolic uses of sporting forms as vehicles of individualized identities (of people and places) has been realized. The importance of sport as a policy area has been further reinforced by the collapse of cultural hierarchies identified by theorists of post-modernity (Featherstone, 1991).

Thus, sport as a legitimate area for urban intervention has been promoted by the restructuring processes which constitute the salient context of urban policy in the 1990s.

Pluralist, Marxist, Elite Theories of Urban Politics and Urban Regime Theory

The urban politics literature has traditionally been characterized by debates between those who have adopted a pluralist, neo-pluralist or hyperpluralist approach on the one hand (Dahl, 1961; Polsby, 1980; Ross *et al.*, 1991), and those who promoted the view that élites invariably control urban politics (Hunter, 1953; Bacharach and Baratz, 1970; Logan and Molotch, 1987), or that urban politics invariably operate to facilitate the interests of capital (Cockburn, 1977; Castells, 1978; Duncan and Goodwin, 1988). The approach associated with the case study of Bilbao reported here is one which argues that the nature of the outcomes of urban politics is a contingent matter, and one which (in principle at least) is open to empirical investigation. This approach accepts Judge's (1995) argument that there is in effect little significant epistemological difference between more radical versions of the pluralist and neo-pluralist accounts, and the accounts of competition between urban élites given by élite theorists.

Urban regime theory is a product of the attempt to get away from theoretical attempts to characterize the exercise of power in urban politics, moving on to consider how the power or control over the policy process is achieved (Stone, 1989; 1993). Regimes are generally coalitions or compromise groups which seek to effect particular types of outcome. Unlike pluralist and élite accounts of urban governance, regime theorists seek to establish how such regimes achieve their goals. In effect they are concerned with questions of how power is gained and exercised to achieve their ends (in Stone's terms, 'power to') rather than how power is exercised in controlling, subverting or excluding other parties in policy processes ('power over'). It might be argued that this implies an amoral approach to social explanation, one in which the moral issues of who should exercise power in certain situations are deemed to be of no significance. However, though the role of social theory may have shifted from the view of the theorist as 'legislator' of values to one of 'interpreter' of values (Bauman, 1992), nevertheless questions such as how power is exercised, and in whose interests, remain of key importance, but will invariably be preceded by questions of how power is exercised, by whom, and how groups exercising power are mobilized.

As Stoker and Mossberger (1994) have indicated, one of the significant contributions which regime theory can make is in the field of comparative studies. They articulate an account of three types of urban regime, and invite a response as to how such regimes emerge, coalesce, proceed, and succeed or fail in certain contexts. These three types of regimes are:

1. *Organic regimes*, which seek to sustain existing conditions within the city, mobilizing themselves to oppose change such as development proposals for the city;
2. *Instrumental regimes*, which promote particular types of urban development, often organized around a central development project.

The primary concern of such regimes is almost invariably with economic development in the city;

3. *Symbolic regimes*: these in effect focus on changing the image or orientation of the city, for example in promoting a service-based profile for the city in the face of deindustrializing tendencies.

Such an approach offers a convenient point of departure for the analysis of Bilbao (and subsequent comparison with other cities). Since what Stoker and Mossberger provide are in effect ideal types, it will be important to establish ways in which the regimes identified in empirical work cohere in their rationale, structures and modes of operation when compared to 'anticipated findings' in respect of their typology. First, however, an account of the investigation of urban governance in Bilbao is given below.

The Bilbao Case Study

The city of Bilbao is at the core of the Metropolitan Area of Bilbao, which covers 372 km² and a population of nearly a million inhabitants. Metropolitan Bilbao is an urban agglomeration of some 30 towns and municipal districts around the Nervion River. This population represents 80% of the Bizkaia Province and 44% of the Basque Country Autonomous Community.

Founded 700 years ago, Bilbao is Spain's fifth-largest city, and the country's second-largest port. It is located at a site on a bend in the River Nervion just inland from its mouth, nestled in a green valley surrounded by steep hillsides which limit the expansion of the city. The industrial revolution arrived in Spain via Bilbao at the beginning of the 19th century. The combination of a long commercial tradition, financial and investment capacity and manufacturing led to the city's rapid industrialization. As a result, considerable capital was attracted to the city, placing Bilbao in a powerful economic position.

At the beginning of the 20th century, commercial and industrial companies such as Euskaladuna, Aurora and Polar Insurance, the Bank of Bilbao, Hidroelectrica Española, Naviera Aznar, and Compañia Maritima of Nervion, together with high-class residential development, grew up around the centre of the city. Over the years, the gradual expansion of the centre has led to an amalgamation of the outlying areas and the expansion of the centre of the city (Ensanche). This expansion, approved in 1876, connects both sides of the Nervion, which became a symbol of the city's industrial landscape. The river divides the city in two and, as such, is the centre-piece of the whole area. The industrialization process not only affected the city physically,

Table 8.1.   Evolution of the population of Bilbao, 1981–1991.

1981	1986	1991	Variation 81/91
393,759	381,506	369,839	–6.1

Source: EUSTAT: Censos de Poblacion and Padrones Municipales.

but led also to the socio-spatial division of the population, with the working-class population situated on the 'left side' of the river, while the business and residential areas were located around the centre of the city and on the 'right side' of the river.

In the 1960s and the 1970s, Bilbao was characterized by rapid industrialization, population growth and unplanned urban develop-ment. During this period the city enjoyed virtually full employment and the highest levels of *per capita* income in Spain. However, the world recession of the 1970s, the loss of jobs to new technology and to low-wage economies, and concerns about investment in the Basque Country because of fears of terrorism, have undermined the local economy with profound effects on the social structure. In the period 1976–1985, 37% of the city's industrial jobs were lost. At its peak in 1986, the unemployment rate in Bilbao stood at 25% and still remains high. According to the Deiker Institute at the city's Deusto University, this deindustrialization process has produced an unemployment rate of more than 50% for those under 25, and 14% of population suffering severe poverty (*Deia*, 11 October 1994). Furthermore, the city itself (see Table 8.1) and the Metropolitan Area have both experienced popu-lation loss and outward migration. This rapid and radical reversal of fortunes has been alleviated only by the city's continuing role as the financial capital for the north of Spain, providing the service base on which regeneration strategies have been constructed.

In cultural terms Bilbao forms, along with San Sebastian and Vitnoria, a key feature of Basque identity. When the new Spanish Constitution came into effect in 1978 after the death of Franco, it awarded special status among the autonomous communities to the Basque Country, as well as creating three tiers of government within the Autonomous Community: the Basque Government itself, the (historic) Provinces – roughly county areas (Bilbao falls within the Province of Bizkaia) – and the local districts. The city of Bilbao is one of 30 district authorities in the Metropolitan Area of Bilbao. Although each of these three tiers of government is controlled by coalitions which incorporate the centre right Basque Nationalist Party (PNV), competencies are not always clearly defined (in particular in relation to the fields of urban planning and culture) for the Autonomous Community, the Province and the District Councils, and there is considerable rivalry and tension between each of the tiers.

The case study of the urban regeneration process in Bilbao focuses on the activities surrounding five key events. The first relates to the development of a *Strategic Plan for Metropolitan Bilbao* produced by the Basque Government and the Bizkaia County Council, but which excluded the City Council from its deliberations. As a consequence, during the period 1987–1990, when Mayor Gorordo was in power, the Bilbao City Council developed a second, alternative, approach to urban development, which when rejected forced his resignation in 1990. The third key event was the establishment of a private–public partnership, Bilbao Metropoli 30, in 1991. This was a coalition of the 30 local authorities of the Metropolitan Area which includes the City of Bilbao, in partnership with the Basque Government, the province of Bizkaia and the private sector. This association was launched to implement the *Strategic Plan for Metropolitan Bilbao* which Gorordo had opposed. The fourth event was the establishment of an organization akin to an urban development corporation, Bilbao Ria 2000 (in 1993), by the Spanish State in conjunction with the local authorities. This organization was responsible for developing two important sites in the city, the Abandoibarra site on the waterfront and Amézola in the interior of the city, and finally, the same year, the fifth key element, a City Urban Plan was approved.

The material presented below relates to an analysis of urban policy in Bilbao over the 1980s and 1990s but focusing on the period of the late 1980s to 1995. Fieldwork was undertaken in Bilbao over the period December to February 1995/96. The key generic research questions related to the identification:

- of strategies for urban regeneration which have been considered;
- of strategies which have been adopted;
- of the rationales for adopting particular strategic options;
- of the groups involved and the tactics employed.

More specifically the research focused on the role of leisure, culture and in particular sport, in the regeneration strategies.

Having identified critical events in the attempts at developing reconstruction plans for the city, a series of in-depth, semi-structured interviews were undertaken with key personnel in organizations implicated in the process. The network of respondents interviewed included Bilbao city councillors, particularly those responsible for the Department of Urban Planning, the Department of Youth, Women and Sports, and the Department of Culture; the politicians, representatives of all political parties on the Bilbao City Council; council officers, particularly those from the Department of Youth, Women and Sports; Bizkaia County Council's officer with responsibility for sport within the Department of Culture; representatives of business groups involved; representatives of the Bilbao Chamber of Commerce; board members of the two associations

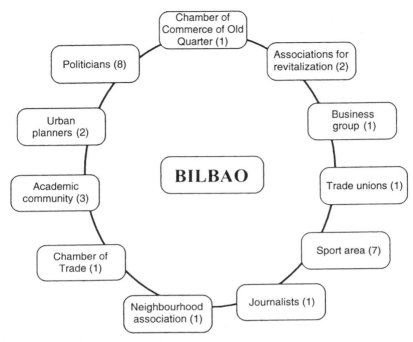

Fig. 8.1. Bilbao interview sample.

for revitalization (Bilbao Metropoli 30 and Bilbao Ria 2000); a representative from local trade unions; representatives from the voluntary sector in the city; representatives of the academic community; a journalist from one of the daily newspapers in Bilbao; and urban planners (see Figure 8.1). In addition to interviews, documentary analysis of materials produced by the local authorities, Bilbao Metropoli 30 and Bilbao Ria 2000, press coverage by local and regional press, policy analysis by independent academic commentators, and central government reports was undertaken.

Approaches to the Regeneration of Bilbao

Despite the assertion that successful contemporary urban governance requires partnership with the private sector in particular, the urban regime underlying development in the case of Bilbao is dominated by the public sector. In effect, the strategies and organizational coalitions developed reflect interorganizational rivalries between tiers of local/ autonomous community government, and between political parties at the local and the Basque Country levels. As we have noted, the material manifestations of the urban regime and the struggle to shape it fall into four distinct projects.

The first is the initiation of a *Strategic Plan for Metropolitan Bilbao* in 1989. This was the product of the Diputaciòn or County Council of Bizkaia, together with the Basque Government. These two levels of government – with little or no consultation with the Bilbao City Council, which forms only part of the Metropolitan Area – produced a strategy for the regeneration of Greater Bilbao. The Strategy essentially revolved around building upon Bilbao's prominent position in the economy of Northern Spain and the Basque Country, to establish itself as a financial and service sector capital in the Atlantic arc of Northern Europe. The strategy was to be spelt out more fully in 1991 following the creation of Bilbao Metropoli 30, a public–private partnership organization with a strategy development function. However, one of the key features of the Plan was the proposal to build a cultural icon, a symbol of Bilbao's regeneration, and something which would declare it as a player in the global field of economic and cultural relations. The Basque Government therefore entered into negotiations with the Guggenheim Foundation, based in New York, to agree the siting of a new European Guggenheim Museum on Bilbao's river-front, negotiations which were successfully concluded in 1990.

The exclusion of the City Council from this process produced a rapid response from the City. Local politicians were concerned about the lack of consultation, the lack of a social dimension to the plan, and the development of a flagship project, the Guggenheim, which had little or nothing to do with Basque identity. The development of the revitalization plan had been entrusted to the Arthur Andersen Consultancy, and the Mayor of the City, Gorordo (a PNV, i.e. a nationalist conservative politician), argued strongly for an approach which more clearly reflected the Basque character of the city. A proposal was put forward for an alternative cultural centre-piece, the building of a 'glass cube' on top of the Alhondiga, a large, stylish and historic building, a former wine store in the centre of the city. The symbolic function of this new building which was to be the tallest in the city, exceeding the height of the Bilbao Bizkaia Bank, was a fusion of the historic (the old winery) and the new (the glass cube), to be designed by a Basque architect. Arguments raged over the relative merits of the two proposals, and Gorordo staked his political career on the building of the cube. He threatened to resign if the City Council would not back his plan, and did so in 1990.

The second stage in the process was the establishing of Bilbao Metropoli 30, a partnership organization which took on the role of developing the strategy for the Metropolitan Area. The organization was established in 1991 by which time it had been recognized that a joint approach, which involved not only the commercial and voluntary sectors but also would involve in partnership all the public sector organizations, was the only likely recipe for progressing plans. The Bilbao Metropoli 30 strategy identified seven key areas to develop:

- investment in human resources;
- a service-based Metropolitan Area in an industrial region;
- mobility and accessibility, the development of an effective transport infrastructure;
- recovery of the environment;
- urban renewal;
- Bilbao as a cultural centre;
- coordination of governmental and private sectors.

Although the organization incorporated local authorities in the Bilbao Metropolitan area, the County Council, and the Basque Government, it did not involve the Spanish Government. Furthermore, those local councils which were not controlled by PNV (the nationalist conservative) tended to take little part since social planning was sacrificed to economic development priorities, and the focus of the plan was on the centre of Bilbao, and in particular on two sites, Abandoibarra (where the Guggenheim Museum and a Convention Centre were to occupy parts of the waterfront site, owned respectively by the Basque Government and the Bizkaia County Council), and the Amézola site. Both sites were owned by the Spanish central state (except for the Guggenheim and the Convention Centre), having been formerly used by government-owned enterprises. Ownership of the land, as we shall see, was to become a key issue.

Although the organization Bilbao Metropoli 30 was only in fact a planning body, that is it took no responsibility for developing projects, and although it incorporated private sector organizations, it was not very successful in attracting private sector funding either for its own running costs (which were in the early years 80% met by public funds) or for the projects which it promoted for development. Nevertheless, having begun with 19 organizations as its membership in 1991, it had risen to a membership of 126 by 1996, including public sector bodies, the universities, business groups and voluntary sector bodies such as the Red Cross.

The seven priorities cited in the strategy were added to in 1993 when, following the pressure of adverse publicity and lobbying by particular local authorities, social development of the Metropolitan Area was cited as an eighth theme. Notwithstanding this new theme, little action has been taken to foster local social development through the actions of Bilbao Metropoli 30.

The third initiative was the establishing of Bilbao Ria 2000. This was created in 1993 and involved partners from Central Government,

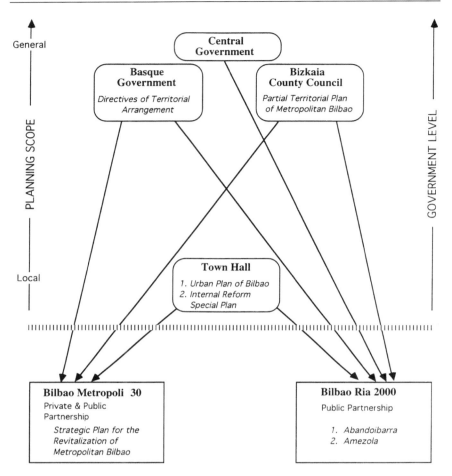

Fig. 8.2. Framework of the Urban Regeneration of Bilbao, including organizations, levels of government and levels of urban planning.

the Basque Government, the Diputaciòn (County Council) and the City Council. The primary thrust of Bilbao Ria 2000 is to generate appropriate infrastructure on two sites, Abandoibarra and Amézola, in terms of transport, office space, etc., to allow regeneration plans to be fostered. The development of this initiative began with Central Government which launched a programme on the Coordination of Action in Cities (following the aid given in 1992 to Barcelona and Seville with the Olympics and Expo) so that cities like Madrid, Bilbao and Oviedo would benefit. Figure 8.2 shows the membership of, and sources of funding for, Bilbao Ria 2000, with 50% of funding from central and 50% from all three levels of local government. Whereas

Bilbao Metropoli 30's function was seen to be the promotion of the Metropolitan Area and of projects for revitalization, Bilbao Ria 2000's function is management of infrastructure change.

Criticisms of Bilbao Ria 2000 echo those addressed at Bilbao Metropoli 30, that is they relate to the geographical centralization of plans on central Bilbao, and the economic focus of the plans with little or no consideration given to social improvement in the city or the wider metropolitan area. More recently there have been proposals to promote development in Barakaldo, a local authority in the Metropolitan Area, neighbouring the City of Bilbao, and lying on the deindustrializing left bank of the river. Such proposals have been insufficient to deflect criticisms about the lack of accountability and lack of social concern of Bilbao Rio 2000.

The fourth initiative in the process of urban revitalization has been the publishing in 1993 of the City Council's own plan for the development of the area under its own jurisdiction. The City Plan certainly does have a social dimension to it. It seeks to enhance the quality of life by, for example, promoting new housing and leisure opportunities for the local population, rather than focusing on attracting inward investment. The plan incorporates economic development proposals, but does so alongside proposals for the physical development of the city (with plans, for example, to promote green space) and the social development of the city with plans for investment in sporting and cultural infrastructure.

However, the funding of social, cultural and physical development in the city is dependent upon the income from economic development activities. In particular, the plan focuses on the development of office space on the Abandoibarra site to fund such schemes as an athletics stadium just outside the city, and a sports stadium in the Alhondiga wine store. Unfortunately, there are problems with this strategy. The city may, in fact, already be over-stocked with office accommodation, but even if this were not the case, the Abandoibarra site (together with the Amézola site) are owned by Central Government which refused to grant the land to the city without payment. Thus the city's proposals for social development are frustrated by virtue of the rivalry between the Central State (controlled by the Socialist Party – PSOE) and the city (PNV-led coalition). It remains to be seen whether the recent change of government will affect this policy.

Sport, Leisure and Urban Regeneration

Just as with planning and cultural policy, responsibility for sports policy is spread across the Diputación and the Town Hall. Funding to sports federations and individual sports organizations is undertaken predominantly by the Diputación; provision of sporting facilities and funding of sporting events is primarily the responsibility of the Town Hall.

In terms of playing a role in the Bilbao Metropoli 30 *Strategic Plan for Metropolitan Bilbao*, sport initially played little part:

> Initially, tourism and sport were not part of the Strategic Plan. The Plan focused on seven or eight areas only to ensure objectives could be met. Later on, tourism and leisure initiatives were included within some areas of the Plan. For example, Urban Renewal Plans include sports facilities, Human Resources Plans consider the relationship between leisure and education, Cultural Plans consider the relationship between hotels and culture.
> *(Interview with representative of Bilbao Metropoli 30, February 1996)*

Culture is rather different from sport in the sense that the construction of a cultural centre-piece for the city was a key element of the regeneration strategy. Culture is significant in the context of Bilbao and the Basque Country not simply as an attraction of inward investment, it is also significant as (potentially at least) a symbol of Basque nationalism. Although parallel arguments could be made in respect of sport, in fact such links have not been made. Certainly Basque Sports are funded, both by the city and by the Diputación, as an aspect of cultural policy. However, élite sports are not supported as a means of city marketing, and Bilbao is regarded as unusual in this respect. There is a tradition of sports sponsorship by municipalities and the semi-public sector bodies (especially the banks). Both politicians from PSOE (the Socialists) and HB (the radical left nationalist party) explained the failure of the city's basketball team to gain promotion to the first division as reflecting a lack of financial support from the public sector, particularly the Town Hall, while a representative of the Sports Federation for Bizkaia (ASFEDEBI) pointed in addition to the financial difficulties of the city's water polo national league team, and the folding of the women's handball team which had competed at national level, as stemming from Bilbao's parsimony in support for élite sport.

The city's priority in terms of sport was said to be 'sport for all' but all parties recognized the city's lack of facilities both in absolute terms, and in comparison with surrounding municipalities in the Metropolitan Area. Furthermore, although there were said to be concessions for use of what municipal facilities there were by clubs, the Sports Federation (AFEDEVI) complained that charges were such that some sports clubs were effectively priced out of facilities. The political group of PNV (nationalist centre right) in the Town Hall were also criticized for failing to acknowledge the relationship between sport for all and élite sport provision by representatives of the Socialist Group.

In fact, élite culture and sports events contribute to the promotion of sport for all and popular culture. Here the PNV ideology does not consider this relationship. It will be necessary to attract sports events to the city. Maybe after the Guggenheim Museum and the Euskalduna (the Convention Centre), sport will be considered more seriously as a way of promoting and marketing the city.

(Representative of PSOE, interview February 1996)

The funding of the Guggenheim Project and associated élite cultural forms appears to have had a considerable effect on the funds available not simply to élite sport projects and to capital projects, but also to revenue funding of sport for all on the part of the Diputación. Sport is funded under two headings of 'sport' and 'youth and community action' and these two combined budgets actually fell in the period 1989–1993 by 33%, while the total cultural budget grew by 47%, much of this growth being attributable to the Guggenheim itself (museum and exhibition funding grew by more than 400% in the period 1991–1993) (Bilbao Metropoli 30, 1993:185).

Despite the generally recognized lack of facilities for sport in the city, the Town Hall's own urban plan was not seen as giving the matter real prominence. There was some discussion at a political level of converting the Alhondiga wine store into a sports stadium, and to covering the bullfighting arena, as well as to building a sports stadium on Artxanda, on top of the hills overlooking the city. However, all plans were predicated upon selling office space or commercial activity space on the Abandoibarra site and, since this remained in the hands of Central Government agencies, development of sporting facilities were unlikely to progress past the 'wish list' stage.

Conclusions

The basis of this chapter has been a discussion of how an urban regime has been established in Bilbao, what its goals have been, and how it has gone about achieving them. It is made abundantly clear by a number of respondents that authorities in Bilbao have been greatly influenced by 'the American model' (perceived primarily as a single, unified approach), with reference to Pittsburgh and Baltimore as examples. The situation in Bilbao is, however, markedly different. The first point to emphasize is that unlike the reported American cases, the regeneration process in Bilbao is rather less a public–private partnership than it is a phenomenon led by the public sector. Bilbao Metropoli 30 as a strategy development agency represents public and private sectors, and its strategy is founded on a private-sector consultancy report by Arthur Andersen Consultants, commissioned by the Diputación and the Basque

Table 8.2. Strategic projects of Bilbao: estimated costs.

Strategic projects	Cost (million pesetas)	Architects
1. Airport	10,000	S. Calatrava
2. Harbour: phase 1:	36,000	
phase 2:	66,000	
3. Underground: line 1:	70,000	N. Foster
line 2:	40,000	
4. Southern by-pass	12,000	
5. RENFE freight terminal	4,500	
6. New railway access to the harbour	5,000	
7. Bilbao passenger interchange	40,000	M. Wildford
8. Guggenheim Museum	20,000	F.O. Gehry
10. Conference and music centre	6,000	F. Soriano and D. Palacios
11. Development of Abandoibarra	5,000	
12. Euskalduna bridge	2,500	
13. Development of Amézola	3,000	
Total	320,000	

Source: Ortega (1995:242) and Bilbao Metropoli 30 (1993).

Government. However, involvement of the private sector in developing strategy has not been complemented by involvement of the private sector in strategy implementation. Table 8.2 cites the major projects developed in the Metropolitan Area and, with the exception of the Guggenheim Museum, all are public-sector dominated in investment terms.

If one defining feature of the urban regime in Bilbao is that it is public-sector-led, a second is that it is characterized by relatively intense rivalry between the four levels of government. This sometimes represents inter-party rivalry, as when cooperation between the socialist-led Central Government and local Basque levels has been limited. The major derelict sites in the city belong, via nationalized industries, to Central Government who will not release these to the city for development. However, the struggles between tiers of government cannot simply be reduced to inter-party rivalries. The PNV is a member of the dominant coalition at city, Diputación and Basque Country levels, yet local opposition to the Metropolitan Area Strategy and its centre-piece, the Guggenheim, was led by the PNV Mayor Gorordo. It has to be remembered that this governmental arrangement is still fairly young and that the relative powers and responsibilities of each of the tiers are still subject to considerable debate.

A further complicating local feature is the significance of issues of culture for the Basque Community. In effect, embracing the globalizing tendencies of inter-city competition was planned around a cultural centre-piece which owed its identity to New York rather more than to the Basque Country. Planners refer to Manhattanization in the Bilbao context (Gonzalez, 1993) but such features of cultural identity are not uncontested. They are in fact contested at two levels. Firstly, as with Gorordo's plan to develop a cultural edifice on the Alhondiga site, they are contested as non-Basque: Gorordo wished to focus on a traditional Bilbao landmark (and to use a Basque architect). Second, such proposals do not reflect the cultural concerns of residents: they are aimed at producing cultural attractions for the new service class rather than for the indigenous population of Bilbao.

The role of sport in the policy process was an important focus of the research. Despite the potential of sport for urban reimaging processes, the city was seen by political and sporting proponents alike as standing out in its failure to subsidize professional/élite teams. The sole major national league team in the city is Athletic de Bilbao, which occupies a profound place in the identity of the city and the Basque Country. Its proud refusal to select any non-Basque players, however, ties it to a traditional sense of Basque identity rather than to a 'modern' identity. Some of the 'new', 'exciting', hyped sports, such as basketball, volleyball, handball and the like, which have enjoyed increased professionalization and media coverage in recent years are thus absent from the portfolio of sports associated with Bilbao.

Support for Basque Sports and for other sporting federations is provided by the city and in particular by the Diputación. However, facilities for both 'sport for all' and for élite sport are relatively sparse in the city, even compared with other, smaller neighbouring authorities within the Bilbao Metropolitan area. To make matters worse, the sporting budget of the Diputación, at least, is suppressed by virtue of the costs of providing for the Guggenheim Project.

In terms of Stoker and Mossberger's (1994) typology of urban regimes, Bilbao's case represents aspects of 'instrumental' and 'symbolic' regimes. It is an instrumental regime in that its project is to restructure the economy of Bilbao, replacing traditional industries by attracting service- and information-based investment into the city. It is symbolic in that it seeks to change the identity of the city. The symbolic change has been contested – as being constructed without reference to local people, and as failing to account for 'local' identity. The hegemony of the regime has thus been under challenge – as an instrumental regime for failing as yet to attract significant commercial inward investment, and as a symbolic regime for promoting an inappropriate or non-democratically derived identity for the city – but the ability of critics of the regime to mobilize alternative strategies has been barely evident in the city during the development of these strategies.

References

Bacharach, P. and Baratz, M. (1970) *Power and Poverty: Theory and Practice.* Oxford University Press, New York.

Bauman, Z. (1992) *Intimations of Postmodernity.* Routledge, London.

Bilbao Metropoli 30 (1993) *Sistema de Indicadores de Revitalizacion del Bilbao Metropolitano 1993.* Bilbao.

Bilbao Ria 2000 (1994) *Bilbao Ria 2000* (promotional document published by Bilbao Ria 2000).

Castells, M. (1978) *The Urban Question.* Arnold, London

Cockburn, C. (1977) *The Local State.* Pluto, London.

Dahl, R. (1961) *Who Governs? Democracy and Power in an American City.* Yale University Press, New Haven.

Defrance, J. and Pociello, C. (1993) Structure and evolution of the field of sports in France (1960–1990): a 'functional', historical and prospective analystical essay. *International Review of the Sociology of Sport* 28(1) 1–21.

Duncan, S. and Goodwin, M. (1988) *The Local State and Uneven Development.* Polity, Oxford.

Featherstone, M. (1991) *Consumer Culture and Post-modernism.* Sage, London.

Galès, P. (1995) Du gouvernment des villes à la gouvernance urbaine. *Revue Française de Science Politique* 45(1), 57–95.

Gonzalez, J. (1993) Bilbao: culture, citizenship and quality of life. In: Bianchini, F. and Parkinson, M. *Cultural Policy and Urban Regeneration: The West European Experience.* Manchester University Press.

Hunter, F. (1953) *Community Power Structures: a Study of Decision Makers.* University of North Carolina Press, Chapel Hill.

Judge, D. (1995) Pluralism. In: Judge, D., Stoker, G. and Wolman, H. *Theories of Urban Politics.* Sage, London.

Logan, J. and Molotch, H. (1987) *Urban Fortunes: the Political Economy of Place.* University of California Press, Berkeley.

Ortega, H. (1995) *Bilbao a la Deriva: Fantasia, Especulacion y Ciudadania.* Txalaparta.

Polsby, N. (1980) *Political Power and Political Theory*, 2nd edn. Yale University Press, New Haven.

Rojek, C. (1995) *Decentring Leisure: Rethinking Leisure Theory.* Sage, London.

Ross, B., Levine, M. and Stedman, S. (1991) *Urban Politics: Power in Metropolitan America.* Peacock Publishers, Illinois.

Stoker, G. and Mossberger, K. (1994) Urban regime theory in comparative perspective. *Government and Policy* 12, 195–212.

Stone, C. (1989) *Regime Politics: Governing Atlanta, 1946–1988.* University Press of Arkansas, Lawrence.

Stone, C. (1993) Urban regimes and the capacity to govern: a political economy approach. *Journal of Urban Affairs* 15, 1–28.

Urban Leisure: Edge City and the New Leisure Periphery

9

Graeme Evans

Director – Centre for Leisure and Tourism Studies, University of North London, Stapleton House, 277–281 Holloway Road, London N7 8HN, UK

Introduction

In the planning and development of urban leisure provision, cities and, increasingly, regions fulfil three distinct and often conflicting roles: the traditional service role as providers of recreational needs for its citizens; as generators of recreational demand upon both the city and wider region; and as destinations for incoming visitors – day-trippers, tourists, both domestic and from overseas (Burtenshaw *et al.*, 1991). In larger urban centres, the definition of 'citizens' and the typology of 'tourists' also present a complex profile from which to assess needs and demands and successfully allocate resources, plan land use and manage provision and development. In metropolitan cities, for example, in-coming commuters mingle with residents and a host of short-term and long-term visitors, from students, business and trade exchange, to family-visitors, day-trippers and holiday-makers.

Travel and movement are therefore central to the spatial and related temporal implications of post-industrial urban society and its leisure. Another key factor arising from the services-based economy evolving since the late 1970s has been the flexibility and fragmentation of working hours, particularly the growth of part-time working and extended opening times, which have removed the traditional separation between day and evening, weekday and weekend, meal times and play times. Responses and enabling legislation contribute to this situation, including the liberalization of licensing hours and admittance of children, Sunday trading, late-night shopping and experiments with club and food licences towards the '24-hour city'.

© CAB INTERNATIONAL 1998. *Leisure Management: Issues and Applications*
(eds M.F. Collins and I.S. Cooper)

Urban Fringe and 'Edge City'

Leisure developments that have both fuelled and responded to this change in time–space demand and supply include the growth of out-of-town and urban fringe centres – often combining leisure, travel and entertainment with retailing – and the commodification of traditional countryside/park. All of this now exists alongside and in competition with home-based and neighbourhood recreation and consumption. One impact from these commercial and public–private partnership developments has been on the workers who service these relocated and all-hours centres. In fact, the market responses to the change in leisure time and space usage have fuelled further fragmentation of leisure time, social atomization and the separation between work, non-work and play, particularly between genders and family groups, and between inner-urban and outer-urban communities.

Urban policy and planning – once dominated by the zoned separation of work, domestic and leisure activity (Clarke and Critcher, 1985; Seabrook, 1988) and a spatial approach to economic development and recreational green space or *lungs* (Abercrombie, 1944) – has therefore had to redefine itself in post-industrial society, where traditional work space, travel-corridors and work–leisure trade-offs no longer apply (Becker, 1965; Gorz, 1989). Castells (1977) defines 'spatial structures' as the particular way in which the basic elements of social structure are spatially articulated; however, the socialist Weberian separation of the economic from other aspects of society no longer holds true in the contemporary urban environment, and certainly not in terms of cultural consumption and leisure behaviour. Technology-induced 'fortress homes' (Henley Centre, 1985, 1990) and the tourist wanderlust present two extremes of this contemporary spatial dimension, and extended commuting and home-based working another. Planning as a historically spatial and normative process has had to adjust to this continuity and change, where culture is consumed (and produced) at home, on holiday (Richards, 1994) and in retail and entertainment centres.

A feature of the 1980s property-led leisure boom was the out-of-town leisure scheme, ranging from multiplex cinemas, theme parks and leisure–retail centres, through to extended heritage attractions and countryside recreation. More recently in the 1990s, computer-branded virtual reality and games centres have transferred the home-based computer technology to the leisure–retail experience. Almost all such developments were planned primarily for the car-borne visitor and require sufficient land, access and scale to achieve commercial viability (even when not-for-profit, or semi-commercial ventures such as stately homes, gardens and independent museums). As Grant observes, this is partly due to land-use planning and economics:

> Out-of-town leisure . . . the relatively land-hungry traffic-intensive forms of development which are forced (or it is more suitable) to locate beyond the areas of city-centre property premiums. Land availability and permissions for development . . . obviously also play a role.
>
> (Grant, 1990:4.4)

Town and city planners, including leisure planners and cultural interventionists, have countered with a renaissance in town and city-centre cultural life, as civic authorities seek to salvage identity, employment and community, against urban decline and fragmentation in the shadow of globalization and post-Fordist forces. A timely recognition of the circle having turned against 'out-of-town' is seen in the UK Environment Minister's proposed revision to Planning Policy Guidance Notes (DoE, 1996, PPGs Nos 1,6 and 13) exhorting local authorities to look favourably on developments that include a mixture of shops, housing, offices and cultural facilities: 'Different but complementary uses during the day and in the evening could reinforce each other, making town centres more attractive to residents, businesses, shoppers and visitors' (Gummer in Walter, 1995:46; and see Comedia Ltd, 1991). However, whilst public policy and planning guidelines seek to revive and rescue urban and town centres, commercial development practice and imperatives continue to focus on the pleasure periphery – urban fringe and 'green belt' areas – for the location of leisure and entertainment centres. In fact in the UK there will be more new out-of-town shopping centres opened in the 1990s than in the planning-liberalized 1980s. Significantly, since the US 'edge city' and mall developments have served as the dominant model in the UK, North American developers are active in both leisure, entertainment and out-of-town leisure 'parks and villages' in the UK.

The Changing Pattern of Cultural Consumption

The 1980s have seen the scale and map of leisure activity shift dramatically due to social, economic, technological and demographic changes, particularly in urban/fringe areas. The growth in leisure time and spending also saw a range of new and recreated leisure experiences and patterns of behaviour and consumption, impacting on holidays, museums and heritage sites, entertainment centres, and sport – formal and informal. This was a case of continuity and change, with switching and substitution between leisure and other consumption, and the transference of time and location of leisure activity. This has all taken place within an underlying growth in leisure participation, albeit unevenly distributed amongst social and income groups. One observation from this period, which also saw greater expansion of leisure time and conspicuous consumption, was that leisure consumption was no longer peripheral, or a luxury activity (the cost of holidays, leisurewear, aerobics and entertainment now form part of the Retail Price Index representative 'basket of items' for household spending). This has meant that such activity is valued (or at least measured) to a greater extent, i.e. people are less inclined to do less or give up such activities in time of recession, preferring to do without other pursuits and expenditure (Henley Centre, 1990).

Whilst economic and employment insecurity has exacerbated the depression in consumer spending generally, leisure has slightly increased as a proportion of household spending over the last 10 years (MINTEL, 1995). None the less, leisure spending has of course suffered significantly during the prolonged recession, with switching to low-cost and 'safe' activities (for example, from theatre/drama to cinema, eating in versus out, low-stake gambling to lottery). This recession has been most acute in the south-east of England with the loss of white- and blue-collar jobs, rationalization in financial and retail services (including the new out-of-town shopping sector), contracting-out and public expenditure/sector decline, which have all led to general job insecurity, part-time working, deskilling and a halt to the decrease in hours worked (Martin and Mason, 1994) – the beginning of the end to the new 'leisure society' (Gorz, 1989).

The changing economic and employment situation has also influenced the temporal and spatial aspects of leisure and cultural consumption, reflected in the need for flexible and extended availability of facilities, services and retailing – manifested in Sunday trading, longer licensing hours, late-night shopping, 'home shopping' and moves towards a 24-hour city. The divide between leisure 'haves' (but with less time) and 'have nots' (time but no money) is widening, with greater pressure for value from precious leisure spending and time (Gorz, 1989). This has particularly affected weekend activity and programming of facilities (e.g. peak, off-peak). A particular shift since the 1980s has been a preference (and imperative) for more time-intensive activities (e.g. visiting homes and gardens, museums), as opposed to money-intensive (e.g. expensive meals, theatre, private health clubs), with implications for time – travel and cost and length of 'stay' at a facility – and therefore the location and range of leisure services and programmes (see Table 9.1).

Table 9.1. New patterns of leisure activity for the late 1990s.

Growing importance	Declining importance
Flexibility in work and leisure time	Traditional working week, holidays, career
Part-time working	Full-time employment
Voluntary work	Expensive professional entertainment
Productive/creative forms of leisure	Casual eating and drinking away from home
Education for and in leisure	Time structuring outings
Time-intensive activities	Money-intensive activities

Source: Leisure Consultants, 1995.

Table 9.2. Consumer expenditure – annual percentage change.

Activity	1993	1994	1995	Forecast 1996	Forecast 1997
Cinema	+9	+4	+1	+2.3	+3.6
Live arts	-1	nil	-0.8		
Spectator sport	nil	+1	nil	+4	+5
Sightseeing	+4	+5	+2		

Source: Leisure Consultants, 1995, 1996.

Home and Away

As the annual change of spending 'out of home' shows in Table 9.2, live arts and entertainment and charged-for leisure facilities have been the worst hit in recent years (Evans, 1996), whilst cinema and visiting stately homes, gardens, heritage attractions, have been the most recession-proof (Henley Centre, 1990).

Urban change – social, environmental (land use, housing), demographic and economic – has also reinforced the divide between the home-based and out-of-home activity. At the same time, active leisure and passive consumption, particularly in out-of-home based activity, increasingly compete with each other. Whilst the stay-at-home preference has been facilitated by social changes and technology (fuelled by home comforts, such as central heating and computers) and the perceived barriers to out-of-home leisure, this has also added value to the desire for (or at least the promotion of) more active pursuits in opposition to the 'couch potato' syndrome. Factors influencing cultural and leisure participation show the growing importance of both private and public transport (Table 9.3). Transport and environmental factors are therefore key to maintaining and expanding usage of facilities and event programmes.

Outside local catchments, leisure-day visits are defined as trips (over 20 miles) made for leisure, cultural and entertainment purposes and of

Table 9.3. Factors influencing cultural and leisure participation.

	% saying 'yes'	
Would you spend more time in away-from-home activities if:	1990	1985
Cultural facilities were more to your liking (comfort, convenience, atmosphere)?	65	55
Facilities catered for the whole family?	58	56
The streets were safer?	54	54
Better parking facilities were available?	43	29
Facilities for a variety of activities were in one small area?	44	41
Better public transport was available?	36	28
Better baby-sitting facilities were available?	24	20

Source: Henley Centre 1990; 1985.

over 3 hours' duration. 'Leisure shopping' dominates, with over 85% as the main purpose of non-regular visits, followed by cinema/theatre and dancing as the most frequently cited motivations to visit urban/fringe centres (OPCS, 1992), while active sports participation accounted for only 25% of such day-trips. Women are twice as likely to undertake leisure day-visits for shopping and for entertainment than men. The appeal of urban fringe and out-of-town leisure activity is of course not new: countryside and mountains have served industrial urban populations and conurbations from the lakes, peaks and dales, to country parks and seaside resorts.

The difference today is the lack of contrast between urban society's recreation and home-based, everyday consumption, and the integration of consumption with 'leisure' activity itself – epitomized in the fusion of 'leisure shopping', i.e. commodification. Modes of transport have also seen the dominance of the collective experience of the train or bus usurped by the individualistic private car – the replacement of the railway with the motorway. Despite this, the day-trip still maintains some special place:

> So long as they can return home the same day, people like to get out of the urban environment. The distance heightens their anticipation, and many regard the journey out from the city – whether by car or other forms of transport – as an important part of the day out.
>
> (Grant, 1991: Section 4.5)

The role and function of the private car is of course fundamental to the realization of this spatial and temporal shift in leisure consumption. Travel distances undertaken and tolerated for differing leisure activities have always varied, and have been influenced by a hierarchy of public provision, particularly parks, libraries, sports and play facilities, as well as arts and entertainment and retail and other amenities. The latter facilities have tended to attract a wider catchment, as Veal (1982) and others established. This travel preference, however, is also determined by supply, past inheritance of facilities, and the inconsistent application of standards or norms of provision between a range of public and private and leisure activities (Evans, 1995). None the less, higher scale facilities and time-intensive pursuits both require and attract a wider travel area:

> The car-borne day visitor may travel some 30 to 60 kilometres for general day recreation but twice that for more specialized pursuits or for weekend activities, thus extending the city's recreational hinterland beyond the sports facilities of the rural–urban fringe and the picnic sites around the conurbations into a 'weekending zone' of second homes, yachtsmen's cottages, camp & caravan sites.
>
> (Burtenshaw *et al.*, 1991:193)

The primacy of the car and the conflicts arising from increased visits to the countryside from urban areas is now a major preoccupation of countryside and conservation agencies, as well as country parks and incumbent local authorities. In discussing future demand for leisure, Veal (1993, 1994) suggests that major changes in car ownership, which might affect leisure demand, seem unlikely. However, the forecasts of car ownership and usage suggest otherwise – car ownership in the UK more than doubled between 1965 and 1995 and the Department of Transport forecasts further growth of between 50% and 80% over the next 30 years (DoT, 1996). On rural roads, overall traffic growth could increase proportionately more – by 127–267% (Countryside Commission, 1992). The out-of-town leisure trend is not the sole cause of such growth, since 60% of car journeys are shorter than 5 miles, and nearly 70% of short trips are between 1 and 2 miles, from taking children to school, to local work, shopping and recreation trips – displacing walking, cycling and public transport usage.

Barriers to out-of-home activity are indicated above (Table 9.3), with safety and public transport of increasing concern. The incidence of car ownership has therefore become a major determinant of leisure participation, access and equity – where public and 'partnership' leisure developments are located in urban fringe and other out-of-town sites (see below), like the commercial leisure and entertainment developments they seek to emulate. Access from non-car owners is largely denied, unless dedicated transport is available, during daytime and evening. The divide in car ownership is seen, for example, in the Lee Valley Regional Park area straddling north-east London and the home counties of Essex and Hertfordshire. Car ownership in the suburban counties was 75% and rising (OPCS, 1991) whilst in the urban riparian boroughs this was as low as 40% (Evans, 1996).

Leisure Shopping

The attraction of out-of-town shopping, and allied leisure and entertainment activity, has been noted in terms of special day-trips, particularly by women (Wigley and Lowe, 1996). In 1994 10% of *all* leisure day-visits cited leisure shopping as the main purpose (OPCS, 1996:vii). A history of the out-of-town shopping centre and 'mall' is beyond the scope here; however, it is interesting to note that the first such development is acknowledged to be the Country Club Plaza, built in Kansas City by J.C. Nichols in 1922. Nichols wrote a guide to mall design in 1947 cautioning against modernist designs that might be quickly outdated (the term 'mall' had been derived from the 16th-century Mall of London's St James's Park; the first city department stores of the 19th century were also places to be seen, where *flaneurs* strolled and paraded, and window shopping gained popular acceptance).

The growth of the urban fringe mall continued to shift trade away from city centres, but niche marketing and mail order also bit into the profits of the big stores; between 1985 and 1989 alone, US department stores lost 5% of their revenues to designer and catalogue sales. The close relationship between developers and large store chains has been unsuccessfully resisted in the USA and the UK – preferential rentals, site allocations and the exclusion of discount and independent shops have continued, perpetuating the homogeneity seen in such centres, irrespective of their location or the vernacular of the local area: 'the cities of the future . . . the nearest thing they have to a centre is the Mall, the retail recreation ground that has replaced any form of municipal life' (Lichfield, 1992:8, and Garreau, 1991). The demise of the town centre, seen in major cities in the UK, is reinforced by this formula and by developers' preference. In 1973 a big shopping centre developer told the *New York Times*: 'I wouldn't put a penny downtown. It's bad. Face it, why should people come in? They don't want the hassle, they don't want the danger . . . stay out in the country, that's the new downtown' (in Sudjic, 1993:243).

The original model for the second generation out-of-town shopping centre, Houston's Galleria, opened in 1970 – 'gallerias' now exist in many cities worldwide: in the UK, for example, The Galleria at Hatfield, Hertfordshire, and Hays Galleria, London. These draw on their association with museums and art galleries and combine commerce with culture in a brash and linked environment, often adorned with obligatory 'public art' installations and water features. Urban fringe sites and reclaimed industrial and quarry locations for these retail–leisure centres are rechristened in order to evoke a more peaceful and idyllic association – Chester Oaks, Lakeside, Meadowhall, Merry Hill, Braehead, Bluewater Park, Cribbs Causeway, White Rose.

The largest centre to date, in this trend towards larger and larger complexes, was built in West Edmonton, Alberta in 1983 and blurred shopping with entertainment even further: 'What they offer is a fair which, instead of travelling the world to reach its audience, sits still on one permanent site and waits for its visitors to come to it' (Sudjic, 1993:246). The ultimate one-stop-shop experience and the shopping-centre-as-theme park and EXPO combined. The scale of such developments continues to grow – in Minnesota the 'Mall of America' is under construction, with an enclosed entertainment mall based on Snoopy characters, 800 shops, 18 cinemas, nightclubs, health club, high-rise hotels and a 70-foot-high artificial mountain. It will have 9.5 million square feet of enclosed shopping, entertainment and hotel space – twice that of a city such as Glasgow. Because of its scale, planners expect that people will spend 2 or 3 days there – as well as hotels, there will be mobile-home hook-ups in the car park, which will accommodate 12,750 car spaces.

In the UK, however, aside from the 'zero sum game' of an unplanned national and regional urban policy, there are likely to be clear losers in those town and other centres who lose employers, trade and economic activity to their neighbours, as already experienced in the 'Docklands effect' (DDC, 1990) and by city centres feeling loss of activity to out-of-town shopping and leisure centres, such as Newcastle to the Metro Centre, or Sheffield city centre to Meadowhall. Between 1961 and 1982 the 580,000 shops in Britain declined in number to 332,000 (down 43%), a decline which paralleled the rise of out-of-town shopping and ownership concentration (Davies *et al.*, 1992). Whilst their spatial and economic impact has been considered, the effects on traditional relationships and amenity-use, and the effect on the relocated retail workers and their own leisure, has largely been ignored:

> Where shopper surveys have been undertaken, they have been used to draw conclusions about the loss or deflection of trade from town centres or other economic aspects . . . they have not gone on to indicate how such trade impacts manifest themselves in the social role of town centres.
> (Whitehead, 1992:5)

In 1980 there was a total of 28 million square feet of out-of-town shopping in the UK, with 9 million under construction; in 1988 a total of 158 million square feet was complete, with 24 million under construction – a fivefold increase.

Another manifestation of the leisure, retail and day-trip phenomenon is seen at British airports, notably at London's Heathrow and Gatwick. Like the multiplex cinema, profits from retailing and ancillary trade exceeds their core airport businesses. British Airports Authority (BAA), a privatized near-monopoly, has 600,000 square feet of retail

Table 9.4a. Employment structure 1981–1993.

	Retail employment	
	1981	1993
Male employment	Full-time 639,000 Part-time 131,000 17% of all employed males	Full-time 645,000 Part-time 199,000 24% of all employed males
Female employment	Full-time 582,000 Part-time 697,000 54% of all employed females	Full-time 506,000 Part-time 872,000 63% of all employed females
Retailing as a % of all part-time employment	40%	48%

Table 9.4b. Retailing activity by selected sector 1981–1991 (thousands employed).

Sector	1981	1991	% Change
Food	564	720	+28
Confectioners, off-licences	159	110	−30
Clothing	149	176	+18
Household goods/textiles	197	270	+38
Filling stations	79	61	−22
Mixed businesses	350	293	−17
Other retail	107	205	+93

Table 9.4c. Employment change 1981–1991 by area/type (thousands employed).

Area type	1981	1991	% Change
Inner London	153	143	−7
Principal cities	193	183	−5
Outer London	165	178	+8
Other metropolitan boroughs	287	312	+9
Other cities	292	309	+6
Districts with new towns	98	134	+37
Mixed urban/rural	329	220	+33
Other rural	176	220	+25
Total	2049	2311	+13

Sources for 4a–4c: *Employment Gazette* (including Historical Supplement 3), Department of Employment, 1992; National Online Manpower Information System.

space – the space is auctioned off to retailers every 3 years – with BAA taking a fixed percentage of profits. As aircraft get larger and larger, boarding and waiting times get longer, so passengers are captive shoppers for longer periods (in the jargon, 'dwell time'). Heathrow has four caviare shops and is the largest single outlet for Havana cigars. One in five bus passengers who arrive at these airport shopping villages do not go near an aircraft. Despite the convenience and speed offered by these one-stop-shops, travel time and frequency have both increased – between 1975 and 1991 the average number of shopping trips grew by 28% and the total distance travelled for shopping by 60%. Following the introduction of the National Lottery in Britain, an additional 12 million shopping trips were generated in 1995 (Henley Centre, 1996). In the 1980s people spent an average of 70 minutes a day shopping, compared with 41 minutes in the 1960s (Lang, 1995).

The changed employment structure created by this period of large-scale, urban fringe leisure–retail development is seen in Tables 9.4a to 9.4c. Retailing is now a significant employment sector – 24% of all male and 63% of all female employment (now more a nation of shopworkers than shopkeepers), accounting for 48% of all part-time employment.

UK Employment in Retailing

The nature of retail provision (see Table 9.4b) also shows a radical shift towards the leisure–retail, as well as household goods/textiles, food and clothing, at the cost of local stores such as confectioners, off-licences and petrol stations (a response here is the redevelopment of stations to include food and 24-hour general stores and lottery ticket sites). The regional shift reveals a decline in real terms in London and Wales, with highest retail employment in the South-east, and the developing regions of East Anglia and the South-west, as well as the Midlands and Yorkshire.

The location of these leisure shopping centres is most marked by a decline in inner London and established cities and below-average growth in other metropolitan areas as shown in Table 9.4c, with the prime growth evident in new town districts, urban/rural fringe (e.g. motorway interchange) zones – the new pleasure periphery (Giddens, 1985; Burtenshaw *et al.*, 1991).

Multiplex Cinemas

The multiplex phenomenon epitomizes the out-of-town leisure, retail and entertainment trend that only recent government planning policy

Table 9.5. UK cinemas, screens and multiplexes.

	Cinema admissions (millions)	Number of multiplexes	Number of screens Total	Number of screens Multiplexes	Multiplex screens as % of the total
1985	72	1	1284	10	<1
1989	96	29	1550	285	18
1990	98	41	1673	387	23
1991	102	57	1777	510	29
1992	104	64	1845	562	31
1993	115	70	1890	625	34
1994	125	76	1969	638	36
1995	121	83	2015	732	37
1996 (est.)	130	not available	2165	not available	not available
2000 (est.)	137	not available	2345	not available	not available

Sources: Screen Digest, 1994; Leisure Consultants, 1996.

has sought to reverse. The multiplex has undeniably been a panacea for the film exhibition industry's revival, the 1550 cinema screens in 1989 are estimated to grow to 2345 by the year 2000 (see Table 9.5). In 1995 one of the top three multiplex operators, UCI, saw a 73% rise in takings in the UK over the previous year.

The multiplex is also a prime example of revival in an activity that was in terminal decline due to the popularity of TV, then video, satellite and lately cable, but has been resurrected, not through a fundamental change to the product (i.e. film), but in the environment and overall experience: food franchising and targeting of a wider family market, rather than the core youth audience (Holder, 1996). Like British Airports, multiplexes rely on non-ticket income, with sales of food, 'souvenirs', videos and advertising exceeding the actual cinema entry fee. Catchments require a population of around 300,000 within a 1-hour drive-time to establish a sufficient market for the £5–7 million capital investment, and location and road transport links are therefore fundamental. The apparent choice offered by several screens effectively substitutes for several traditional cinemas and allows for longer runs of films.

In the north London Borough of Enfield, for example, the Lee Valley Regional Park Authority leased a site adjoining their flagship sports and leisure centre at Pickett's Lock to multiplex operator UCI, creating a 12-screen cinema with franchised fast-food outlets (the Park is not empowered itself to operate commercial facilities). The Park's decision to host a multiplex cinema on a 125-year lease was a major departure in policy and planning terms (and outside both the Park and Enfield Borough statutory plans). Attracting an estimated 1 million visits in its first year, usage exceeds the total visitors to the Park's Leisure Centre and Ice Rink combined, both suffering declining usage. Here the core, frequent user includes black and white youth, primarily paying by cash rather than credit card, which is atypical for UCI, although nationally 90% of young people's consumer spending and 60% of adults' is still by cash. Although this multiplex is perhaps atypical (normally they are built on greenfield sites located on urban fringe/motorway interchanges), none the less, the impact on existing local provision was still evident: '. . . the Borough is now served by one cinema where previously there were seven' (Enfield, 1993).

Traditional town centres have been the main victims of such leisure–retail developments, and so has increasingly neighbourhood recreation and community provision (CELTS, 1995), as public authorities focus on flagship and multi-use centres (e.g. leisure pools rather than traditional swimming pools), aping the commercial centres and urban fringe locations. This is seen no more starkly than in the city imaging and urban regeneration strategies, such as in Birmingham, Sheffield, Liverpool and in London boroughs (Loftman and Nevin, 1993; Evans, 1993). In France, however, where the battle against American 'cultural imperialism' has been fought out between the French cinema and Hollywood, the government has stepped in to restrict the growth of large multiplexes. Prior to the opening of a 17-screen, 3000-seat 'Megarama' on the outskirts of Paris, the Culture Minister announced plans to increase subsidies to small town-centre cinemas. The French parliament had just passed a law limiting new multiplex cinemas to 2000 seats. In contrast, the world's third-largest cinema complex is planned for the site of a former power station near Birmingham's infamous Spaghetti Junction, with outline planning permission for a 30-screen development.

The retailing by film production companies has been another phenomenon; the Disney and Warner Brothers empires were the first to take their basic product and extend it to a successful consumption experience via theme park and store (much as off-site museum and National Trust shops and mail order business has grown). Their stores can be viewed as the ultimate shopping and entertainment mix, and they have become increasingly popular in UK shopping centres. A less obvious but growing example of this leisure/retailing blurring is football clubs. As football has become increasingly commercialized, it has sometimes moved 'out of town', with the old club shops becoming superstores open 6 days a week and crammed with everything from club duvets, to gnomes, aftershave, jeans, teddy bears and mountain bikes (Longmore, 1994). Manchester United, for example, plans to open stores in Tokyo and Sydney, to add to its branches in Plymouth, Dublin, Belfast as well as central Manchester. These stores 'boast loyalty that

other retail brands would die for' (Longmore, 1994). United's commercial
marketing generates £24 million a year – their latest brand product is
'Manchester United Premium Blend Whisky'. Football museums and
shops are, of course, most developed on the Continent – Barcelona FC's
club ground and museum is one of the most popular visitor attractions
in Spain.

Family Entertainment

Demographic change in Britain over the last 10 years shows a decline
in the youth market, but increase in the family formation and middle-
aged and retired segments, whilst overall populations have been static
or in slight decline. The decline in the youth market, whilst progressing
to the 20–24 age group over the next 5 years, is set to reverse for 15–
19-year-olds, and with 5–10% growth in under-11s generating an
increase in school rolls during this next period. The demand for family-
based leisure experiences has not only been driven by demands for
families, parents and children, but by their dissatisfaction with traditional
leisure and entertainment that is not attractive (in cost, ambience,
'attitude', facilities – Henley Centre, 1990) to children or their carers, or
to young adults.

A particular commercial response, in addition to (and often in
collaboration with) family entertainment centres, has been the further
'theming' of pubs, capitalizing on their growing popularity for family
outings. This has been facilitated by the relaxation of planning and
licensing, particularly Sunday ('all day') trading and extended opening
hours. Allied Domecq's plans to create 200 theme pubs and restaurants
('Big Steak Pubs') includes supervised 'play barns' for children, whilst
Whitbread's Brewer's Fayre pubs are attached to 'Charlie Chalk Fun
Factories'. The impact of licensing liberalization is significant – up to
30% of customers at Whitbread's pubs brought children in 1994,
compared with only 18% in 1991.

At the same time, the demand and supply of 'family entertainment'
suggests that the trend towards US-style arenas and sites for a mix of
sport, music and entertainment (e.g. ice shows, 'Gladiators', spectacu-
lars, opera) is compelling (Kelly, 1996) – the move towards all-seater
football stadia has accelerated this trend. Whilst only a few arenas have
been developed in the UK (such as the London Arena, Docklands, in
receivership, and in Birmingham, Sheffield, Manchester and planned
in Cardiff and Bradford), it has largely been high land costs and
planning constraints that have limited their development in the South-
east. Smaller stadia and tracks which were inherited from previous
uses, such as greyhound racing, are barely surviving commercially (e.g.

at Walthamstow and Hackney in East London) – there are parallels here with pre-war music halls and theatres, and their marginal re-use as cinemas, bingo halls and latterly Quasar centres, followed by a move to 'out-of-town'.

Another entertainment (rather than 'sport') activity that has gone through a revival is ten-pin bowling. First imported from the USA in the 1960s, it largely failed to gain hold, not adapting to the UK market and being relatively expensive and club-member dominated. In 1981 there were 49 bowling centres in the UK and gradually some of these were refurbished and modernized, so that by 1989 60 were in operation. The market again shifted to families and mixed groups aged 20–40 years. By 1990 over 100 were in operation, and bowling has been established as a family leisure activity, on the back of automated technology, designed interiors and food and drink. Significantly most of the original bowling sites have been replaced by those better located. New centres combine bowling on two floors, several bars, other games (e.g. pool) and a fitness centre. Bowling and multiplex developments have the same key criteria for success – location, branding and 'quality' (i.e. standardization) of service/management and, increasingly, extended/late-night opening.

The pursuit of value for money and quality in the service and experience has also demanded that operators have had to counter the pull of home-based entertainment and neighbourhood facilities (and short-breaks/holidays) and the factors limiting out-of-home activity – weather, safety, cost – and offer instead excitement, social interaction, cultural diversity and an educational experience. This is seen most clearly in the growth of educational and theme-museums such as Eureka! in Halifax, Snibston Discovery Park, Cardiff Techniquest and other science and interactive museums – what Disney terms 'edutainment'. The replication of the small screen and games in the new branded 'interactive' virtual reality centres (such as Cyberspace, Sega World) further blurs the distinction between home-based and out-of-home leisure activity targeted at children and families. The physical environment is therefore of particular importance, as is the range of facilities and services on offer, since this will directly influence the length of stay and catchment area of visitors and the average group size (e.g. family, friends, organized groups). Entertainment centres can therefore be divided between three main types:

1. The traditional (sports) leisure centre with 'add-ons': pools, ice rink, sports halls with catering, clubs, small shops/boutiques, fitness/health, conference facilities, etc.;
2. Entertainment zones (e.g. The Point, Milton Keynes): high-tech sport and leisure, cinema, bowling, leisure pool, nightclubs/disco, entertainment hall;

3. Virtual entertainment centres: driven by home-based computer entertainment and games, audio-visual wizardry and the technology of omnimax cinema and theme-park 'rides'.

Examples of these suburban/urban-fringe centres in the UK include Leisure World, Hemel Hempstead (Rank); Bass's Hollywood Bowls, and their new development at The Edge, Harrow (cyberspace); and, in central London's tourist zone, Sega World at the Trocadero. Prime locations here, as for multiplex and retail–leisure centres, are out-of-town/fringe and transport interchange sites, and most recently, urban town and city shopping centres.

Parks as Places of Entertainment

The core function of parks has developed from their role as 'green lung' and as a buffer to encroaching urbanization and industrial life in the 19th and early 20th centuries. The importance of natural and green spaces is still paramount, although the pressures of urbanization, population growth and manufacturing industry have declined. Pressure for the use of green belt land for housing and other developments has, however, placed more emphasis on the retention of urban/fringe parks, as has the loss of playing fields and other recreational land (Comedia HMSO Ltd, 1995).

The core purpose of urban parks was evident from user research of visitors to the nine Royal Parks in London (n=33,000), carried out between 1993 and 1995 in the central London parks of Hyde Park/Kensington Gardens, Regent's, St James's and Green Parks to the suburban parks at Greenwich, Richmond, Bushy and Primrose Hill (Curson and Evans, 1995). Here the value of the parks was reaffirmed: 'Open Space, Like the Country, Beauty' being the most quoted, followed by 'Convenience and Variety of activity/experience'. Again the features parks users particularly liked: 'Large/open space; Flora/fauna; Tranquil/relaxing; and Landscape' not surprisingly dominated. From the author's study for the Lee Valley Regional Park (Evans, 1996) this sentiment was echoed: 'There is so much countryside and such a variety of birdlife right in the middle of our environment' and 'Personally I like the peace and quiet [so to me to have any play facilities for children would put me off]'.

This raises the fundamental issue of potential conflict of use between more intensive activities associated with public events, organized sports and entertainments. This periodic conflict encompasses both the impact on the park landscape and 'fabric' itself, to noise, parking and other intrusion, reducing the amenity for regular parks visitors seeking the traditional peace and quiet. Examples range from the banning of roller-blading in Hyde Park (but approval of VE-Day and concert events), and conflicts between festival promoters and locals/police, to residents tying themselves to trees in Melbourne's Albert Park to prevent the 1996 Grand Prix track under construction there, despite an A$100 million state-aid package for the park. This is more of a problem with single-space parks where one such activity precludes other usage and where environmental impacts are felt to be excessive – one reason for Greenwich Park refusing permission for Millennium celebrations despite its prime location as the 'home of time'.

There follow some examples of fringe park and leisure village developments:

Leisure World, Hemel Hempstead

Located at Jarman Park, a former refuse tip used for football pitches, 5 minutes from the M1, 10 minutes from the M25 and less than 1 mile from the centre of the town. Dacorum Borough Council's aim was to achieve for its 132,000 residents a modern leisure scheme at no revenue cost to the Borough. Ladbroke and Rank were chosen to develop the site, as a mixed-use development – Tesco, McDonald's drive-thru', athletics track, and later a hotel. The Leisure World itself combines in one large building a wide range of attractions to appeal to a wide range of people: families, groups, young and old. The under-one-roof concept means that there is no obvious separation between local authority facilities and commercial attractions.

Within 180,000 square feet is contained an eight-screen Odeon cinema; *Hotshots* – 20 lanes of bowling, with bar and table games, fast-food outlet and large video screens with non-stop sporting footage; a Silver Blades Ice Rink with largely non-competition skating; and an Aqua Splash leisure pool with a Mayan theme (!) with many water rides. There are two nightclubs each aimed at different age and market sector, but interlinked, and a bar with major live entertainment – comedy, music – every night of the week. The Play Zone is a small-children's activity area for 150 at a time. As well as food franchises (Pizza Hut, Burger King), there is an indoor green bowls area that operates as a members' club. This one-stop-leisure facility appeals to a wider catchment with a critical mass of activity and services, linked by a central mall. Rank is now actively seeking other sites, to replicate the Leisure World concept, as is Bass Leisure. Sites require around 200,000 square feet with parking for 2000 cars.

Kettering Leisure Village, Northants

Here a regional centre for sport, leisure and entertainment was located in a rural area of Northamptonshire with funding via a capital receipt (land in kind) and planning gain accruing to Kettering Borough Council from a residential development of 100 acres on the edge of the town. Twenty acres of the site were designated for a leisure complex to be developed by a private consortium of house builders. The site was leased by the Council to a new company on a 125-year lease, which then sublet back to the Council half of the site. The Council's 'contribution' funded a 2000-seater entertainment hall (which can also be used for 12 badminton courts), an ancillary hall, a gymnastics training centre, a dance studio, a crèche, a public meeting room and a three-court tennis hall. The commercial facilities include a leisure pool, ice rink, bowling and Quasar centre, snooker club, catering, health suite and a wine bar. A private company, Redelco, managed the entire complex, including the public facilities, on a 15-year management contract (currently the local authority has taken back the facility, the operator being in liquidation).

Parc de la Villette, Paris

This park was developed from reclaimed land and derelict sites and industrial buildings on the outskirts of Paris. Formerly the location for slaughterhouses serving Paris, the park is approached via canal, underground or car/coach and bus, and covers 86 acres. As well as public art, covered walkways (ground and raised), squares with cafés and play areas, the park contains a grand hall/exhibition centre (1500 capacity) and a theatre arena (seating 6400). There is also a museum/entertainment quarter containing an Omnimax cinema and a science/children's museum (with planetarium and aquarium, and with a 'hands on'/experiential approach) attracting school/educational usage, families, traditional park users, groups, etc. The performance element – in addition to the hall, a former industrial building – is supplemented with outdoor events, including giant outdoor film screenings. The development received considerable national funding (as a *Grand Projet*) and is now one of the city's main attractions for locals, Parisians and visitors – no mean feat given its unlikely urban fringe/industrial wasteland location, and competition from tourist honeypots. In its first year the park attracted 3 million visitors.

Event 'games'

A particular development in the 1980s, initially on farmland and woodlands, has been the growth of war games and competitions such as paint balling (the indoor equivalent, Quasar, and other laser centres have been an urban development). Over 400 rural sites now exist for such activities, from a 40-acre plantation at Billericay, Essex, to Trickey Coppice, Warwickshire. The use of a site for war games is exempt from planning permission provided no more than 28 days use a year is made. Hire rates range from £50–100 a day to £10,000–15,000 a year for a 'regular' site. Concern has been expressed by the CPRE and English Nature about the impact of war games on sensitive sites and, if these are restricted, sites may be sought on less sensitive areas in future. The growth of indoor Quasars may have peaked, however; the novelty has worn off and their obsolescence has been accelerated by the high-tech entertainment centres noted above.

Arts Festivals

The growth of arts festivals and outdoor events (e.g. concerts, open-air theatre, rock festivals, 'Pavarotti in the Park') has also placed pressure on parks and outdoor sites for regular events. Where these are furnished with buildings and sites of particular interest, such as stately homes, museums, natural attractions (e.g. canals, rivers, lakes), the scope for events is even greater, whilst the pressure for large theme-park and arena developments is still evident in and around London (e.g. London Docklands, Battersea Power Station, MGM 'Universal Studios' at Hillingdon) despite the leisure property depression and succession of failed schemes, as Middleton notes: 'the urban visitor attractions field is littered with the debris of over-optimism, overrated projects and written-off loans' (Middleton, 1994:88). Other leisure and entertainment facilities which have been developed within public parks include adventure/nature type projects, such as at Roundhay Park, Leeds and Walsall Metro Park. Of course many gallery and museum spaces are located within park settings, such as the Burrell Collection, Glasgow. Examples of successful arts centres located within public parks include the Midlands Arts Centre, Cannon Hill Park, Birmingham and South Hill Park Arts Centre, Bracknell.

Festivals have been a considerable growth area for public performance and visitor attraction in the UK, often focusing on a particular art form or theme and most successfully linked to particular venues and sites with natural and heritage associations. There are over 500 arts festivals taking place in the UK, more than half of them originating in the 1980s. Although a small number of major international festivals such as Edinburgh and Chichester attract a large number of visitors from outside the area, two-thirds of arts festivals largely attract a local audience (Rolfe, 1991). Most of these festivals take place on an annual basis, with July the most popular month, followed by May, August and June, and they generally last between 2 and 7 days. Large-scale music

Table 9.6. Major rock festivals.

Location	Attendance	Duration (days)	Promoter
Finsbury Park, North London – *Fleadh*	30,000	1	Mean Fiddler
Rivermead Leisure Centre	17,000	3	WOMAD
Reading, Berkshire	50,000	3	Mean Fiddler
Luton Hoo, Beds – *Tribal Gathering*	35,000	1	Mean Fiddler
Phoenix, Stratford-upon-Avon	45,000	4	Mean Fiddler
Donnington Park, Leics – *Monsters of Rock*	70,000	1	Midland Concerts
Strathclyde Country Park, Scotland	35,000	2	Tennants Beer
Glastonbury	90,000	3	Landowner

festivals taking place in large park and rural locations developed from the 1970s rock festivals, and some survive today, such as Reading and Glastonbury (see Table 9.6). Increasingly, such music festivals take place in parks, in city fringes and on rural sites, with pressure for larger audiences and sites (Evans, 1996).

Park Villages

Finally, another land-intensive development more for leisure than entertainment, is the expansion of holiday park/villages in rural and scenic locations. Center Parcs' latest development at Longleat covers 400 acres of Longleat Park – the 'village' will feature chalet/lodges, an all-weather leisure centre, shops, restaurants and other sporting and recreational activities – with capacity of 3500 a week or 250,000 a year. The importance of the quality of the environment and the need for conservation alongside development is a balance that needs to be struck in such schemes. Despite opposition from the CPRE and local groups, and the fact that the development is located in an Area of Outstanding Natural Beauty (AONB), following a public inquiry the Secretary of State gave consent for the Center Parcs development, arguing that screening and associated traffic management was adequate, and that the creation of 750 jobs was in the 'national interest' (CPRE, 1994). This is the third Center Parcs scheme in the UK – all were greeted with environmental and local opposition and all have been based in 'unspoilt rural locations'; the basis of their appeal. Several additional Parcs are planned, and both the English Tourist Board and government argue that 'there is potential demand for a dozen or more such holiday villages in England alone' (NEDC, 1992).

Some Conclusions

The pleasure periphery is expanding both in terms of lei̲___
tion and physical usage, and in terms of land use and traffic gen̲ᴇ̲ɪ̲ᴜ̲
Since 1944, the south-east of England has increased its urban area by
44% (470,000 acres), an area more than the size of Greater London itself
(CPRE, 1993). By the same token, government attempts to bring back
into use derelict land in existing urban areas, through the Derelict Land
Grant scheme, have so far failed: since its inception in 1974 only 6% of
designated derelict land has been brought into use. The quality of
experience and symbolism presented by this commodification of countryside and out-of-town also represents a converging of home-based
entertainment, consumption and *recreation*, where in industrial society
they were complementary, or even the antithesis of each other, in time,
place and purpose. Richard Sennett (1996) made the observation that:
'The spatial relations of human bodies obviously make a great deal of
difference in how people react to each other, how they see and hear one
another, whether they touch or are distant.' In a commentary on the
urban fringe transformation and population shift to 'thinner more
amorphous spaces', after viewing a film he goes on to comment: 'If a
[cinema] in a suburban mall is a meeting place for tasting violent
pleasure in air-conditioned comfort, this great geographic shift of people
into fragmented spaces has had a larger effect in weakening the sense of
tactile reality and pacifying the body' (Sennett, 1996:17).

Urry describes the shift to post-Fordist consumption in his *Consuming Places* (1995:150–151), with greater consumer dominance, segmen-
tation ('niche marketing') and rejection of mass production in favour of
more customized products and services and aesthetic tastes (and see
Glennie and Thrift, 1992; 1993). However, the commercial imperatives
of scale economies, branding and replication through franchising and
uniformity, suggest otherwise. The obsolesence and high capital costs
of maintaining consumer and leisure popularity, evident in the short
shelf-life of leisure-entertainment centres, suggest that as a public
partnership and land-use option they are not sustainable – with 125-
year leases demanded from private operators, the lesson of ghost 'out-
of-towns' as seen in the US and in the failure of surplus malls and
yesterday's theme and leisure parks should be heeded. The technological determinism that has featured in modern society since the 19th
century continues to influence leisure forecasters, not least the transfer
of technologies to leisure experiences and facilities outside of the home
and workplace. Again, how far these applications will sustain and
impact on leisure and cultural consumption remains to be seen – the
futuristic scenarios have not proved to be robust in the past and the

ume lag between technological discovery, commercial replication and mass consumption should not be underestimated (in a recent national survey on the impact of technology in the USA, the highest ranked items were not the Internet, cable or satellite TV, but the humble video recorder and microwave oven!).

One impact of post-Fordist production and the transfer of manufacture to developing countries and low-cost workforces has been the separation of industries from their traditional locations, communities and skill-base, leaving the areas ill-prepared for new forms of working (and enforced 'leisure' – un/under-employment) and severed relationships between work, home and recreation. The out-of-town drift, Edge City settlements and the growth of part-time employment has certainly reinforced the effects of such structural change. With the shift towards out-of-town leisure and shopping centres, the urban areas are losing this collective consumption role, but instead serve as both generators of consumers and visitors, and ghettoes for those who are less able to escape to the pleasure periphery. One observation here is that black and ethnic minority groups are substantially lower participants in countryside recreation (Evans, 1996).

With North American models and capital formation directly influencing this change in the UK, experience there is of significance, as has been noted above:

> The hallmarks of these new urban centers are not the sidewalks of New York of song and fable . . . But if an American finds himself tripping the light fantastic today on concrete, social scientists know where to look for him. He will be amid the crabapples blossoming under glassed-in skies where America retails its wares.

(Garreau, 1991:3)

Britain's urban concentration, with 92% of the population living in cities and towns, suburban zones and large 'villages' – the entire population of Britain lives on 10% of the land – suggests that in terms of spatial and other 'hierarchies of need', amenity and other planning strategies are not comparable with other western countries. In Italy, France and the USA only 74% of populations are urbanized and even the urban densities of cities in smaller countries such as Belgium and The Netherlands do not compare with the urban concentration of mainland Britain (World Bank, 1987). However, intraregional scale development now transcends the local, urban or even regional sphere, with mega leisure–retail developments proposed in Northern France, exploiting the channel tunnel link and traffic, with drive-away capability for large items, and, like their American counterparts, becoming settlements in their own right.

The central question about the out-of-town leisure-consumption phenomenon is whether it is its form that dictates the nature of urban living, or if it is the post-modern city that in fact dictates how the pleasure periphery has developed. The answer appears to be somewhere in between. Vast sheds that serve (some but not all) people from more than one city or conurbation (or country) demonstrate that urbanism has already become an amorphous landscape in which mobility allows anything to happen anywhere. Paradoxically, while the city itself has decentralized, the pleasure periphery has in all senses become ever more concentrated.

References

Abercrombie, P. (1944) *The Greater London Development Plan*. HMSO, London.

Becker, G.S. (1965) A theory in the allocation of time. *Economic Journal* 75(3). Royal Society for Economics, London.

Burtenshaw, D., Bateman, M. and Ashworth, G.J. (1991) *The European City: a Western Perspective*. David Fulton Publishers, London.

Castells, M. (1977) *The Urban Question*. Edward Arnold, London.

Centre for Leisure and Tourism Studies (CELTS) (1995) *You Don't Know What You've Got 'Till It's Gone, Survey of Leisure Services Budgets in England & Wales*. Evans, G.L. (ed.) Association of Metropolitan Authorities and Centre for Leisure and Tourism Studies, University of North London, London.

Clarke, J. and Critcher, C. (1985) *The Devil Makes Work*. Macmillan, London.

Comedia Ltd. (1991) *Out of Hours: A Study of Economic, Social and Cultural Life in 12 Town Centres in the UK*. Comedia, London.

Comedia HMSO Ltd. (1995) *Park Life*. Comedia, Stroud.

Countryside Commission (1992) *The Countryside Commission and Transport Policy in England*. CCP 382. Cheltenham.

CPRE [Council for the Protection of Rural England] (1993) *The Lost Land*. CPRE, London.

CPRE (1994) *Leisure Landscapes: Leisure Culture and the English Countryside: Challenges and Conflicts*. CPRE, London.

Curson, T. and Evans, G.L. (1995) *People in the Parks – Annual Report 1995*. Royal Parks Agency, Centre for Leisure and Tourism Studies, University of North London Press, London.

Davies, R. *et al.* (1992) *The Effect of Major Out-of town Retail Development*. HMSO, London.

Docklands Consultative Committee (1990) *The Docklands Experiment: A Critical Review of Eight Years of the London Docklands Development Corporation*. Docklands Consultative Committee, London.

DoE (1996) *Planning Policy Guidance Notes (Revised)*. Department of the Environment, London.

DoT (1996) *Transport: The Way Ahead*. Department of Transport, Cmnd 3234. HMSO, London.

Enfield, L.B. (1993) Unitary Development Plan 13.3.3. Enfield Environmental Services, London.

Evans, G.L. (1993) Leisure and Tourism Investment Incentives in the EC: Changing Rationales. *International LSA Conference*, Loughborough.

Evans, G.L. (1995) The National Lottery: planning for leisure or pay up and play the game? *Leisure Studies* 14. E. & F.N. Spon, London.

Evans, G.L. (1996) *Arts Culture and Entertainment Topic Study*. Lee Valley Regional Park Authority: 10 Year Plan (1996–2005). LVRP, Waltham Abbey.

Garreau, J. (1991) *Edge City: Life on the New Frontier*. Anchor Books, New York.

Giddens, A. (1985) Time, space and regionalization. In: Gregory, D. and Urry, J. (eds) *Social Relations and Spatial Structures*. Macmillan, London, pp. 265–295.

Glennie, P.D. and Thrift, N.J. (1992) Modernity, urbanism and modern consumption. *Society and Space* 10, 423–443.

Glennie, P.D. and Thrift, N.J. (1993) Modern consumption: theorizing commodities and consumers. *Society and Space* 11, 603–606.

Gorz, A. (1989) *A Critique of Economic Reason*. Verso, London.

Grant, A. (1990) Out of town leisure developments, London. *UK Leisure Property Conference* 4(4).

Henley Centre (1985) *Social Change and the Arts*. National Association of Arts Centres, London.

Henley Centre (1990) *Leisure Futures*. February, Henley Centre, London.

Henley Centre (1996) *Lottery Fallout II*. Henley Centre, London.

Holder, J. (1996) The inter-war heyday of cinema design. On 'Cinema in Britain – the development of cinema architecture', exhibition at Heinz Gallery, RIBA London. *Architect's Journal*, 14 March, London, p. 54.

Kelly, P. (1996) Family entertainment centres – family circle. *Leisure Management*. January, pp. 23–24.

Lang. T. (1995) *Off Our Trolleys?* Thames Valley University, Greenwich.

Leisure Consultants (1995) *Leisure Forecasts 1995–1999*. (Volume I – *Home Leisure*; volume II – *Away from Home Leisure*). Leisure Consultants, Sudbury.

Leisure Consultants (1996) *Leisure Forecasts 1996–2000*. (Volume I – *Home Leisure*; Volume II – *Away from Home Leisure*). Leisure Consultants, Sudbury.

Lichfield, D. (1992) *Urban Regeneration for the 1990s*. DLA, London Planning Advisory Committee, London.

Loftman, P. and Nevin, B. (1993) *Urban Regeneration and Social Equity: A Case Study of 1986–1992 Birmingham*. University of Central England in Birmingham, Birmingham.

Longmore, A. (1994) Football puts its skill on profit. *The Times*. 19 December, p. 27.

Martin, B. and Mason, S. (1994) Current trends in leisure: taking account of time. *Leisure Studies* 13(2), 133–139.

Middleton, P. (1994) Urban tourism 90s style – or a new search for pixie dust! *British Urban Regeneration Association News*. London, pp. 5/88–89.

MINTEL (1995) *British Lifestyles*. MINTEL, London.

NEDC (1992) *Tourism – Competing for Growth*. National Economic Development Council, London.

OPCS [Office of Population Censuses and Surveys] (1991) *Census 1991*. HMSO, London.

OPCS (1992) *Leisure Day Visit Survey 1991/2*. Office for Population Census and Statistics, London.

OPCS (1996) *Day Visits Survey 1994* (draft). Centre for Leisure Research, Edinburgh.

Richards, G. (1994) Cultural tourism in Europe. In: Cooper, C. and Lockwood, A.L. (eds) *Progress in Tourism Recreation and Hospitality Management*. Volume V. Wiley Press, London.

Rolfe, H. (1991) *Arts Festivals in the UK*. Policy Studies Institute, London.

Screen Digest (1994) *UK Multiplex Cinemas: Phase I Near Maturity*. September. London.

Seabrook, J. (1988) *The Leisure Society*. Basil Blackwell, Oxford.

Sennett, R. (1996) *Flesh and Stone: the Body and City in Western Civilization*. Faber & Faber, London.

Sudjic, D. (1993) *The 100 Mile City*. Flamingo, London.

Urry, J. (1995) *Consuming Places*. The International Library of Sociology. Routledge, London.

Veal, A.J. (1982) *Planning for Leisure: Alternative Approaches*. Papers in Leisure Studies No. 5, May. Department of Extension Studies, Polytechnic of North London, London.

Veal, A.J. (1993) Planning for leisure: past, present and future. In: Glyptis, S. (ed.) *Leisure and the Environment: Essays in Honour of Professor J.A. Patmore*. Belhaven Press, London. pp. 85–95.

Veal, A.J. (1994) *Leisure Policy and Planning*. Longman/ILAM.

Walter, J. (1995) Planning policy update. *Architect's Journal*, October. London, p. 46.

Whitehead, A. (1992) *Decisions in a vacuum – local authorities and out-of-town shopping 1980–1992*, Centre for Local Economic Strategies Summer School. Northern College, Barnsley: CLES.

Wigley, N. and Lowe, M. (1996) *Retailing, Consumption and Capital: Towards the New Retail Geography*. Longman, Harlow.

World Bank (1987) *World Development Report*. Oxford University Press, Oxford.

A Model of Alternative Forms of Public Leisure Services Delivery

10

Troy D. Glover and Thomas L. Burton

Faculty of Physical Education and Recreation, University of Alberta, Edmonton, Alberta T6G 2H9, Canada

Introduction

The creation of the Welfare State during the 40 years or so following the end of World War II greatly influenced public leisure service provision throughout the developed world. The widespread adoption of Keynesian economic principles led to large-scale government involvement in the provision of leisure and recreation programmes, facilities and services (as in other fields), and considerable public acceptance of such involvement (Henry, 1993; Ravenscroft, 1993; Andrew *et al.*, 1994). However, this pattern is now strongly criticized on both philosophical and practical grounds (Osborne and Gaebler, 1992). Much of this criticism has to do with perceived inefficiency and waste in government service provision, and is linked to financial problems faced by national, subnational and local governments affected by severe fiscal imbalance, deficit funding and accumulated debt. As a result, governments have sought alternative methods to deliver public services, including leisure. This has led, in turn, to the development of a wide array of methods of providing public services, but little understanding of how these fit within a broader philosophical and management framework. The intent here is to present a model of public service provision. We will begin with the construction of a theoretical framework upon which the model will be based. Then, a typology will be presented, outlining a range of public service delivery options. Finally, the model itself will be presented.

© CAB INTERNATIONAL 1998. *Leisure Management: Issues and Applications* (eds M.F. Collins and I.S. Cooper)

Theoretical Framework

In Canada (and, indeed, in most of the developed world), municipal governments have traditionally adopted one or more of five distinct roles in the provision of leisure services. The particular role or roles adopted by any municipal agency have been dependent on three factors: the client group; the type of service being provided; and the philosophical orientation and values of the policy makers (Searle and Brayley, 1993).

Burton (1982) describes the first role as the *direct provision of services*: that is, a government department or agency develops and maintains leisure facilities, operates programmes and delivers services using public funds. For example, city-operated swimming pools are typically built, maintained and operated by a city's Leisure Services or Parks and Recreation Department.

The second role that Burton (1982) identifies is that of *an arm's-length provider of services*. This requires the creation of a publicly owned special-purpose agency that operates outside the regular apparatus of government. An arm's-length organization is funded by a government and has a government-appointed board of directors. Crown corporations, such as the Canadian Broadcasting Corporation, and regulatory commissions are examples of arm's-length agencies through which a government provides services. However, such agencies are rarely found at the municipal level.

The third role of government is as *a coordinator of services* (Burton, 1982). In this role, a municipal Leisure Services or Parks and Recreation Department identifies agencies that provide leisure services and encourages and helps them to coordinate their efforts, resources and activities. This is typically achieved through leadership training and government-supported consultation services.

The fourth role involves the Leisure Services or Parks and Recreation Department acting as *a supporter and patron of leisure service organizations* (Burton, 1982). A government may recognize that an existing organization already provides a valuable service and can be encouraged to continue doing so through specialized support, especially (though not exclusively) through monetary grants. Recipient organizations may be from the not-for-profit or commercial sectors. Many cultural organizations receive this kind of support from public agencies.

Finally, a government invariably acts as *a legislator and regulator of leisure activities and organizations* (Burton, 1982). Using its authority to create laws and establish regulations, a government exercises control over agencies and individuals engaged in the provision of leisure

Table 10.1. A typology of public goods.

Consumption	Exclusion	
	Non-excludable	Excludable
Non-rival	1. Public	2. Toll
Rival	3. Common pool	4. Private

Source: Peston (1972).

services. In addition, it regulates personal behaviour in leisure environments such as national and local parks.

Burton's five roles of government are helpful in discerning how a municipal Leisure Services or Parks and Recreation Department would control or provide public leisure services. Regardless of the particular method of service delivery, one or more of these roles can be used effectively as a means of control. However, when determining the specific delivery of a public service, municipal governments must also consider the types of goods and services to be provided. Peston (1972) has identified four basic kinds: *public*, *toll*, *common pool*, and *private* goods and services (Table 10.1).

The first kind, *public goods*, refers to commodities or services that are non-excludable and non-rival. Non-excludable means that the provider does not discriminate among the people who consume the service. Non-rival refers to a good that is provided by one organization exclusively. Given these definitions, a public good can be perceived as a commodity or service provided by a government with the intention of making it available to anyone without discrimination. For example, municipal governments develop and manage parks in communities for the enjoyment of their citizens. These are provided by a municipal Leisure Services or Parks and Recreation Department and are generally available for the use of everyone in the community.

The second kind, *toll goods*, refers to commodities or services that are excludable and non-rival. Excludable means that the provider of the good or service controls who can and cannot consume the good. Therefore, a toll good is a commodity or service provided to consumers who meet predetermined requirements, by an organization that controls its distribution. For example, a municipal government may authorize a commercial agency to provide a paddleboat service at a small lake within the city limits. The firm that is awarded the permit monopolizes the delivery of the service and only those who can afford to pay the fee for the rental of the boats are allowed to take part in the activity.

The third kind, *common pool goods*, includes commodities or services that are non-excludable and rival. Rival refers to products or services that are provided by more than one organization. Thus, a common pool good is a commodity or service that is delivered by various suppliers who do not control access to consumption. For instance, a municipality may operate a community centre, which competes against various kinds of centres provided by commercial and not-for-profit organizations. However, unlike those in the other two sectors, the publicly operated community centres are open to all members of the community – at least in principle, though, in practice, it doesn't always work out that way!

The fourth quadrant, *private goods,* refers to commodities or services that are excludable and rival. Thus, a private good is a commodity or service that is delivered by various providers who control its consumption. These providers may come from any of the three sectors. An example of a private good would be aerobics classes. Such classes might be offered by several private fitness clubs, not-for-profit organizations such as the YMCA and YWCA, and, even, a city Leisure Services Department. However, a fee is charged to the participant which excludes those who cannot (or choose not to) pay.

Using Burton's five roles of government and Peston's four kinds of goods leads to the conclusion that municipal governments should consider three significant variables when determining the choice of a method for delivering public leisure services: the level of competitive forces; the nature of the goods; and the amount of government control. The first variable, *level of competitive forces*, refers to the level of competition involved in providing a public service. For example, compulsory competitive tendering (CCT) in Britain involves a tendering process whereby public, private and not-for-profit organizations are permitted to bid for a contract to provide a public service (Henry, 1993). The bidding involved in obtaining a contract and the attempt to renew it after its expiration encourages a firm to fulfil the expectations of the client. In other words, in principle, competition motivates the firm to provide quality services. In contrast, competition is absent from public services that are provided directly by a municipal government because the government monopolizes delivery. Competitive forces can be conceptualized along a continuum whereby competition is *high* at one end and *low* at the other. Obviously, there are many degrees of competition which appear on the continuum.

The second variable, *nature of the good*, allows for differentiation between social and private goods. A social good is perceived as a product available for all, or most, to consume. The notion of equality is implicit in the provision of the service, as the provider avoids controlling its consumption. For example, outdoor hiking trails in Edmonton, Canada, may be considered a social good because they are available for everyone to use at no direct cost to the user. Conversely, a private good is market-driven. That is, it is available only to consumers who can afford to pay for the service. A theatrical performance is a private good because spectators who wish to watch it must pay a stated price to attend. Consequently, people who cannot afford to pay are unable to attend.

Finally, the third variable, *amount of government control,* provides a continuum along which the degree of government regulation is measured. At one end of the continuum is total control; at the other, minimal control. Total control involves complete regulation over a given service. For instance, direct public provision is completely regulated by government: that is, the government plans, implements and manages the service. In contrast, minimal control describes a situation in which services are provided outside the public sector and are subject only to the overall control that government exercises over all commercial activities; for example, taxation. A small private business that offers guided trips in wilderness environments is virtually independent of public sector control. It is expected to adhere to the laws and regulations set out for small businesses, but beyond this it has no connection with the public sector. Together, the level of competitive forces, the nature of the goods, and the amount of government control are important factors to consider when deciding on a particular method of delivering public leisure services.

A Typology of Public Service Delivery

Broadly, there are four specific categories of public service delivery. First, there are *governmental arrangements*, which have been the dominant form of delivering public services in many Western countries for several decades. A governmental arrangement can be defined as any arrangement whereby public sector agencies alone provide a public service. Such arrangements include service provision by means of municipal departments and agencies, arm's-length organizations, internal markets and intermunicipal partnerships. Second, *cross-sector alliances* have been used to deliver public services. A cross-sector alliance consists of a contractual relationship between a public sector department or agency and a private or not-for-profit organization. There are two predominant forms of such alliances: partnerships and contracts. Third, *regulated monopolies* exist to supply public goods and services. A regulated monopoly occurs where, by agreement, a non-public agency organization is granted a monopoly to directly provide public services. These agreements principally take the form of franchises. Finally, the public sector occasionally turns to *divestiture* to deliver services. Divestiture occurs when public services, lands or facilities are sold or leased to private or not-for-profit agencies. After the sale or lease, the good or service that is sold no longer belongs to the public sector.

What follows is a outline of each of these four categories of public leisure service delivery, by reference to the dominant modes of delivery within each category. In total, there are nine distinct modes of service delivery identified. The discussion will provide a definition of each, and will indicate who arranges for the service to be produced, who actually produces it, and who pays for it. As well, an example will be given of each mode. The entire discussion is summarized in Table 10.2.

Governmental arrangements

Direct provision

Direct provision is the traditional method of public leisure service delivery. Essentially, it is an arrangement by which a government delivers a service directly to consumers: that is, a government agency arranges, produces and pays for the provision of a specific service. An example of direct provision would include a municipal baseball or football (soccer) field. They are built, maintained and financed by municipal Leisure Services and Parks and Recreation Departments. The rationale for this method arises directly from the welfare approach to service delivery. Equity and social welfare are pursued to rectify market imperfections in order to achieve collective goals. In this mode of service delivery, direct public provision is deemed necessary because market forces cannot achieve the desired distribution of recreational opportunities.

The notion of equity is paramount to the Welfare State. Governments attempt to provide services in an equitable manner by granting citizens social rights which subsequently affect policy within the public sector. Social rights refer to the idea that members of society share an equal claim to citizenship (Ravenscroft, 1993). As a result, claims are made on the state in the name of equity. For example, citizens claim the right to recreational opportunities, regardless of their socio-economic status. Governments respond by providing affordable leisure opportunities directly to the community.

Arm's-length provision

The arm's-length provider of services is an autonomous agency or organization created by a government to operate separately from the regular bureaucracy, but which is answerable to the government for its overall operations and expenditures. A government arranges for a service to be provided, the arm's-length agency produces it and the government pays for its provision. For example, the City of Edmonton has established an Arts Council, separate from its Parks and Recreation Department and accountable directly to City Council. The individuals hired to operate the Arts Council are employed by the city, but the council remains a separate, autonomous entity from the Parks and Recreation Department.

Internal markets

An internal market is an arrangement whereby one government department contracts another to supply a service. More specifically, Walsh (1995) identifies internal markets as having three important characteristics: the development of clear and independent roles for both the purchaser and the supplier of services; the creation of internal quasi-contracts and trading agreements between purchaser and supplier; and the development of charging and accounting systems. Basically, internal markets separate the purchaser from the supplier of services within a government. The intent in developing internal markets is to decrease the overproduction of goods and services, and to keep the bureaucracy small (Walsh, 1995). For example, the Culture and Heritage Department in a municipal government may contract the Parks and Recreation Department to provide maintenance services for a public park during a city festival which it has organized.

Intermunicipal partnerships

Intermunicipal partnerships occur when one government collaborates with another to provide a particular service jointly. This arrangement involves a scenario where two or more municipalities arrange a service, one or more municipalities produces it, and each partner contributes to the cost of its provision. The Capital Region Forum in Edmonton has identified four specific types of partnerships between or among municipalities in the Greater Edmonton area (Capital Region Forum Ltd., 1995). First, *regional partnerships* are those in which several municipalities combine their activities to address regional issues or problems: 'Decision-making is interdependent and is the responsibility of all participating municipalities, with the goal being to achieve a consensus'. For example, the Alberta Municipal Safety Codes Service Commission consists of elected representatives from participating municipalities and provides inspection services to all. Second, *local partnerships* occur where municipalities work jointly to deliver local services or to address local problems. Essentially, a local partnership is a regional partnership, but with fewer participants. For instance, the towns of Bon Accord and Gibbons in Alberta deliver joint recreation programmes to residents of both municipalities. Events and activities are coordinated to ensure that there is cooperation instead of competition between the municipalities. Third, *sharing* is a mutually beneficial strategic alliance which involves municipalities sharing personnel, facilities and resources to deliver public services. Sharing is different from the other intermunicipal partnerships because it

Table 10.2. The range of public leisure service delivery.

Category	Mode of delivery	Definition	Arranges the service	Produces the service	Pays the producer	Example
Governmental arrangements	Direct provision	A government directly delivers a leisure service	Government	Government	Government	A City Parks and Recreation Department offers leisure programmes to the public
	Arm's-length provision	A government creates an autonomous agency, separate from its regular bureaucracy but responsible to it	Government	Autonomous agency	Government	A City establishes an Arts Council to operate its arts programmes
	Internal markets	A government division contracts a separate government division to supply a service	Government	Government	Government	A municipal Police Department contracts a Parks Department to maintain its property
	Intermunicipal partnerships	A government collaborates with one or more other governments to provide a service	Government	Government	Government	A rural School Board with no High School pays another to take its students

Category	Form	Description				Example
Cross-sector alliances	Contract	A government contracts a private firm or non-profit organization to supply a service	Government	Private firm or non-profit organization	Government	A municipality pays a private firm to collect refuse
	Partnerships	A government collaborates with a private firm or non-profit organization to supply a service	Government	Government and private firm or non-profit organization	Government and private firm or non-profit organization	A private firm contributes capital dollars to build a recreational facility with a municipality
Regulated monopoly	Franchise	A government awards a monopoly to a private firm	Government	Private firm	Consumer	A government allows only one utility company to supply natural gas to consumers
Divestiture	Lease	A government leases land to a private firm or non-profit organization to provide a service	Government	Private firm or non-profit organization	Consumer	A theatre company leases public land to build a community theatre
	Sale	A government sells surplus land, or facilities or the rights to provide services to a private firm or a non-profit organization	Private firm or non-profit organization	Private firm or non-profit organization	Consumer	A provincial government sells its liquor stores to private firms

involves more independent decision-making. The libraries in the towns of Calmar and Devon, Alberta, illustrate this form of partnership as they both accept library cards from either municipality. In each case, the cost is shared between the two libraries, but the decisions regarding individual service are made locally. Finally, *service provision* describes a formal agreement whereby municipalities cooperate by providing and supporting services through various funding arrangements. The more consumers who purchase a service or commodity, the more economical it is for the supplier to provide the service. Without the purchase, the commodity or service might not be offered, unless it is deemed to be an essential service. For example, the City of Leduc, Alberta, contracts its building inspector to the towns of Thorsby and Calmar. Neither of the latter is large enough to be able to afford its own inspector. These types of partnerships are specific to Alberta and the Edmonton Region and are not necessarily generalizable to the rest of Canada and other countries because of differences in government structures. As well, it is a simplified typology of the kinds of cooperation that exist among local governments. Nevertheless, it serves to provide a general idea of what is involved in intermunicipal partnerships.

Cross-sector alliances

Contracts

Contracts (often referred to as contracting out) refer to the process whereby a government, as a client, contracts a private firm or non-profit organization, as a contractor, to provide a public service. This involves the government arranging the service, a private or non-profit organization providing it, and the government paying for it. Walsh describes contracting as 'a move from a hierarchical to a market-based approach to the organization of public services, in which the roles of principal and agent are clearly separated and property rights more explicit' (1995:110). A clear example of contract service provision is where a municipal Leisure Services or Parks and Recreation Department contracts park maintenance services to a private firm or not-for-profit organization. Sometimes, internal workers may also be allowed to bid on contracts in competition with private and not-for-profit organizations. This latter situation is found extensively in Britain under CCT (Henry, 1993; Coalter, 1995).

The argument in favour of contracts is based on the notion that it is better to produce goods and services from the market than from within a government organization (Walsh, 1995). Contracts make responsibilities explicit because the expectations of service delivery must be specifically outlined for the contractor. In addition, contracts introduce competitive pressures which are more likely to ensure quality of provision as contractors work towards the renewal of the contract. Furthermore, contracts create a clear separation between management and policies, as the bureaucracy is removed from direct provision and concerns itself with setting service strategy and specifiying the parameters of the service (Walsh, 1995).

Partnerships
Partnerships involve a contractual relationship between a government and a private firm or not-for-profit organization to supply a public service jointly. Typically, it is a comprehensive arrangement covering all aspects of infrastructure development, including design, finance, construction, ownership and operation. The government arranges the service, the private firm or not-for-profit agency and the government jointly produce the service, and the government and the private firm or not-for-profit agency both pay for its delivery. For example, a city Parks and Recreation Department might seek the involvement of a private firm or not-for-profit organization in the construction or renovation of a major leisure facility in the city. As a partner, the private firm or not-for-profit organization contributes money and other services to the venture. Thus, a partnership gives the public sector access to such things as capital, revenue enhancement, the division of risk, and (often) new technology.

Oliver (1990) identifies several critical contingencies that explain why an organization chooses to establish a partnership. First, a partnership can be established out of necessity: that is, it can be involuntarily established to meet necessary legal or regulatory requirements. Second, reciprocity can motivate an organization to create a partnership. Reciprocity emphasizes cooperation, collaboration and coordination among organizations and is rooted in exchange theory whereby both partners benefit from a partnership. Third, efficiency motivates the establishment of a partnership. Efficiency is internally rather than externally orientated as organizations attempt to improve their internal input/output ratios by entering into partnerships with other organizations. Fourth, organizations establish partnerships to achieve stability. Stability is an adaptive response to environmental uncertainty. Alliances serve as '. . . coping strategies to forestall, forecast or absorb uncertainty in order to achieve an orderly, reliable pattern of resource flows and exchanges' (Oliver, 1990). Finally, partnerships are formed to improve an organization's legitimacy. Legitimacy demonstrates or improves an organization's reputation, image, prestige or congruence within its institutional environment. It is important to note that the formation of partnerships is typically motivated by more than one contingency.

Regulated monopoly

Franchise
A franchise is simply an agreement by which a government awards a monopoly to a private firm (or, occasionally, a not-for-profit organization). The government arranges the service, a private firm provides it and the consumer pays for its provision. For example, paddleboats are offered for rent to visitors to Hawrelak Park in Edmonton by a franchised vendor. No other vendor is permitted to rent paddleboats. As a result, the vendor monopolizes the supply of paddleboats for rent. The service is provided through an agreement between the vendor and the City's Parks and Recreation Department. But, while the Department arranged for the service to be available, it does not pay for the service – the patrons do.

Divestiture

Lease
A lease is an arrangement whereby a government rents public land or facilities to a private firm or not-for-profit organization to provide a service. It divests itself of its rights in those lands or facilities for the specified period of the lease. The government arranges the service, a private firm or not-for-profit organization produces it and the consumer pays for it. For example, a city may lease parkland to a private firm that is interested in building a curling facility. The agreement usually includes a provision requiring that the land, and the facilities built on it, be returned to the city after the lease expires. Allen (1980) suggests that the concession or lease approach to cooperation has several advantages. Noteworthy among these are: the provision of revenue-producing park facilities without capital improvement expenditures and without operating and maintenance costs; the production of non-tax funds that can be used to support other non-revenue-producing park units; the potential for private enterprise to lease public facilities for general public use; and finally, the potential to be employed for any facility or service for which fees and charges can be levied.

Allen (1980) also suggests that a lease holds the following advantages for both the community and the entrepreneur. First, the community benefits from getting a 'luxury' facility with no investment. Because facilities usually have a low municipal priority with respect to other needs, the concept of a lease permits the development of a facility that might otherwise be years away. Second, the community receives private investment and expert management to ensure an effective operation. Third, a lease provides an annual income for the park agency, which usually comes from a percentage of the receipts. Finally, after the lease period has expired, the facility can become the property of the community if this provision is written into the lease.

From the perspective of the private entrepreneur, first, a profitable opportunity is secured without the need to purchase land. Second, by building on leased land, the entrepreneur avoids excessive costs in time and money spent obtaining zoning changes. In some instances, this can be very high. Third, the entrepreneur saves on construction costs because the facility can usually be placed in a park to take advantage of existing access and egress roads, parking and an aesthetic setting. Fourth, despite paying a lease fee, the cost is usually less than the property taxes on private development. Fifth, a park location is usually strategically placed from the standpoint of patrons, with good access to the park. Finally, outside maintenance is likely to be handled by the public park staff, while internal maintenance personnel can often be hired at rates lower than those required by the municipality.

Sale
Sale involves the permanent divestiture by a government of land, facilities or the rights to provide services to a private firm or not-for-profit organization. A private firm or not-for-profit organization obtains ownership of a public asset and produces a service for which the consumer pays. For example, a city may sell lands that it has accumulated through the development of new neighbourhoods or through tax-delinquent possession. The private firms and not-for-profit organizations that purchase such lands are then entitled to use them for whatever purposes they choose (within zoning categories), as the city has given up its right to regulate the service that is provided.

A Model of Public Service Delivery

In order to simplify understanding of the concepts and forms of service delivery discussed here, a model has been created which depicts the interrelationships among the three defining variables: (i) the level of competitive forces, (ii) the nature of the good, and (iii) the degree of government control (Fig. 10.1). The model is diamond shaped with four quadrants. Each quadrant includes one of the four categories of public service delivery that were identified earlier: (i) governmental arrangements, (ii) cross-sector alliances, (iii) regulated monopolies, and (iv) divestiture.

In the first quadrant, *governmental arrangements* reflect social goods, characterized by a low level of competition and maximum government control. Direct provision, arm's-length provision, internal

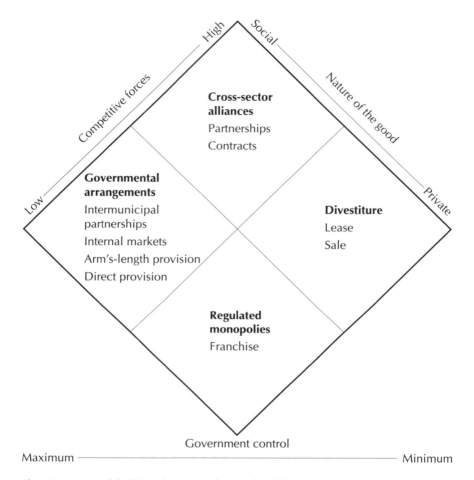

Fig. 10.1. A model of the alternative forms of public leisure services delivery.

markets and intermunicipal partnerships fall into this group. They are similar because the nature of each good is social; however, the level of competitive forces and the amount of government control differs for each governmental arrangement, affecting its position within the quadrant. Direct provision involves the lowest possible level of competition, followed by arm's-length provision, internal markets, and intermunicipal partnerships in that order. In the same order, direct provision involves the highest degree of government control, followed by arm's-length provision, internal markets and intermunicipal partnerships. The position of each arrangement in the quadrant must be considered in order to identify differences among them.

It is our contention that the remaining three quadrants all involve some degree of privatization of public service delivery. Traditionally, privatization has been equated primarily with sale. However, this explanation excludes several modes of public service delivery that involve private or not-for-profit organizations. For instance, when a municipal government contracts a private firm to manage an arena, essentially they are privatizing that facility, as it is no longer operated by public employees. Again, if a government enlists the aid of the Boys and Girls Club, a not-for-profit organization, to provide after-school day care, thereby acting as a patron of leisure services, this, too, can be perceived as privatization, because direct service delivery is offered by a non-governmental organization, despite receiving subsidy from the public sector. In this regard, the authors concur with Servos (1989) and Savas (1987), the latter of whom defines privatization as '. . . a wide range of alternatives to the direct provision of public service(s) by governments using their own employees.' In other words, that which is not a governmental agreement can be considered a form of privatization.

Therefore, in the second quadrant, *cross-sector alliances* are really specific methods of privatization. They are employed to provide social goods, characterized by a high level of competition and a moderate level of government control. Partnerships and contracts are both intended to secure the provision of social goods, but the competitive forces are somewhat higher for a partnership than for a contractual relationship. In addition, partnerships involve less government control than do contracts. However, the government control over cross-sector alliances is less than that involved in governmental arrangements, although more than is found in divestiture.

In the third quadrant, *regulated monopolies*, such as a franchise, are employed to provide private goods, characterized by a low level of competition and a moderate level of government control. However, as was the case for cross-sector alliances, franchises involve greater government control than divestiture and less government control than governmental arrangements.

Finally, in the fourth quadrant, *divestiture* is used to provide private goods, characterized by a high level of competition at a minimum level of government control. Lease and sale are similar in that both are employed to provide private goods and involve equally high levels of competition, depending on the specifications of the agreement. However, a lease involves more government control than a sale as the service is turned back to the public sector after the period of the lease. Divestiture involves greater competition and less government control than cross-sector alliances, regulated monopolies and intergovernmental arrangements.

Conclusion

The model presented in this chapter can be a helpful tool for government decision-makers as it identifies a typology of a range of alternatives for the delivery of public leisure services and indicates the level of competitive forces, the nature of the goods, and the amount of government control for each particular form. It should be noted, however, that the lines that divide the four quadrants of the model are porous. As Burton (1996) has noted, dichotomies and continuums are essential to the overall understanding of a concept, but they are only approximations of reality. Clearly, exceptions to each of the proposed categories are possible and, indeed, more than likely. The interpretation of each method of service delivery is dependent on the specifications of the agreement. Nevertheless, the various forms of governmental arrangements, cross-sector alliances, regulated monopolies, and divestiture identified here describe viable options for the delivery of public services, depending on the shifting philosophical, political and economic underpinnings of the public agency.

References

Allen, S.E. (1980) Public–private cooperation. *Parks and Recreation* 15, pp. 41, 44, 89.

Andrew, C., Harvey, J. and Dawson, D. (1994) Evolution of local state activity: recreation policy in Toronto. *Leisure Studies* 13, 1–16.

Burton, T.L. (1982) The Roles of Government in the Leisure Services Delivery System. Paper presented at the VIIth Commonwealth and International Conference on Sport, Physical Education, Recreation and Dance, Brisbane, Australia.

Burton, T.L. (1996) Safety nets and security blankets: false dichotomies in leisure studies. *Leisure Studies* 15, 17–30.

Capital Region Forum Limited (1995) *Newsletter* 1, November.

Coalter, F. (1995) Compulsory competitive tendering for sport and leisure management: a lost opportunity? *Managing Leisure* 1, 3–15.

Henry, I.P. (1993) *The Politics of Leisure Policy*. Macmillan Press, London.

Oliver, C. (1990) Determinants of interorganizational relationships: integration and future directions. *Academy of Management Review* 15(2), 241–275.

Osborne, D. and Gaebler, T. (1992) *Reinventing Government: How the Entrepreneurial Spirit is Transforming the Public Sector*. Addison-Wesley Publishing Company, New York.

Peston, M. (1972) *Public Goods and the Public Sector*. Macmillan Press, London.

Ravenscroft, N. (1993) Public leisure provision and the good citizen. *Leisure Studies* 12, 33–44.

Savas, E.S. (1987) *Privatization: The Key to Better Government.* Chatham House, Chatham, New Jersey.

Searle, M.S. and Brayley, R.E. (1993) *Leisure Services in Canada: an Introduction.* Venture Publishing, State College, Pennsylvania.

Servos, P. (1989) Alberta Recreation and Parks. Privatization of Park Operation and Maintenance Services. MA thesis, University of Alberta, Edmonton.

Walsh, K. (1995) *Public Services and Market Mechanisms.* Macmillan Press, London.

The Value and Structure of Commercial Leisure

11

Dominic Irvine and Peter Taylor

Leisure Management Unit, University of Sheffield, Hicks Building, Hounsfield Road, Sheffield S3 7RH, UK

Introduction

In leisure studies there are some major, worrying gaps in the description of the field which so many researchers are busy analysing. This chapter reports continuing research at Sheffield University which is attempting to clarify one of these major gaps – just what is the commercial leisure sector, how big is it and how is it structured? In order to fulfil this unashamedly descriptive purpose, this chapter considers problems of both definition and data and attempts a consensus description of the commercial leisure sector. It then uses a hitherto unexploited resource, commercial market reports, to construct estimates of the size and structure of the commercial leisure market.

Commercial Leisure in Leisure Literature

In 1979 John Roberts noted that only just over 9% of listed publications on leisure were concerned with the commercial leisure sector, concluding, 'It appears that, quantitatively and with regard to the vast scope of the sector, it is under-researched.' Of the many academic studies of leisure since 1979, few of the approaches have embraced commercial leisure as a discrete entity worthy of consideration. Green *et al.* (1987) for example, despite detailed critical analysis of contemporary sociological theories, dismiss commercial leisure in two sentences:

© CAB INTERNATIONAL 1998. *Leisure Management: Issues and Applications*
(eds M.F. Collins and I.S. Cooper)

Not surprisingly, the drive for profit within the commercial sector has seen the public sector lagging behind and often serving to fill in some of the gaps left by the market. Obviously, commercial leisure provision is about the selling of leisure services and goods to consumers who can afford them.

(Green *et al.*, 1987:183)

Rojek (1989) is a little less dismissive, but still limits reference to the commercial leisure sector to a few references of which this is an example:

The leisure industry consists of the conglomerate of business units which aim to produce and reproduce consumer demand for leisure goods and services. Its branches include tourism, catering, sport, outdoor recreations, and the huge area of mass communications, including pop music, video, television, radio magazines and books. The leisure industry seeks to organise leisure activities on strict market principles; i.e. in pursuit of the accumulation of profit rather than the satisfaction of social need.

(Rojek, 1989:21)

Leaving aside substantive issues such as the extent to which social need is actually met by the market, such a statement leaves many definitional questions unanswered. For example, does catering include meals eaten as part of corporate entertaining? Is sponsorship a commercial activity and part of 'strict market principles' or is it altruism and therefore not commercial? Does tourism as commercial leisure include business travel? What is the relationship between strict market principles and the provision of staff leisure facilities – are they commercial? Statements such as the two above fail to provide a satisfactory explanation of commercial leisure, let alone an appreciation of its role in the issues under common discussion in analysis of leisure.

The identification and analysis of commercial leisure is a 'ghetto' area of leisure studies, with a few notable reports (e.g. Roberts, 1979; Gratton and Taylor, 1987; Martin and Mason, 1989). This is worrying because many of the issues of leisure participation and provision can be better explained and understood by a fully informed appreciation of differences *and similarities* between public, voluntary and commercial sectors. To do this it is necessary to identify and analyse commercial leisure as a perspective in its own right.

Commercial Leisure

A common starting point is a dictionary definition of 'commercial': 'being engaged in commerce – financial transactions; the buying and selling of merchandise on a large scale where profit is the primary aim rather than artistic or altruistic goals' (*Concise Oxford Dictionary*, 8th edition, 1990). A commercial leisure organization is primarily concerned with generating profit from leisure. Given that a profit is generated by businesses through the provision of products or services, commercial leisure refers to those leisure *activities* which depend on goods and services commercially provided. In accepting activities as the basis for defining leisure, the well-documented ambiguities detailed in sociological texts have some relevance. The choice of activities as the basis for defining commercial leisure was adopted by Roberts (1979), Gratton and Taylor (1987), Martin and Mason (1989) and Tribe (1995).

It is perhaps useful at this point to clarify the distinction between the commercial leisure market and the commercial leisure industry, because the two are not synonymous. The commercial leisure market refers to those leisure activities which require a financial transaction to have taken place between the participant (or on behalf of the participant) and a commercial organization. Whilst the commercial organization supplying the goods or services is part of the leisure market, it may well be that the leisure-related aspect of their business is a minor part of their operation. A focus on the commercial leisure industry would be on those businesses whose *core business* is the provision of goods and/or services for the leisure market. As such, the leisure industry may not represent the whole of the leisure market. Therefore, to understand fully commercial leisure, it is necessary to adopt a market-based rather than an industry-based focus.

Given that commercial leisure refers to activities dependent on the provision of goods and services by commercial organizations, Crossley and Jamieson's (1988) definition of commercial recreation would appear to be a reasonable one, assuming that recreation and leisure are synonymous: 'the provision of recreation related products or services by private enterprises for a fee, with the long-term intent of being profitable' (Crossley and Jamieson, 1988:6).

This definition leaves open to interpretation what is or is not a recreation-related product or service. To answer this, a useful starting point is to examine the range of activities in which commercial organizations are involved and which are claimed to be leisure. For the purposes of this exercise the range of activities which are considered leisure will be defined by those supplying the market. Such information is provided in a number of market research reports (e.g. Jordans, 1992; Key Note, 1992) and in two academic reports (Roberts, 1979; Martin and Mason, 1989) which provide an interpretation of what is meant by the leisure market. By relying on more than one source it is possible to compare and contrast the various approaches to determine whether the concept of commercial leisure is consistent. This would be demonstrated if the same activities appeared in all the reports examined. The greater the recurrence of activities the more consistent the concept. The validity of the concept can then be established through conceptual analysis.

The four sources that form the basis of this process have been set out in Table 11.1 (Roberts, 1979), Table 11.2 (Key Note, 1992), Table 11.3 (Jordans, 1992), and Table 11.4 (Martin and Mason, 1989).

Table 11.1. Leisure activities provided by the commercial sector.

LEISURE Common elements Transport: Private car Cycling Motor- cycling Coaches Private rail Air Water	Arts	Home- based	Newspapers and magazines Books Radio Television Records, cassettes, hi-fi Indoor games		
		Outside home	Music Theatre Cinema *Museums and art galleries* *Libraries* *Parks, country homes* *Education*		
	Tourism	Accommo- dation	Hotels Holiday camps Camping, caravanning Second homes Boat holidays *Historic*		
		Attractions	Sightseeing Wildlife and amusement parks Zoos		
		Operators	Travel agents and tour operators		
	Sport	Active	Indoor	Tenpin bowling Ice-skating *Swimming and diving* Tennis *Table tennis*	*Squash* Darts Billiards and snooker, etc.
			Outdoor	Yachting and boating Fishing	Horse and pony riding Golf, hockey

Table 11.1. (*cont.*)

Sport	Active	Outdoor	*Skateboard-ing* *Roller skating* *Tennis*	Football Flying and gliding *Athletics*, etc.
	Equipment providers			
	Spectator	Indoor	Boxing and wrestling Show jumping	Tennis Table tennis
		Outdoor	Football Cricket *Athletics* Show jumping	Speedway Tennis Horse and greyhound racing, etc.
Recreation and social-ising	Gambling		Amusement arcades, pools, bingo, betting, casinos, lotteries	
	Eating		Restaurants, cafés, snack bars, street stalls, home entertainment	
	Drinking		Pubs, hotels, off-licences, home brewing	
	Tobacco			
	Shopping		Window shopping, special displays (e.g. Christmas sales, etc.) comparison shopping, exhibitions	
	Dancing		Ballrooms, discotheques, dance schools	
	Home environment		Hobbies, home-making, gardening, DIY, car maintenance, pets, promotional parties, knitting and sewing circles	
	Health and beauty		Health spas, saunas, beauty parlours, slimming aids, cosmetics	

Table 11.1. (*cont.*)

Recreation and social ising	Other	Drug-taking, fun fairs, dating and marriage bureaux

Items in *italics* are marginal
Source: Roberts, 1979.

Table 11.2. Types of UK leisure-dependent businesses.

Transport	**Other leisure services**
Railways	Cinemas
Bus operators	Theatres, music halls, etc.
Taxis and private hire	TV and radio services
Sea transport	Film and recording studios
Air transport	Performers and performing groups
Travel agents	Radio and TV relay services
	Dance halls and dancing schools
Leisure goods wholesalers	Sport
Alcoholic drink	Other recreations
Brown goods, records and tapes	Betting and gaming
Musical instruments	Photography and photographic
Photographic goods	processing
Toys	Public museums, libraries and galleries
Travel and fancy goods	
	Leisure goods manufacturers
Leisure goods retailers	Motor vehicles and parts
Off-licences	Other transport equipment
Radio and electrical shops	Food and drink manufacture
Radio and rental shops	Reading material, etc.
Hardware and DIY shops	Musical instruments
Leather goods, sports goods, toys, and fancy goods shops	Photographic processing laboratories
Music shops	Toys and games
Pet and pet food shops	Sports goods
Motor trades	Brown goods, records and tapes
	Photographic equipment
Catering companies	Other
Hotels and residential establishments	
Holiday camps, camping and caravan sites	
Restaurants, cafés and snack bars	
Public houses	
Clubs (excluding sports and gaming clubs)	
Catering contractors	

Source: adapted from Key Note (1992).

Table 11.3. Britain's leisure industry.

THE PRIVATE SECTOR

Firms and corporate organizations mainly involved in:

- Hotels and other forms of accommodation
- Restaurants and derivative eating and social drinking establishments
- Health and fitness clubs and studios
- Cinemas
- Theatres
- Sports centres
- Visitor attractions including theme parks and amusement centres
- Discotheques and night-clubs
- Gaming, gambling and casinos
- Mixed retail and recreation centres or 'leisure villages'.

Source: adapted from Jordans (1992).

Table 11.4. Extent of commercial leisure provision.

Sector	Commercial role
Reading	Most books, newspapers and magazines
Viewing and listening	Virtually all equipment and software Some Broadcast Services
DIY and gardening	Virtually all products and tools
Hobbies and pastimes	Virtually all products and services
Formal entertainment	Many venues and events, e.g. cinema, theme and amusement parks, some theatres and sports events
Sport and active recreation	Most sports equipment and clothing. specialist sports facilities and health clubs, management of facilities
Alcoholic drink	Virtually all products and services
Leisure catering	Most hotels, restaurants, fast-food outlets, holiday resorts, etc.
Holidays overseas	Most holiday packages and travel services

Source: Martin and Mason (1989).

Testing Consistency

The definitions of commercial leisure in Tables 11.1–11.4 demonstrate a remarkable degree of inconsistency. Only a few categories are listed in all four, namely theatre and concerts, cinema and sports participation. Two of the more curious entries are public museums, libraries and galleries (Key Note) and education (Roberts).

From the descriptions of leisure and commercial leisure detailed in Tables 11.1–11.4 it is possible to create an aggregate classification of leisure activities (Table 11.5). In this instance, a number of assumptions were made. These mostly relate to whether the activity included in one

Table 11.5. Summary of the commercial leisure market.

Area	Field	
Arts	Reading material	Theatre and concerts
	Brown goods	Cinema
	CDs/records/tapes	Television relay services
	Radio relay services	Photography/films/processing
	Musical instruments	Music, video tapes
	Galleries	
Sports	Participation	Clothing and footwear
	Equipment	Spectating
Attractions	Country houses	Amusement parks
	Historic attractions	Wildlife parks
	Zoos	Theme parks
Travel	Travel agents	Tour operators
Transport	To and from participating in leisure activities, or as a leisure activity in its own right, e.g. motoring for pleasure, rail, boat trips	
Accommodation	Hotels	Holiday camps
	Leisure villages	Caravanning
	Boats	Camping
	Second homes	
Eating	Restaurants	Eating as occasion
	Fast food	Snack bars
	Take-away	Clubs
Alcohol	Off-licence	Licensed premises
	Home brewing	
Gambling	Amusement arcades	Pools
	Bingo	Betting
	Gaming	Lotteries
	Casinos	
Dancing	Dance schools	Night clubs
	Discos	Dance halls
Tobacco	All tobacco products	
Home environment	Home computers	Games
	Gardening	Hobbies
	Toys	DIY
	Car maintenance	Pets and pet foods
	Art and antique	
Sponsorship		

table can be assumed to mean the same as an activity defined using similar but not identical terms. Even where the same terminology is used, such as 'eating in restaurants', it is not possible to be certain that the type of catering establishments referred to in one report are the same as those defined as restaurants in others. For example, does one or the other include roadside catering vans?

Each of the market research reports has taken a different approach to classifying the markets. The Key Note (1992) report breaks down the market in terms of manufacture, wholesale and retail, whereas Jordans (1992) details a list of 'private sector activities'. In some instances it is possible to reduce a section to its core element. For example, Roberts (1979) breaks down sport into five categories; active sport (indoor and outdoor), spectator sport (indoor and outdoor), and sports equipment providers. This can be reduced to three areas – sports participation, sports spectating, sports equipment – with an additional sector created for sports shoes and clothing. Further, there are areas of overlap, such as establishments which offer food and those that sell alcohol such as restaurants and pubs. Tourism, which is given a separate section under Roberts (1979), is a combination of several areas including accommodation, attractions, eating, drinking and transport.

Another difficulty is the reliance on creating a list of activities as done by Roberts (1979). The results of this method can date when some activities have a short lifespan, whilst new activities appear. In so doing, the essence of the concept has not changed, merely the range of activities which is covered by that concept. It is inevitable that an updated classification will cover more or different activities as new activities develop and become popular. Given that all four reports took varying approaches to describing the leisure market and accepting the assumptions made, the inconsistency of entries is not surprising. Table 11.5 represents the summary classification of commercial leisure. Approximately a third of the categories in Table 11.5 were only listed in one of the separate sources in Tables 11.1–11.4.

Validating the Concept

The process of developing a concept is facilitated by establishing contrary cases or examples which fall in the grey area. The issue under exploration in such an instance is whether the concept developed is sufficiently narrow in its criteria that contrary examples are excluded. For example, the types of questions which might be asked are: '. . . if "X" goes with "Y" can we also find evidence that "X" can go with "non-Y"? The second type of evidence does not invalidate the first, but by considering both we protect ourselves against spurious generalizations'

(Bendix, 1963:536). The examples which are borderline, or in the grey area, provide an opportunity to revisit the original criteria and develop them further. The process can be summarized as one which alternates 'back and forth between tentative clause and tentative definition, each modifying each other so that in a sense closure is achieved when a complete and integral relation between the two is established' (Turner cited in Bulmer, 1984:252).

Given the complexity of the nature of leisure it is unlikely that complete closure can ever be achieved: however, that is no justification for not being as accurate as is possible within the objectives of the research. Many of the closure issues are more to do with the question 'what is leisure?' than 'what is commercial?'.

Direct and indirect spending

An interesting example is window shopping, which whilst a leisure activity does not involve any expenditure in its own right, but may require transport to get to the shops which involves expenditure to commercial organizations. If secondary activities such as transport, eating and drinking are included in the concept then it would be included. If the focus is on the primary activity, window shopping, then it would be excluded. By focusing on what is directly consumed rather than indirect consumption, attention is limited to those activities that are purely commercial leisure. Kelly (1990) made such a distinction but in relation to the supply side, rather than consumer purchases:

> In general, there are two types of recreation business. The first type is the *direct* supplier of goods and services related to recreation. The second is the *indirect* provider. Direct suppliers provide the equipment and environments that make recreation activity possible . . . Indirect suppliers are a step removed from our experience with the recreation occasion. For example, they advertise the products, edit trade periodicals for the business managers, and provide capital for new and expanding businesses.
>
> (Kelly, 1990:324–325)

Thus watching television would be included because it requires the viewer to purchase or rent a television in the first instance; whereas window shopping would be excluded – it does not require the individual to purchase a shop! Secondary leisure spending associated with window shopping should be included in other categories, such as travel or eating.

Obligated spending

The lack of areas such as personal hygiene and sleeping in Table 11.5 implies that activities which are of a mundane nature or obligated are excluded. Food and drink manufacture (in Key Note, 1992), beauty and slimming aids and cosmetics (in Roberts, 1979) and drugs (in Roberts, 1979) are excluded as being conceptually on the wrong side of the divide – i.e. more obligated than leisure. Determining what is or is not an obligated activity can be a grey area, for example 'eating'. Eating as social occasion is included and incorporates eating at home as a social occasion. The implication would appear to be that not all eating can be considered a leisure activity. As eating can be considered an obligated activity in order to stay alive this would make sense. The difficulty is in attempting to determine when a meal is eaten as social occasion and when it is eaten merely as part of existence, identifying the two not only conceptually but also empirically.

Another example of ambiguity is the consumption of tobacco products. For those addicted to tobacco products it could be argued that their consumption is part of everyday existence, i.e. obligated. However, it could be argued that as there are individuals who do not have a dependency on the product, its consumption in principle cannot be considered essential. Further, the increase in smoking-free workplaces would appear to add credence to the argument that smoking cannot be considered as part of work and therefore is a leisure activity. Similar arguments apply to drinking and gambling and hence they too are included. On the other hand, drugs are treated as obligated because of their addictive qualities, although soft drugs could be treated as commercial leisure products, even if they are illegal.

Such markets as eating, tobacco and drugs may be marginal conceptually but they are not marginal in terms of their market value. Another significant area of expenditure which is traditionally excluded in measures of commercial leisure spending is the cost of the home. Given that much of leisure takes place in the home, it could be argued that an element of the cost of accommodation should be included; however, since the primary purpose of a home is likely to be more obligated than leisure, we have followed convention and excluded it.

Profit

Profit as a primary objective does not exclude those activities undertaken by a commercial organization which are loss-making and are cross-subsidized using the profits from other areas. It is assumed that such a situation is temporary in that the organization either: (i) abandons its efforts; or (ii) is undertaking such an exercise to gain an initial foothold in the market. In both these instances the focus is generating profit, but in the first it has failed and in the second a longer-term view is being taken of the market.

It is this focus on profit that enables the distinction to be drawn between sponsorship and patronage. Altruistic social enterprises are excluded from the analysis because the primary focus is not the pursuance of profit. However, sponsorship of leisure activities is part of the profit-making process, therefore:

> Sponsorship is one aspect of a company's marketing mix. The growing sophistication of sponsorship as an activity and the greater awareness of the benefits that can be gained from sponsorship have been reflected in the increasing importance of its role in the marketing mix.
>
> (MINTEL, 1994:4)

Thus a local authority fun run (which may well have been organized to satisfy social objectives) whose total costs are met by commercial sponsors would be considered to be a commercial activity. Where the activity is only partially sponsored, then only a part of the activity can be deemed to be commercial. Conceptually, this makes sense as it reflects the differing agendas that organizations may have in choosing to involve themselves in an activity. Empirically, too, the measurement of sponsorship money is more appropriate than the total costs of a sponsored event. However, sponsorship lies outside normal definitions of commercial activity, such as Crossley and Jamieson's (1988) cited above, because no fee is paid by the leisure customer to the commercial company.

There is therefore a range of issues briefly alluded to here which affect whether an activity can be classified as commercial leisure. In any research process, if for no other reason than pragmatic consider-ations, a degree of ambiguity or vagueness is tolerated. The concept of vagueness on first reckoning might appear to be a strange state of affairs to accept in research. Vagueness offers the opportunity to declare a con-cept invalid, but provides a chance for the theorist to further enhance understanding through the analysis of the concept. In some instances a term, whilst vague, is intellectually useful (Guba, 1990). It is argued that this is the case here. The ambiguities surrounding leisure are inevitable given the complex interrelation of issues involved in the concept. Refining the concept is a continual process.

Determining the Value of the Commercial Leisure Market

Using government data organized by Standard Industrial Classification codes to determine the value of commercial leisure not only commits the error of being industry- rather than market-focused, it does not separate activities into leisure and non-leisure use. Some reports were identified which purported to provide a value for the leisure sector. For example, the Cabinet Office Enterprise Unit (1985) produced a report which addressed the tourism and leisure sector, in which they valued tourism and leisure as having an annual turnover of £10 billion. No sources were cited for these data. There is also doubt as to whether it includes only those activities mentioned in the report or whether it represents all leisure activities: no reference was made to a number of key leisure areas such as sports participation or spectating, do-it-yourself (DIY), hobbies and other leisure activities undertaken at home – as these were not mentioned they were presumably left out of the calculation.

In Banks (1985) the word 'tourism' is adopted as the all-embracing term incorporating leisure. In valuing the tourism and leisure industry, a figure is given for tourism but not for other areas of leisure. As with the Cabinet Office report, Banks fails to identify all aspects of the leisure industry. In contrast, Leisure Consultants (1996) in conjunction with the Leisure Industries Research Centre provide the most comprehensive coverage of the leisure industry. However, even in this report there are areas of the leisure industry that are excluded, for example no mention is made, either in general or under DIY, of car maintenance; similarly, whilst television, videos and compact discs (CDs) all feature, radio relay services do not, neither do musical instruments, nor the tobacco industry. As well as directly echoing the conceptual problems reviewed earlier of identifying all relevant leisure areas, these reports also do not distinguish clearly between commercial and other provision.

The value of the commercial leisure market is a reflection of total leisure turnover of commercial organizations in the leisure market. This should not be confused with the value of the leisure industry which is an expression of the value of businesses whose core activity is leisure. By determining the total expenditure it is possible to compare the commercial leisure sector with other markets. A common medium for comparison is market size in relation to gross domestic product (GDP).

Ideally, information on the value of each sector would be obtained firsthand from those involved in the sector. On this basis an attempt was made to obtain the data on how much each sector was worth by contacting the various trade organizations that represent each area. It was found that, with the exception of tourism as represented by the British Tourist Authority and alcohol as represented by the Brewers' Society, most trade organizations do not have such data.

There appears to be no one source which provides a value on the whole of the commercial leisure market. As a consequence, it was decided to investigate secondary information contained within commercial market-research reports. These often have access to unpublished trade information from the industries concerned, and sometimes they commission specific primary research. They are generally of unknown quality, however. Nevertheless, there is a considerable volume of such reports, many specific to individual industries. A search in the British Library for reports specific to leisure industries and markets revealed over 230 commercial reports covering the period 1990 to 1994.

Many of the problems in determining the value of the market depend on avoiding double counting. This is because of the complex interrelationship between the many forms of leisure activity. For example, part of the commercial leisure market includes tourism. This can embrace a wide variety of activities including eating out and using sports centres to name but two. In both of these cases their leisure use can be attributed other than to tourism. Simply accepting a figure for tourism and using that as indicative of all use may be to undervalue the sector. Conversely, using a value for tourism and then a value that represents the total for eating out will double count markets, thus exaggerating the value. In valuing the commercial leisure market it is desirable to have a value for the total of each sector and an aggregate total that has been adjusted for double counting.

The technique used for determining the value has to be able not only to deal with the problem of under- and overvaluing the sector but also must be of sufficient accuracy to be able to distinguish between non-leisure and leisure. This can be problematic. To illustrate this, consider the example of gardening, and in particular the market for gardening tools. There is considerable blurring between tools used for the recreational garden and those used in horticulture. The 'sit on' mower might be used by the recreational gardener and the small hand mower might be used by the professional gardener as noted in Key Note: 'although regarded as a leisure industry, gardening is broadly based. At one end of the scale it has associations with horticulture, whilst at the other end it borders on DIY and home improvement' (Key Note, 1993:2). Problems similar to this can be found in virtually any aspect of the leisure industry and affect the choice of source selected.

A major difficulty of relying on secondary information such as that contained within commercial market-research reports is that little explanation is provided about the methodology used for determining the data. Thus it is not possible to determine its validity or consistency. Therefore, all the figures from the market-research reports have to be treated with caution. That said, collectively they provide a comprehensive amount of information. Using Table 11.5 as a framework, the value for each of the sectors was sought. The findings are set out in Table 11.6, which covers the year 1990, the year for which reliable information was available for the most number of leisure markets. A

Table 11.6. Total value and aggregate value of the commercial leisure sector.

Area	Example	Total value 1990 (£m) of each market segment	Aggregate value 1990 (£m)
Arts	Reading material	4437	4437
	TV – retail	790	790
	TV – rental	640	640
	Video – retail	530	530
	Video – rental	370	370
	Hi-fi and stereo	695	695
	CDs, records and tapes	1183	1183
	Video tapes	1123	1123
	TV relay services	2554	2554
	Radio relay services	160	160
	Musical instruments	Unknown	Unknown
	Music	Unknown	Unknown
	Theatre and concerts	283	Included in tourism
	Cinema	295	Included in tourism
	Photography	1361	1361
	Galleries	Included in tourism	Included in tourism
Sports	Participation	805	805
	Equipment	470	470
	Clothing	1176	1176
	Footwear	792	792
	Spectating	260	Included in tourism
Attractions	Country houses	Included in tourism	Included in tourism
	Historic attractions	Included in tourism	Included in tourism
	Zoos	Included in tourism	Included in tourism
	Amusement parks	Included in tourism	Included in tourism
	Wildlife parks	Included in tourism	Included in tourism
	Theme parks	Included in tourism	Included in tourism
Travel	Travel agents and tour operators	5018	Included in tourism
Transport	Transport	Included in tourism	Included in tourism
Accommodation	Hotels	Included in tourism	Included in tourism
	Leisure villages	Included in tourism	Included in tourism
	Boats	Included in tourism	Included in tourism
	Holiday camps	Included in tourism	Included in tourism
	Caravanning	Included in tourism	Included in tourism
	Caravan – retail	25[a]	25[a]
	Camping	Included in tourism	Included in tourism
	Camping equipment (retail)	121[a]	121[a]
	Second homes	Unknown	Unknown

Table 11.6. (*cont.*)

Area	Example	Total value 1990 (£m) of each market segment	Aggregate value 1990 (£m)
Eating	TOTAL	30,672[b]	7668[b,d]
	Restaurants	3906	Included in the above figure
	Fast food and take-away	4162	Included in the above figure
	Contract catering	2059	Included in the above figure
	Public houses	10,154	Included in the above figure
	Hotels	Included in the total	Included in the above figure
	Holiday camps	Included in the total	Included in the above figure
	Snack bars	Included in the total	Included in the above figure
	Clubs	Included in the total	Included in the above figure
Alcohol	TOTAL	21,738[b]	5435[b,d]
	Off-licence	Included in the above figure	Included in the above figure
	Home brewing	Included in the above figure	Included in the above figure
	Licensed premises	Included in the above figure	Included in the above figure
Gambling	TOTAL	3108[c]	3108[c]
	Amusement arcades	Included in the above figure	Included in the above figure
	Bingo	Included in the above figure	Included in the above figure
	Gaming	Included in the above figure	Included in the above figure
	Casinos	Included in the above figure	Included in the above figure
	Pools	Included in the above figure	Included in the above figure
	Betting	Included in the above figure	Included in the above figure
	Lotteries	Included in the above figure	Included in the above figure

Table 11.6. (*cont.*)

Area	Example	Total value 1990 (£m) of each market segment	Aggregate value 1990 (£m)
Dancing	TOTAL	2074[c]	2074[c]
	Dance schools	Included in the above figure	Included in the above figure
	Discos	Included in the above figure	Included in the above figure
	Night clubs	Included in the above figure	Included in the above figure
	Dance halls	Included in the above figure	Included in the above figure
Tobacco	Tobacco products	8683	8683
Home environment	Gardening equipment	261	261
	Plants	790	790
	Toys/games/home computers	1599	1599
	Car maintenance	Unknown	Unknown
	Hobbies	Unknown	Unknown
	Pets and pet foods	1980	1980
	D.I.Y.	1472	1472
Tourism	Day trips	13,350	13,350
	One night or more	20,285	20,285
Sponsorship		265	265
Total aggregate value (£m)			83,937
GDP			478,886
Commercial leisure as a % of GDP			17.5%

[a]The value referred to is in addition to the segment value included in Tourism.
[b]Includes expenditure for work/business purposes.
[c]There may be some overlap with the Tourism figures.
[d]25% of the market segment values for eating and alcohol have been allocated to the aggregate value to cover expenditure not otherwise included in the aggregate Tourism data.

number of assumptions had to be made to arrive at the data contained within Table 11.6. Additionally, assessing the validity of data by comparing and contrasting it with other sources was not always possible because of the different methodologies used and the different ways in which the sectors were broken down.

Accepting these limitations, the data represent as accurate a picture as has been possible to obtain of the value of the commercial leisure market. The first column of data in Table 11.6 represents each separate market, whilst the final column of data is the best available aggregate picture, after eliminating some double counting in the first column of data. There are six missing elements in Table 11.6, however, so the aggregate total is likely to be an underestimate. Nevertheless, the results do present a 'bottom line', which is that the commercial leisure sector represents at least 17.5% of GDP in the UK.

It was considered prudent not to provide separate market value estimates for many of the individual markets under the attractions and accommodations sectors, because of grey areas and possible double counting between them and because the primary purpose was to assemble the aggregate figure. We therefore report the tourism figure which embraces these attractions and accommodation markets.

As with determining the nature of commercial leisure, different market research organizations divided the market up into different sections. For example, Jordans (1991) in their analysis of the British television and radio industry detailed the information about the value of the sector in terms of the top 20 organizations as defined by turnover. What was not specified was whether each organization was concerned with radio or television or both. In contrast, the Economist Intelligence Unit's report (1991) into commercial radio simply listed all the commercial radio stations at the time the report was being written and included turnover as part of that information. Thus, to obtain figures for both sectors it was necessary in the first instance to sum the turnover of the radio stations detailed in the Economist Intelligence Unit report to ascertain the value of the market. Because the Economist Intelligence Unit report was only concerned with radio stations, it was then possible to determine which was a television or radio station in the Jordans (1991) listing, thus enabling the value of the television broadcasting industry to be determined. As nearly all companies at the top of the list in the Jordans ranking were television companies the assumption was made that this represented the bulk of the television broadcasting sector. Decisions analogous to this had to be made throughout the analysis.

Because most of the data was for 1990, this year was chosen as the base year for the estimates, against which it was possible to determine the percentage of GDP attributable to the commercial leisure industry. Inevitably, the size of the market will have changed since 1990, perhaps the biggest shifts being the introduction of the National Lottery and the results of recent legislation governing radio and television companies which has increased significantly the number of companies operating. However, as the data gathered for 1990 are the most detailed available, they provide the best indication of the value of the commercial leisure market. Because of the ambiguity in attempting to compare a report from one organization with that of another organization, it is a possibility that there is still overlap and/or areas missed out in the coverage of the various reports.

In some instances, the figures detailed in Table 11.6 cover more than one area. Where this is the case, the amount is detailed adjacent to the section heading and it can be assumed that all the items within that section are incorporated within the figure detailed. Where there are separate figures for specific areas these are detailed adjacent to the relevant activity. For some areas it has been possible to obtain an aggregate figure from one report but not specific figures for each example within that area. In other instances it has been possible to obtain figures specific for individual activities but not for the sector as a whole. Where this has occurred, the aggregate figures for each section have been used in working out the total value of the sector. Where a report covers more than one area, the reference to the relevant section is detailed in the value column. Wherever possible, for the purposes of accuracy, the most detailed data have been used.

The Structure of the Commercial Leisure Industry

Fifteen of the markets detailed in Table 11.5 were selected as the basis for determining industry structure. The choice of markets was based on the availability of market research reports in the area and also to ensure a broad mix of manufacturing and service industries. The sample frame is thus a non-probability sample. The sources of the data were the ICC Financial Survey, ICC Business Ratios and ICC Business Ratios Plus reports. An important distinction between the three types of report is that the Business Ratios and Plus reports exclude businesses with a turnover of less than £4 million. This limitation does not apply to the Financial Survey reports which include all companies whose activities are considered to fall within the scope of the report and are actively trading. In all three cases, only those companies registered at Companies House are included. The analysis does not therefore represent the distribution of all companies and this affects the generalizations that may be drawn from the data.

The turnover, number of employees, holding company, and ultimate holding company were recorded for each company detailed in the 15 reports which provided an initial sample of 6302 companies.

To avoid double counting, where a holding company featured in the reports as well as the subsidiary, the subsidiary was deleted. In 100 such instances it was not clear whether the turnover detailed was attributable solely to the holding company or the subsidiary. For example, where a company had two or more subsidiaries, in some instances the combined turnover exceeded the turnover of the holding company. In such instances, to remove the subsidiaries may be to undervalue the company, but to include them may overvalue the company. To overcome this potential source of error primary data was sought direct from the companies concerned in the form of company reports. Of the 100 companies contacted where there was uncertainty about which company to attribute the turnover detailed, 20 responded and of these 15 provided company reports. Two reports contained insufficient information to be able to determine which was the correct figure and one supplied reports for the wrong years. The remaining 12 provided sufficient information to be able to determine which was the correct figure. These reports also provided an additional method of checking whether the figures detailed in the ICC reports were accurate. Of the remaining 80 companies, whichever was the higher figure was accepted as being that which represented the turnover of the group. In two instances turnover was expressed as a negative figure, so they were deleted.

The 15 markets investigated are listed in Table 11.7, which is also the key for Fig. 11.1, which presents evidence of the market concentration in these sectors. Market concentration is a major indicator of market structure, demonstrating the size distribution of firms supplying a market, in particular the extent to which supply of a particular product is concentrated in a few large firms.

In Fig. 11.1 the most widely used measure of market concentration is reported, the five-firm concentration ratio, which measures the percentage of market output supplied by the largest five firms. Table 11.7 indicates a high level of market concentration in the 15 leisure markets examined. Even in the least concentrated markets, DIY and book publishers, over 30% of market production is by the largest five firms. More commonly in the sectors examined, 50% or more of production is controlled by the largest five firms. The most concentrated markets in Fig. 11.1 are airlines and airports, and photography, with over 70% of output in the hands of the largest five suppliers. Clearly this is evidence to verify the suggestion that leisure, like most markets in the British economy, is oligopolistic, with market power in the hands of a few major companies. The equivalent five-firm concentration ratio for British industry in 1983 was just over 50%.

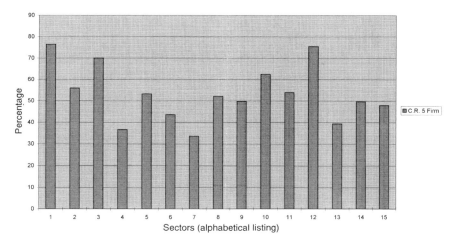

Fig. 11.1. Five-firm concentration ratio.

Table 11.7. Leisure sectors investigated for market structure.

	Sector	Five-firm concentration ratio
1	Airlines and airports	76.39
2	Antiques and fine art	55.9
3	Betting and gaming	70.01
4	Book publishers	36.6
5	Brewers, bottlers and soft drinks	53.26
6	Caravans	43.56
7	DIY	33.54
8	Film and television	52.18
9	Hotels and leisure complexes	49.81
10	Music	62.42
11	Newspaper publishers	53.97
12	Photography	75.39
13	Sports equipment	39.36
14	Toys	49.65
15	Travel agents and tour operators	49.97
	Average	**53.33**

Conclusion

This essentially descriptive exercise will provide some comfort to those who have been suggesting on the basis of no evidence at all that the commercial leisure industry is important, and that it is highly concentrated in a few hands. However, the evidence in this chapter is only the start of an analysis of the size and structure of the commercial leisure industry. A major adjustment needs to made to the measure of market concentration to account for the effects of international competition – in 1983 the five-firm concentration ratio for British industry fell from 50% to 36% when adjusted for the effects of international competition in British markets.

Furthermore, the market power held by the largest five firms in any commercial leisure market sector, as measured by the concentration ratio, may conceal more healthy competition in a variety of ways, including ease of entry into the market for new firms, and changing identities over time of the largest five firms. However, it has been noted elsewhere (Gratton and Taylor, 1987) that the largest five firms in different sectors are often the same companies, operating with market power in a number of sectors, which implies greater market concentration than is apparent in Table 11.7.

As regards more substantive issues of firms' market behaviour consequent upon their market power, it is worth reminding those keen to jump on the simplistic bandwagon of 'more market concentration is always bad', that this is not necessarily the case. Oligopoly gives rise to a large variety of companies' behaviour and competitive conditions in leisure markets as in other markets, and the net result is not always against the consumer or public interest.

References

Banks, R. (1985) *New Jobs from Pleasure*. London.
Bendix, R. (1963) Concepts and generalizations in comparative sociological Studies. *American Sociological Review* 28(4), 532–539.
Bulmer, M. (1984) *Sociological Research Methods*. Macmillan, London.
Cabinet Office Enterprise Unit (1985) *Pleasure, Leisure and Jobs*. HMSO, London.
Crossley, J.C. and Jamieson, L.M. (1988) *Introduction to Commercial and Entrepreneurial Recreation*. Sagamore, Champaign, Illinois.
Economist Intelligence Unit (1991) *UK Radio – a New Era*. EIU, London.
Gratton, C. and Taylor, P.D. (1987) *Leisure Industries: an Overview*. Comedia, London.
Green, E., Hebron, S. and Woodward, D. (1987) *Leisure and Gender*. Sports Council, London.
Guba, E.G. (ed.) (1990) *The Paradigm Dialog*. Sage Publications, Newbury Park, California.
Jordans (1991) *Britain's Television and Radio Industry*. Jordan & Sons Ltd, London.
Jordans (1992) *Britain's Leisure Industry*. Jordan & Sons Ltd, London.
Kelly, J.R. (1990) *Leisure*. Prentice Hall, Englewood Cliffs, New Jersey.
Key Note (1992) *Leisure and Recreation*, 4th edn. Key Note, London.

Key Note (1993) *Garden Equipment*. Key Note, London.

Leisure Consultants (1996) *Leisure Forecasts 1996–2000*. Leisure Consultants, Sudbury.

Martin, B. and Mason, S. (1989) Commercial leisure provision, its nature and role. In: White J. (ed.) *The Leisure Industry*, LSA publication 41. Leisure Studies Association, Brighton.

MINTEL (1994) *Leisure Intelligence*, volume 3. Mintel, London.

Roberts, J. (1979) *The Commercial Sector in Leisure*. Sports Council, London.

Rojek, C. (1989) *Leisure for Leisure*. Macmillan, London.

Tribe, J. (1995) *The Economics of Leisure and Tourism*. Butterworth-Heinemann, Oxford.

12

The Casino in the Post-industrial City: the Social and Economic Impact of the Sydney Casino[1]

Rob Lynch and Anthony J. Veal

School of Leisure and Tourism Studies, University of Technology, Sydney, PO Box 222, Lindfield, NSW, 2070, Australia

Introduction

Since the opening of the first legal casino at Wrest Point in Tasmania in 1973, a further 12 have been developed around Australia, so that casinos now operate in each of the country's six states and two territories, as shown in Table 12.1. These developments have been part of a remarkable growth in casino development over the last two decades, in Australia and worldwide. (Note: there were approximately $A1.99 to £1 sterling at time of writing.)

Equally remarkable is the paucity of systematic studies of the social and economic impacts of these often massive developments, either in Australia or elsewhere in the world.[2] The need to research the social and economic impacts of the development and growth of the casino industry in Australia has been recognized for some time, and has been mentioned in numerous government reports over the years.[3] On the international stage, a major reference work on casinos by Eadington and Cornelius (1991) does not contain any social impact studies, supporting the conclusion that research work in this area remains to be done. As McMillen (1995:23) notes, the literature which does exist in this area 'has tended to focus on disparate elements of gambling development, without a rigorous or comprehensive assessment of their socio-economic impact'. Developers and operators conduct research on the actual and potential markets for casinos, but the commercial sensitivity of the data from such studies means that this research is generally not available in the public arena.

Table 12.1. Casinos in Australia.

Casino	Location	Year opened/ opening	Number of gaming machines*	Number of gaming tables*	Annual revenue per table[†]$
Wrest Point	Hobart	1973	490	30	320,000
Diamond Beach	Darwin	1979	376	29	308,000
Country Club	Launceston	1982	315	14	360,000
Lasetters	Alice Spring	1982	188	19	95,000
Jupiters	Gold Coast	1985	1003	112	1,100,000
Burswood	Perth	1985	1117	117	2,520,000
Adelaide	Adelaide	1985	876	86	656,000
Breakwater	Townsville	1986	202	34	346,000
Canberra	Canberra	1992	0	50	959,000
Christmas Island	Christmas Island	1993	43	26	3,084,000
Crown Galleria[†]	Melbourne	1994	1300	180	—
Treasury	Brisbane	1995	1224	102	1,350,000
Sydney Temporary[†]	Sydney	1995	500	150	—
Reef Casino	Cairns	1996	540	48	1,631,000 (est.)
Crown Casino	Melbourne	1997	2500	200	1,570,000 (est.)
Sydney Casino	Sydney	1997	1500	200	2,200,000 (est.)

Source: SHC Prospectus, via Byrne (1995), and McMillen (1991:158).
*Casino Operators will from time to time vary the number of gaming machines and
   number of gaming tables in response to patron demand.
[†]A temporary casino which closed when the permanent facility opened in the
   respective city.
[‡]Byrne (1995) and McMillen (1991:158).

This chapter outlines the background to a study which aims to
explore the social and economic impact of the Sydney Harbour Casino,
a $A1.2 billion[4] development, including a hotel and entertainment
facilities, currently under construction on a central harbourside site.
The study is designed to focus on three areas: the New South Wales
registered club industry, which is a major, well-established provider of
gambling and other leisure services in New South Wales; the inner-city
residential neighbourhood of Pyrmont–Ultimo, immediately adjacent
to the casino site; and tourism to Sydney, including domestic and overseas visitors. The chapter discusses in turn the following topics: the
development of gambling in Australia and New South Wales; the New
South Wales club industry; the development of casinos in Australia;
the development of the Sydney Casino; casinos as a tool of economic

development; and a theoretical perspective on the impact of the Sydney casino.

Gambling in Australia

Prior to the arrival of the British convict ships in 1788, there is no evidence of gambling existing among the Aboriginal population of Australia. Sport flourished in the Australian colonies in the 18th and 19th centuries and betting accompanied a wide range of activities, including cockfights, fist-fights, horse racing and rowing (O'Hara, 1981:72). Towards the end of the 19th century a campaign against gambling, led by the Protestant churches, resulted in the enactment of no less than 22 gambling regulation bills in the New South Wales parliament alone (O'Hara, 1981:75). By the 1920s, however, state activity had changed from a sole concern with regulation to include a concern for ways of raising state revenue from legalized gambling – a concern which continues to this day.

Historians such as O'Hara (1987) and Ward (1966) confirm the existence of a strong gambling tradition in Australia, both legal and illegal, and involving a wide range of activities, including horse racing, greyhound racing, harness racing, foot races, lotteries, lotto, bingo, two-up,[5] cards, casino games, poker and other amusement machines.

Gambling in its various forms is therefore big business in contemporary Australia. As Fig. 12.1 indicates, between 1972 and 1995 net expenditure[6] grew threefold in real terms and now accounts for over $A8 billion a year in net consumer expenditure. Of the $A8 billion expenditure in 1994/95, almost $A3 billion flowed to State and Territory governments in the form of taxes. Current developments, stimulated by State governments, assume a significant growth in the importance of gambling, both as a source of economic development and jobs and also as a source of government revenue.

In the period 1972–1995, the adult population of Australia grew by 50%, so, in terms of social impact, aggregate growth of expenditure can be somewhat misleading. In Fig. 12.2, therefore, expenditure per head of adult population is shown. This indicates a doubling of expenditure per head in real terms over the 22-year period. It is possible that some of the growth came from overseas visitors, but that will, to some extent, have been offset by overseas gambling expenditure by Australian residents. Fig. 12.2 also shows that this growth came initially from 'other' gambling, such as lotteries, then from casinos, and more recently, as a result of legislation in the States of Queensland and Victoria, from gaming machines, which include 'one-arm bandits' or poker machines. Racing, the traditional gambling outlet in Australia, established since

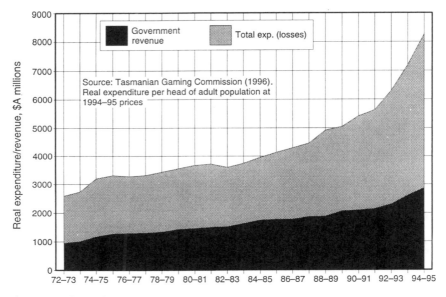

Fig. 12.1. The scale of gambling in Australia, 1972–1995.

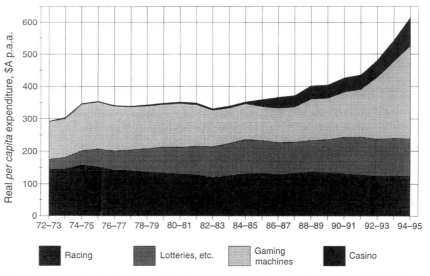

Source: Tasmanian Gaming Commission (1996).   Real expenditure per head of adult population at 1994–95 prices

Fig. 12.2. Gambling expenditure per head, Australia, 1972–1995.

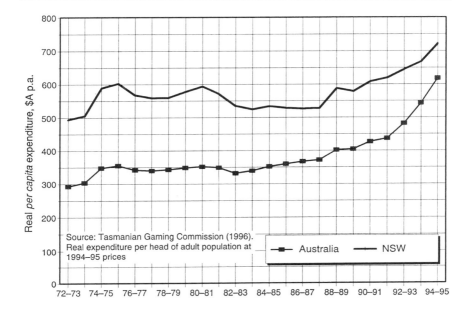

Fig. 12.3. NSW/Australia gambling expenditure, 1972–1995.

the early days of European settlement, has experienced a decline in expenditure per head.

In Australia, the control of gambling lies with State and Territory governments. Legislation as to which forms of gambling are permitted therefore varies across the country. The aggregate picture is determined largely by the two most populous states, Victoria and New South Wales, which contain more than half the national population. Thus the increase in gaming machine income in the 1990s is due to such machines being permitted in the State of Victoria for the first time. Casinos have only recently opened in Victoria and New South Wales and the statistics do not yet reflect this major change.

The research described here focuses on developments in Sydney, the capital city of New South Wales. New South Wales, with a population of 5 million, contains just under a third of the total population of Australia. The State capital, Sydney, has a population of almost 4 million. New South Wales is the most highly developed gambling market in Australia. Fig. 12.3 shows that gambling expenditure in New South Wales has been much higher than in the rest of Australia for at least the last 20 years. The reason for this lies in the unique role played by registered clubs in the State.

The New South Wales Registered Clubs

During the second half of the 20th century, registered clubs have emerged to become the major providers of leisure services, including gambling, in New South Wales. An outline of this emergence follows.[7] Registered clubs are the equivalent of licensed clubs in the UK and are non-profit mutual organizations controlled by their members.

In 1905 a number of small, exclusive New South Wales sporting and business clubs formed an association (Registered Clubs Association of NSW, 1985). A political/welfare organization, the Returned Services League (RSL) was formed in 1916 following the return of wounded soldiers to Australia from Gallipoli. This organization later gave birth to the leisure organizations that now constitute the many RSL social clubs across Australia.

The Registered Clubs Association (RCA) was formed in 1921 in response to problems in the industry. Caldwell (1983) traces the development of the club industry in New South Wales, noting the effects of key pieces of legislation relating to liquor licensing and to the 1956 Gaming and Betting (Poker Machines) Act, which legalized the use of poker machines in registered clubs exclusively. There is unanimity that this last development was the crucial and most far-reaching event in the history of New South Wales clubs. In 1954 there were 452 clubs; following the two developments of 1954 and 1956, this number had increased to 1052 in 1956 (Caldwell, 1983) and to 1570 in 1988, making the New South Wales club industry arguably the largest provider of leisure services in the state.

Following its turn-of-the-century élite origins, the industry developed into a working-class institution catering largely for older people (Caldwell, 1983; RCA, 1983:3). Although clubs are largely a working-class phenomenon, there is evidence of conflict and of clubs being implicated in a post-war split between so-called 'respectable' and 'rough' working classes. During the Second World War, pub drinking conditions had deteriorated – as evidenced in the fights, jostling and swilling that accompanied the infamous '6 o'clock swill'. The legalization of poker machines in 1956 and the ensuing large injection of finance into club development created a new, pleasantly furnished, carpeted and extended-hours drinking environment for club patrons. Late in 1950, access to club facilities had been extended to women which, according to Caldwell (1972), saw the beginning of a social revolution in New South Wales drinking habits. The clubs, with their strict codes of conduct, became the leisure havens of a 'respectable' post-war working-class, while the pubs largely remained a single-sex domain of the 'rough' and 'rowdy'.

Legal and illegal gambling, intraclass tensions, conflict between clubs and hotels, a contentious Act of Parliament and amendments to the Liquor Act have accompanied the emergence of registered clubs as providers of leisure in New South Wales. The Registered Clubs Association of New South Wales has a membership of 1378 of the 1549 registered clubs in the state. These clubs have a combined annual income of $A2500 million, a combined staff of 62,000 and membership in excess of 2 million. The New South Wales clubs make yearly donations in excess of $A400 million in direct support of charitable, community and sporting organizations. A substantial proportion of club income is derived from gaming activity and poker machines in particular. This activity generates net profits for clubs each year of some $A1500 million of which $A300 million is paid to the New South Wales government as taxes on poker machine revenue (Registered Clubs Association, 11 May 1994, personal communication).

By any measure, the New South Wales Club industry is a major provider of leisure to the citizens of the state. In recent years the industry has been affected by the introduction of poker machines into the neighbouring states of Victoria and Queensland. The clubs have been concerned about the development of a Sydney casino and have been actively involved in negotiations with the State Government with regard to the legislation for the casino. This concern is not surprising as the Sydney Harbour Casino, even in its temporary form, is in direct competition with the club industry, in particular the inner-city club establishments. Prior to the opening of the casino, a major study (Swan, 1992) predicted that the clubs would lose up to $A82 million in annual net income to the casino.

Casino Development in Australia

Casino development in Australia has been rapid since 1973 (see Table 12.1). Prior to this date, illegal casinos had been in existence since the early years of the first penal colony in New South Wales in the late 18th century. Since 1973 there have been two growth phases; the first from 1979 to 1986 and the second from 1992 to the present. The first stage saw casinos developed in the smaller cities of Hobart, Launceston and Darwin, and subsequently in medium-sized cities such as Adelaide and Perth. As McMillen (1987:20) points out, these developments were in sparsely populated states, which were in a relatively weak position in the national economy and were most vulnerable to the early stages of the economic downturn of the 1980s. Developments in the second phase include casinos in Australia's three biggest cities – Sydney, Melbourne and Brisbane – reflecting the desire of State governments to ensure that they too receive economic benefits from the flourishing gaming industry. Eight key features of the Australian casino industry can be identified.

1. The development of casinos is occurring within a nation which has a well-developed gambling ethos and patterns of expenditure. Australia also has remarkably liberal gambling laws and opportunities for legal (as well as illegal) gambling (O'Hara, 1987).
2. Casinos have generally developed in large cities, rather than resorts. The Australian industry is therefore highly decentralized and lacking in the 'strips' of the USA, for example.
3. When the current 14 casinos are operating in 1998, in excess of 67% of the national population will have a casino within their local geographic region (Sydney Harbour Casino Holdings Ltd, 1995:28). This potentially reduces the reliance of the industry on a tourist base.
4. When they are fully operational, the Sydney and Melbourne casinos will be among the largest in the world, in terms of table games allowed.
5. Casino licences are granted by the relative state or territory government and these allow the owner a period of exclusivity. In return for exclusive rights, licence holders pay certain costs/fees to governments including: up-front licence fees ($A376 million in the case of Sydney), annual licence fees, taxes on gambling revenue, government cost recoveries, provision of infrastructure, and community benefit levies. These costs are additional to corporate tax and other normal corporate fiscal imposts (Sydney Harbour Casino Holdings Ltd, 1995:29).
6. Payments made by Australian casino licence holders to governments are amongst the highest in the world; however, the exclusive rights of each (except Gold Coast and Brisbane) mean that they do not have to compete with other casinos in their local region (Sydney Harbour Casino Holdings Ltd, 1995:29).
7. Australian casino regulations are arguably some of the most stringent in the world and the industry is generally perceived to be free of corruption and criminal activity.
8. The third wave of casino development after 1990 introduced a new style of operation, which was commercially more ambitious than the earlier casinos. Casino development is now accepted as an integral part of state tourism and economic development strategies and the moral voices in opposition to such large-scale gaming, while audible, have lacked the power or the government backing to override the widespread cultural acceptance of gambling in Australia, as did similar expressions of objection to the new UK lottery in 1992–94.

Development of the Sydney Casino

For over two centuries illegal gaming houses have operated in Sydney where there is a well-established legal and illegal gambling culture (Lynch, 1995). In the late 1970s, the Premier of New South Wales, Neville Wran, announced the intention of the NSW government to permit the building of a casino in Sydney. However, due to opposition allegations of organized crime, the proposal was shelved (*National Times*, 11 July 1986:20). In 1981 the New South Wales conference of the Australian Labour Party moved in favour of State-run casinos and in 1985 Wran announced such an establishment to be built in Darling Harbour (*National Times*, 11 July 1986:20). Tenders were called in 1986, but following bribery investigations into the successful consortium, Hooker-Harrah, approval was cancelled (*Sydney Morning Herald*, 30 June 1991:11). In a second round, two bidders were refused on the basis of a Police Board report and a third round followed. Nine starters took part in the third round, which was aborted due to the election of a Liberal–National coalition State government under the premiership of Nick Greiner. The new government initially proposed a smaller, more exclusive casino run on European lines, then in 1988 announced that the casino would not proceed (*Sydney Morning Herald*, 30 July 1991:11). This decision was reversed in 1989 with a proposal for one large casino at Darling Harbour or the inner-city suburb of Pyrmont and a smaller, 'boutique', operation in the city centre.

Following an inquiry into the establishment and operation of legal casinos in New South Wales (NSW Government, 1991), the New South Wales Casino Control Authority was formally constituted on 23 September 1992. One of the first major tasks of the Authority was to report on the location, size and style of the proposed Sydney Casino. After assessing 19 potential sites, the Casino Control Authority recommended the disused, government-owned, Pyrmont Power Station site as the only one which met all assessment criteria (NSWCCA, 1993:1–2).

In keeping with earlier developments, the site of the casino proved contentious, as did the bidding process, the size and style of the proposed gambling operations, and the design of the building itself. Tender bids closed in October of 1993 and included on the list were a consortium involving media magnate Kerry Packer and the US casino operators Circus Circus, and a partnership between Leighton Constructions and another US casino operator, Showboat. This latter consortium, named Sydney Harbour Casino, was announced as the winning bid in May 1994, ahead of the Packer-backed Darling Casino Ltd.

Under the terms of the tender, Sydney Harbour Casino has a 12-year monopoly on the casino market in New South Wales and a 99-year licence to operate the Sydney Casino. Sydney Harbour Casino was to be floated on the Sydney Stock Exchange to raise about $A125 million (*Sydney Morning Herald*, 7 May 1994:37). Following the tender announcement, further controversy ensued. The New South Wales Royal Commission into the Building Industry raised concerns about collusive tendering practices of a Leighton subsidiary. The concerns were quashed by the Casino Control Authority (*Sydney Morning Herald*, 17 May 1994). The Labour opposition then announced probity concerns over Showboat's New Orleans partners in a riverboat casino, suggesting a Mafia link. This led to a public inquiry which in turn produced evidence of unfair tender practices by Leighton *(Sydney Morning Herald*, 3 December 1994). After some restrictions being placed on Leighton (no power to appoint members to the casino company board), fresh controversy emerged as police in the US moved to suspend the Showboat riverboat licence. In November of 1994, Packer and Darling Casino challenged the awarding of the casino licence to Sydney Harbour Casino. The challenge took place in the Supreme Court and the Land and Environment Court (*Sydney Morning Herald*, 16 December 1994:1).

Sydney City Council was also opposed to various aspects of the proposed casino and, in July of 1994, considered a report to go to the New South Wales Minister for Planning. The City Council is responsible for the Pyrmont area as one of its urban precincts; however, planning control for the Pyrmont Casino site itself lies with the New South Wales Government and its City West Development Project (*Sydney Morning Herald*, 11 July 1994:3). The council threatened to mount a court challenge to stop the casino being built on the Pyrmont site, but the design was modified and the New South Wales government gave the go-ahead for the development in October 1994 (*Sydney Morning Herald*, 10 December 1994:4). In April 1995 the Court dismissed the Packer challenge against the Sydney Harbour Casino consortium and, against this backdrop of controversy, a temporary casino opened its doors on Pyrmont Wharves 12 and 13 on 13 September 1995, while work on the massive $A1.2 billion permanent casino began nearby.

The temporary casino contains 500 gaming machines, 150 gaming tables, cocktail lounges, restaurants and on-site parking for over 400 vehicles (Sydney Harbour Casino Holdings Ltd, 1995:3). The permanent Sydney Casino is scheduled to open late in 1997 with 1500 gaming machines and 200 gaming tables, making it one of the largest casinos in the world (Sydney Harbour Casino Holdings Ltd, 1995:4). Features of the Sydney Casino complex will include:

- a maximum 1500 gaming machines and 200 gaming tables installed on the main casino gaming floor and in a premium player area;

- 12 bars and 14 restaurants, ranging from casual coffee shops to fine dining;
- banquet facilities for 600 guests and meeting-room facilities for up to 1000 guests;
- a 1350-room international hotel;
- a separate building containing 140 luxury serviced apartments;
- a 2000-seat lyric theatre for musicals, ballet, opera and other entertainments;
- a 700-seat showroom theatre for cabaret-style shows and other entertainment;
- a podium of terraced roof gardens and water features;
- a retail arcade and food hall;
- underground parking for 2500 cars; and
- a light-rail station connecting to all facilities by lifts and elevators.

The Sydney Harbour Casino is a major leisure development on a world scale. Thus far, controversy has characterized the 20-year saga preceding the opening of the temporary casino and, given the scale and history of the development, it will not be surprising to see further controversy. The Sydney Harbour Casino management is, however, active in promoting its good citizenship in the local and regional area. This is particularly evident in their appointment of community and government liaison personnel. Another example of 'good citizenship' is that, under the legislation, 2% of the taxation income generated by the casino will accrue to a Casino Benefit Trust Fund to be spent on socially beneficial projects, including counselling services for problem gamblers.

Sydney Harbour Casino is just one example of this relatively new phenomenon of State governments in Australia fostering massive casino developments as a source of economic development and revenue.

Casinos as a Tool of Economic Development in the Post-industrial City

The deliberate use of casinos as a tool of economic development is not new. Turner and Ash (1975) describe the mid-19th century development of Monte Carlo as a tourist resort, using a casino as its major attraction. To compete with the already well-established resorts of Cannes and Nice, in attracting the British upper-class tourists of the time, the ruler of Monaco was nevertheless advised of the 'necessity of disguising a gambling resort as a spa' (Turner and Ash, 1975:64). The casino, opened in the Villa Bellevue, was not, however, an immediate success. In fact, Turner and Ash point out that the project:

. . . was nearly a disaster, an object lesson in injudicious investment and incompetent tourism planning . . . Monaco was without adequate communications with the neighbouring French resorts and had few hotels. The Villa Bellevue was dilapidated and the casino was soon losing as much as £2800 a day. Between 15th and 20th of March 1857 it received only one visitor who left with the princely sum of two francs in winnings . . . The casino somehow survived and in 1859 began to make a profit of £50 a day.

(Turner and Ash, 1975:64–65)

The 20th-century development of Las Vegas based on casinos and tourism is universally known, with Atlantic City a later American example. Turner and Ash (1975:103) also report that, in the early 1960s, the Batista regime in Cuba sought to turn Havana into the 'Las Vegas of Latin America' with tax breaks and other inducements being offered to American casino and hotel investors. Following the revolution and the subsequent economic isolation of Cuba, casino-based tourism in the Caribbean developed in the Bahamas.

For many years casinos remained a comparatively rare phenomenon, shunned by governments around the world because of moral pressures brought by church and other groups and, no doubt, self-interested pressures brought to bear by existing gambling outlets, such as racing and football pools. Today, casinos are being developed at a rapid pace around the world. Because of the legal controls on gambling, the decision to permit the development of a casino in a given jurisdiction is always a government decision. The change of governmental attitudes towards casinos in recent years has been brought about primarily by the increasing involvement of governments in the competitive enterprise of tourism development. The growing importance of tourism in non-peripheral economies can be seen as an indicator of post-industrial change. Casinos are part of that trend.

Casinos, gaming and other leisure developments are arguably replacing, in both symbolic and material senses, the former reliance on manufacturing and industrial production as the economic base of the nation. Post-industrialism involves the economic base shifting from manufacturing and heavy industry to service industry. In western societies in the 1960s and 1970s this shift was largely towards large-scale, labour-intensive 'infrastructure' services, such as education, health and welfare in the public sector, and banking and finance in the private sector. As, during the 1980s and 1990s, these services have become increasingly mechanized, privatized and 'downsized' and have consequently declined as a source of new employment or investment opportunities, there has been a further shift towards what some have termed the 'quaternary' sector[8] (e.g. Kahn and Weiner, 1967). Industries which make up the 'quaternary' sector include information processing, and leisure and tourism services. Barry Jones (1995) has called this stage of development the 'post-service' economy.

To call Sydney *post-industrial* is somewhat incongruous since it has never been a major manufacturing centre in world terms. However, the recent closure of the city's only car manufacturing plant, with the loss of some 750 jobs, on a site immediately adjacent to the Sydney 2000 Olympic site, which is itself likely to generate several thousand permanent jobs in the sport and entertainment industries, provides a graphic illustration of the post-industrial shift.

Western societies have always been uneasy with the post-industrial idea. In the early 1980s the British Prime Minister, Margaret Thatcher, lauded a proposal to open a theme park on the disused site of the old Corby steel works in Northamptonshire (a project which never eventuated) and, in a magazine interview, made her famous comment that 'There is much industry to be had from people's pleasures' (Thatcher, 1983:22). The front-page headline in the *Daily Mirror* the next day was: 'Maggie's Mickey Mouse Jobs Plan: Thatcher Backs a Leisure Boom to Cut Dole Queues' (*Daily Mirror*, 26 August 1983). The idea that a theme park could replace a steel works as a provider of wealth was clearly seen, by the fourth estate at least, as a bit of a joke.

Such sentiments are partly based on a popular economic paradigm which sees 'real jobs' and 'productive jobs' as being associated with primary and secondary industries only. Services are seen as 'consumption' rather than 'production'. Such sentiments are perhaps a natural legacy of the pre-industrial and industrial eras. Even within the value system of those eras the view is, however, somewhat paradoxical in that, for example, the manufacture of television sets is seen as serious, 'productive' activity, whereas the production of programmes to be shown on those television sets is seen as less serious, less 'productive' activity.

In addition to, but linked with, the 'economic paradigm' is a moral dimension, which can be traced back at least to the Protestant ethic. Leisure scholars are familiar with the Protestant *work* ethic, but have tended to ignore religious or moral evaluations of *leisure activities*. Historical research, particularly that relating to the 19th century, has examined the tensions caused by religious moral objections to certain activities, such as drinking, gambling and the theatre (e.g. Bailey, 1978), and papers referring to non-Western religions, such as Islam and Buddhism, have drawn attention to the moral dimension of leisure activities as viewed by those religions (e.g. Ibrahim, 1982). However leisure studies literature arising from Western societies with a largely Christian heritage, particularly Europe and North America, has tended to ignore moral issues and appears to assume a shared secular, vaguely humanistic, moral code. In such a scenario, those in the community who condemn certain leisure activities on moral grounds are seen as conveniently marginal – ethnically, politically or geographically.

A wide range of leisure activities lie on the 'margins of conventional morality' (Lynch and Veal, 1996:290–301), including the consumption of alcohol and the use of other recreational drugs, prostitution and gambling. Some of the objections to such activities are based on rationalistic arguments about their potentially damaging effects: others are based on given moral codes, which may have a spiritual or rationalistic basis.

Thus the uneasiness of contemporary societies with post-industrial developments is exacerbated by moral misgivings when governments and the community at large appear to be embracing and profiting from certain activities which have, hitherto, been banned or restricted. Despite the strong tradition of gambling in Australia, in a recent national opinion poll, some 48% of respondents were reported as believing that gambling was harmful because of the social problems it causes, while 21% thought it was harmful, but that the good effects outweighed the bad (Murphy, 1996). Community concerns about gambling have often been mollified by the use of profits or taxation income for specific public benefits – such as the funding of hospitals or the building of an opera house (as in the case of the lottery-funded Sydney Opera House). In New South Wales, this phenomenon has taken the form of the granting of exclusive rights to certain gambling income to non-profit clubs, which in turn provide community leisure facilities. Casinos are, however, for private profit – even though they also generate considerable tax income.

The Impact of the Sydney Casino

The controversy surrounding the development of the Sydney Casino and others in Australia and elsewhere in the world arises partly from the usual range of environmental concerns which are common to any large-scale developments, but is also complicated by the uneasiness arising from both post-industrial change and moral concerns. The economic impact of a casino may be relatively easy to conceptualize and research, and assessment of certain social impacts – such as noise, congestion, crime levels and the incidence of problem gambling – can be equally straightforward, but taking account of the effects on society's moral sensibilities and concerns about global and local trends in the economy and the labour market adds considerable complexity to the task of social impact assessment.

Notes

1. The research upon which this paper is based is supported by the Australian Research Council, Tourism New South Wales, Sydney City Council and the Registered Clubs Association of New South Wales. The authors acknowledge the assistance of Michelle Toms in the conduct of surveys and compilation of information for the study.
2. At the WLRA Cardiff conference we became aware of Patricia Stokowski's (1996) forthcoming book, which deals with casino development in Colorado.
3. See, for example, Tasmanian Government (1978), South Australian Government (1982), Victorian Government (1988), Australian Capital Territory (1988), and New South Wales Government (1991).
4. The Australian dollar is worth approximately $US0.70 or £0.50 at time of writing.
5. A uniquely Australian activity involving betting on the spin of two coins.
6. *Net expenditure* is the total losses incurred by gamblers, and includes the returns to the gambling organizations and the government. Actual amounts staked are much higher than this, being estimated at $61 billion in 1994–95 (Tasmanian Gaming Commission, Annual).
7. This section draws extensively from Lynch (1990:189–192).
8. The primary sector is agriculture and mining; the secondary sector is manufacturing; and the tertiary sector is services.

References

Australian Capital Territory (1988) *Casino Development for Canberra.* Government Printer, Canberra, ACT.

Bailey, P. (1978) *Leisure and Class in Victorian England*. Routledge and Kegan Paul, London.

Byrne, A. (1995) All bets off as the casino war widens. *Sydney Morning Herald* 23 October, p. 4.

Caldwell, G. (1972) Jackpot: the NSW club. *Current Affairs Bulletin* 49(4), 115–127.

Caldwell, G. (1983) The provision of leisure in Australia – some observations. In: *National Leisure Seminar Discussion Papers*, Victorian Government Printer, Melbourne, pp. 47–62.

Eadington, W. and Cornelius, J. (eds) (1991) *Gambling and Public Policy: International Perspectives*. Institute for the Study of Gambling and Commercial Gaming, University of Nevada, Reno.

Ibrahim, H. (1982) Leisure and Islam. *Leisure Studies* 1(2), 197–210.

Jones, B. (1995) *Sleepers Wake! Technology and the Future of Work*, revised edn. Oxford University Press, Melbourne.

Kahn, H. and Weiner, A.J. (1967) *The Year 2000: a Framework for Speculation on the Next Thirty Years*. Macmillan, London.

Lynch, R. (1990) Working class luck and vocabularies of hope among regular poker machine players. In: Rowe, D. and Lawrence, G. (eds) *Sport and Leisure: Trends in Australian Popular Culture*. Harcourt Brace Jovanovich, Sydney, pp. 189–208.

Lynch, R. (1995) On the basis of chance: crime, gambling and casino development. In: McMillen, J., Sturevska, S. and Walker, M. (eds) *Lady Luck in Australia*. National Association for Gambling Studies, Sydney, pp.156–169.

Lynch, R. and Veal, A.J. (1996) *Australian Leisure*. Longman, Melbourne.

McMillen, J. (1987) Gambling for high stakes: Australian casino developments. *Current Affairs Bulletin* 64(4), 20–25.

McMillen, J. (1991) Casinos and tourism: what's the big attraction? In: Carroll, P. *et al.* (eds) *Tourism in Australia*, Harcourt Brace Jovanovich, Sydney, pp. 153–172.

McMillen, J. (1995) Social impacts of urban casinos: the Australian experience. *Proceedings of the National Association for Gambling Studies Conference*. NAGS, Fremantle, pp. 23–37.

Murphy, D. (1996) Come in suckers: gambling special report. *The Bulletin* 116(6031), 30 July, pp. 20–24.

New South Wales Government (1991) *Inquiry into the Establishment and Operation of Legal Casinos*. Government Printer, Sydney.

New South Wales Casino Control Authority (NSWCCA) (1993) *Report on the Location, Size and Style of the New South Wales Casino*, CCA, Sydney.

O'Hara, J. (1981) The Australian gambling tradition. In: Cashman, R. and McKernan, M. (eds) *Sport in History: the Making of Modern Sporting History*. University of Queensland Press, St Lucia, Queensland, pp. 68–85.

O'Hara, J. (1987) *A Mug's Game: a History of Gaming and Betting in Australia*. University of New South Wales Press, Kensington, NSW.

Registered Clubs Association of New South Wales (1983) *There's a Club Everywhere You Go! and You're Always Welcome*. RCA, Sydney.

Registered Clubs Association of New South Wales (1985) *History of the Registered Clubs*. RCA, Sydney.

South Australian Government (1982) *Select Committee Report on the Casino Bill*. Government Printer, Adelaide.

Stokowski, P.A. (1996) *Riches and Regrets: Betting on Gambling in Two Colorado Mountain Towns*. University of Colorado Press, Niwot, Colorado.

Swan, P. (1992) *Report on the Likely Effect of Slot Machines in a Casino on the Operations and Viability of the Registered Clubs and Hotel Industries*. Report to the Chief Secretary. NSW Government Printing Service, Sydney.

Sydney Harbour Casino Holdings Ltd (1995) *Prospectus*. SHC, Sydney.

Tasmanian Gaming Commission (Annual) *Australian Gambling Statistics*. TGC, Hobart.

Tasmanian Government (1978) *Interdepartmental Committee Report on Casinos*. Government Press, Hobart.

Thatcher, M. (1983) Interview in *The Director*, September.

Turner, L. and Ash, J. (1975) *The Golden Hordes: International Tourism and the Pleasure Periphery*. Constable, London.

Victorian Government (1988) *Board of Inquiry into Casinos*. Government Printer, Melbourne.

Ward, R. (1966) *The Australian Legend*. Oxford University Press, Melbourne.

Sports and Safety: Leisure and Liability

13

Steve Frosdick

Director, IWI Associates Ltd, Hounslow TW3 2PR, UK

Introduction

Emphasis on safety in the British sports and leisure industry has sharpened in recent years. Disasters such as Hillsborough and the Dorset canoeing tragedy have promoted this. Venue owners and operators should be increasingly concerned about the extent of their liability if disaster should strike. This chapter will argue five main points:

1. British football has shown the failure of 'legislation by crisis' as public policy;
2. The problems of disasters and near misses in Britain are not confined to football;
3. The owners and operators of British sports and leisure facilities are unequivocally responsible for the safety of their customers;
4. When the next disaster strikes, the climate of risk as blame will mean that owners and operators will be called to account for the adequacy of their arrangements for public safety; and
5. Proper management of risk is a useful tool for beginning to be satisfied that safety arrangements are sufficient to withstand the scrutiny of civil and criminal actions.

Whilst the chapter focuses on the British experience, I believe that the issues have considerable relevance to international debate about management in the world of leisure and recreation.

© CAB INTERNATIONAL 1998. *Leisure Management: Issues and Applications*
(eds M.F. Collins and I.S. Cooper)

Table 13.1. British stadia disasters.

Year	Location	Deaths	Injuries
1902	Ibrox Park, Glasgow	25	500+
1914	Hillsborough, Sheffield	0	80
1914	Burnley	1	?
1923	Wembley Cup Final	0	1000+
1946	Burnden Park, Bolton	33	400
1957	Shawfield	1	50
1961	Ibrox Park, Glasgow	2	?
1971	Ibrox Park, Glasgow	66	'100s'
1985	St Andrews, Birmingham	1	250
1985	Valley Parade, Bradford	56	'100s'
1989	Hillsborough, Sheffield	95	400+

Adapted from Scarff *et al.* (1993).

The Failure of 'Legislation by Crisis'

Throughout the 20th century, considerable numbers of people have been killed or injured in sports and leisure disasters of all kinds. British stadia, however, and particularly British football grounds, have been strongly represented in the history of such disasters. This prominence has arisen for a variety of historical, economic and social reasons, including the overall popularity of football as a symbolic form and focus of collective identification (Dunning, 1989; Critcher, 1991), dilapidated grounds, hooliganism, poor leadership (Home Office, 1989, 1990) and general neglect of supporters' safety and comfort (Taylor, 1991:12).

The catalogue of British stadia disasters (De Quidt and Chalmers, 1993) is set out in Table 13.1. Crowd pressure, either direct or leading to structural collapses, was the immediate cause of all except the Bradford and Birmingham tragedies. Accumulated refuse caught fire at Bradford, whilst the disorder commonly associated with football was the immediate cause of only the Birmingham disaster. Ten official reports have been commissioned into safety and order at British football grounds. In reviewing the reports and some recent incidents, I am seeking to demonstrate the ineffectiveness of the 'legislation by crisis' response to crowd-related disasters.

The Shortt Report (Home Office, 1924) followed the near-disaster at Wembley in 1923 and included recommendations about responsibility, licensing, stewarding and fire safety. Inattention to the two latter were contributory factors at Bradford in 1985.

The Moelwyn Hughes Report (Home Office, 1946) arose from the Bolton overcrowding disaster. Recommendations about calculating maximum capacities and coordinated counting of numbers admitted were not pursued. Had they been so, the Hillsborough disaster may have been avoided.

The growth of football hooliganism prompted the Chester Report (Department of Education and Science, 1968), Harrington (1968) Report and Lang Report (Ministry of Housing and Local Government, 1969). Harrington reviewed previous reports and noted that their helpful suggestions had often been ignored. He went on to comment on the lack of legislation covering standards of safety and amenity at grounds. Lang included references to the benefits of closed circuit television (CCTV) and the impact of alcohol on behaviour.

The Wheatley Report (Home Office, 1972) was prompted by the 1971 Ibrox disaster in Scotland and resulted in legislation requiring safety certificates at designated grounds. The first edition of the *'Green Guide' to Safety at Sports Grounds* was also published. It had been 50 years since Shortt first recommended such action.

The McElhorne Report (Scottish Education Department, 1977) was concerned with spectator misbehaviour in Scotland. Recommendations included legislation to control alcohol, spectator segregation, perimeter fencing, CCTV, improved amenities, stewarding, club membership and club community involvement. Set up following disorder at England matches abroad, the Department of the Environment (1984) Working Group repeated similar recommendations for English clubs.

The Popplewell Reports (Home Office, 1985, 1986) dealt with the Bradford and Birmingham disasters and the Heysel tragedy in Belgium. Many recommendations echoed the 1977 and 1984 reports. The Football Trust funded the installation of CCTV, the *Green Guide* was revised and there was considerable legislative activity. The range of grounds and stands requiring safety certification was increased. Exclusion and Restriction Orders were introduced to keep convicted hooligans both away from British grounds and unable to travel to matches abroad. A national membership scheme for fans and the establishment of a National Inspectorate and Review Body were both provided for.

Following the fatal crushing of 95 Liverpool supporters at Hillsborough Stadium on 15 April 1989, the Taylor Reports (Home Office, 1989, 1990a) proved to be the catalyst for radical change. There was swift implementation of changes in planning, responsibilities, testing and improving the fabric of stadia, involving considerable energy and expense for clubs, local authorities, police and others. Other key areas of change included the revision of the *Green Guide* (Home Office, 1990b), the scrapping of the proposed national membership scheme and the establishment of the Football Licensing Authority and Football Stadia Advisory Design Council. New criminal offences of pitch invasion, racist chanting and missile throwing were also created. The police role shifted to concentrate on crime, disorder and major emergencies

(Wilmot, 1993), whilst the clubs appointed safety officers and began to improve the quality of their stewarding schemes (Football League *et al.*, 1995).

The most notable change involved the elimination of standing accommodation at all Premier and Football League stadia, although the all-seater requirement was subsequently relaxed for the lower division clubs. As Stevens (1991) has pointed out, there are only 115 designated sports grounds in England and Wales, yet the Taylor Report, the implementation costs of which will exceed £600 million (Inglis, 1996:13), gave rise to the overnight appearance of a thriving industry offering a diverse range of services and products.

I want to argue that, notwithstanding the post-Hillsborough changes, there is continued good evidence of potential disasters in and around British football grounds since 1989. A comprehensive analysis of club accident records, inspections, police match reports, media reports, anecdote and my own experiences as a researcher in the field would reveal many examples of such near misses. Four examples must suffice to make the point.

1. In April 1993 I was present in the control room at a North-east derby match when away supporters experienced crushing both whilst queuing at the turnstiles before the match and on leaving the ground afterwards. In fact, they burst a huge gate open to get out of the ground.

2. On 5 May 1993, the *Daily Mail* reported that several Newcastle United fans had been treated on the pitch after crushing problems at Grimsby Town.

3. The same month, after the Arsenal vs. Sheffield Wednesday FA Cup Final at Wembley Stadium, I was one of many people crushed in the crowds making their way off the concourse to the underground station. On the following Monday, the *Daily Telegraph* expressed its concerns in a story headed, 'A Disturbing Crush Down Wembley Way'.

4. The early rounds of the 1993–94 FA Cup saw intense crowd pressure cause structural failure in the pitch perimeter walls at two non-league grounds. The 1994–95 season saw a similar incident at Tiverton Town for their first-round FA Cup match against Leyton Orient. Viewing the television newsreel, it was remarkable that nobody was seriously injured.

In addition, I have not mentioned any of the risks to public safety posed by the hostile pitch invasions and/or disorderly behaviour seen at grounds such as Millwall, Chelsea, Lansdowne Road in Dublin and, at the end of the 1995–96 season, at Brighton.

Looking at this chronology of disasters, reports and continued near misses, we can see that the whole approach comes from the unitary perspective of a world organized by rules. Each report has been commissioned to serve the political purpose of being seen to have done something in response to the disaster. This has been achieved by each post-disaster report proposing further rules and prescriptions, ostensibly to prevent future disaster. There are problems with this 'disaster . . . inquiry . . . legislation' approach. It is centrally orientated, remote from the ground, ignores the more frequent near misses from which learning could take place and results in piecemeal, generalized and short-term panic measures. As Canter *et al.* (1989:92) have argued, 'it has all the quality of closing the stable door after the horse has bolted. An accretion of legislation adds in a piecemeal fashion to previous controls. As a consequence there is never any possibility of examining the system of legislation as a whole.'

Critically, as I have indicated, the disasters and near misses have continued to occur. A Channel Four television documentary on 12 October 1994 claimed that British football grounds remain 'An Accident Waiting to Happen'. Much of that documentary was mischievous, but the underlying point is, I believe, still true of a number of stadia.

The Problems are not Confined to the Football Industry

Whilst football grounds are most prominently represented in the history of British sports and leisure disasters, there have also been fatalities in at least three other leisure contexts (not including transportation disasters such as Zeebrugge and the *Marchioness*):

1. 1973 – Summerland, Isle of Man – 50 dead;
2. 1988 – Castle Donnington Concert – two dead;
3. 1993 – Dorset Canoeing Centre – four dead.

If we examine the media reports of other incidents, we can find plenty of examples of near misses too. Let me mention four quite prominent cases to illustrate the point.

1. The Pavarotti Concert in Hyde Park in 1991 was expected to attract 250,000 people. Sir John Wheeler, MP, wrote to *The Times* on 21 August 1991 to report the absence of proper safety and stewarding arrangements and to suggest that '. . . the Government may well have been saved from a Hillsborough disaster by the wet weather which deterred so many people from attending'.
2. In the world of motor racing, a near disaster resulted from the mass celebratory circuit invasion after Nigel Mansell's victory in the 1992 British Grand Prix at Silverstone.
3. During 1993, crushing problems were reported at pop concerts at the Hammersmith Palais, Crystal Palace and in Birmingham City Centre,

where 300 girls needed medical treatment during a Bad Boys Inc. concert.

4. In 1995, the injuries to spectators caused by a motorcycle leaving the circuit during the TT races on the Isle of Man were widely reported.

Let us be clear, then, that the problems of disaster and continued near misses are not confined to the football industry. Public safety risk management is an important issue for the whole of the sports and leisure industry.

Responsibility for Safety

Some readers will have sporting events in their venue. The Department of National Heritage (1997) *Guide to Safety at Sports Grounds* – commonly referred to as the *Green Guide* – is quite clear that 'the responsibility for the safety of spectators lies at all times with the ground management.' Others will have pop concerts and the like in their venue. The Health and Safety Commission and Home Office (1993) *Guide to Health, Safety and Welfare at Pop Concerts and Similar Events* – the *Purple Guide* – tell us that 'anyone who is directly responsible for the undertaking . . . will have responsibilities for the health and safety of third parties affected by it, including the audience.' Many will have crowds in their venue, and the Crowd Safety Guidance from the Health and Safety Executive (1996), still in draft at the time of writing, opens with the following sentence: 'Ensuring crowd safety is a basic responsibility of venue managers, owners and operators.' Let us therefore be clear that the responsibility for safety starts at the top, with the Chairman and Board of Directors, or their public sector equivalents, of the company or body running the venue concerned. It could be your responsibility.

Risk as Blame

So what? Well there is now a view that, because the world is a more individualist place, and because individual people feel a greater need to be protected from the effects of the world, the concept of risk has moved on from probability and consequences into the idea of risk as accountability, or risk as blame and liability, even without fault. According to Priest (1990), 'the more precise statement of the first principle of civil liability today is that a court will hold a party to an injury liable if that party could have taken some action to reduce the risk of the injury at a cost less than the benefit from risk reduction.'

The newspapers carry almost daily stories of large payments being awarded in civil damages for injuries sustained. And since many such cases appear to be settled out of court, there is a suspicion that ability to pay is as important an issue as negligence in any pre-trial discussions about liability.

But it is not now just a matter for the civil law. In December 1994, British legal history was made. An outdoor activities company and its managing director were convicted of manslaughter following the deaths of four teenagers during a canoeing trip in Dorset. The managing director was jailed for 3 years, later reduced on appeal to 2 years. But he went to jail. And many more companies and individuals could find themselves facing criminal prosecution if the Law Commission's (1996) proposals for a new offence of corporate killing are adopted.

Let's not be coy about this. The days of insuring against civil liability are now behind us. There is no insurance policy on the market that will nominate somebody else to grip the rails in the dock at the Old Bailey. If it's your event, if disaster strikes, and if you were negligent in your preparations, then the trial by media and scapegoating processes will ensure that the criminal accountability is firmly down to you.

Venue owners and operators need to be sure that their arrangements, in this context their safety arrangements, are capable of withstanding the closest public scrutiny. So they need to know how to assess and manage risk. They need to know how to document the process so they can produce the evidence to show their insurance company, a Civil Court, the police, a Coroner's inquest or even the jury in a criminal trial, that they did everything that they could reasonably be expected to do. At the same time, they don't want to overreact with measures which are disproportionately expensive or which damage their customers' legitimate enjoyment of the event or activity.

The Management of Risk

The overall management of risk process (Scarff *et al.*, 1993) shown in Fig. 13.1 comprises the three main components of analysis, management and monitoring, each of which has a number of subsidiary processes. This offers us a framework for identifying hazards, estimating their likely frequency and consequences and evaluating their acceptability. We call this part of the process risk analysis. Where appropriate, we can go on to plan what needs to be done. We allocate resources to progress the plans and thus take the necessary management measures to control the risk, whether by reducing it, avoiding it altogether or perhaps transferring it to another party. Finally, we monitor how we are doing. Each of the management of risk processes can result in a report.

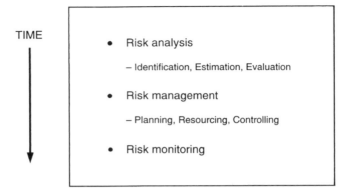

Fig. 13.1. Management of risk framework.

So by carrying out these processes, we can end up with a robust and comprehensive set of documents which demonstrate our commitment to managing risk in a concerned and competent manner.

What I want to do now is to run through these processes and, as we go along, to demonstrate their practical application through a simple worked example. But first let me say something about the nature of risk itself. For such a little word, risk is a complex concept, the meaning of which has evolved over time (Douglas, 1990) and is now the subject of disagreement between natural and social scientists (Royal Society, 1992). In 20th-century engineering and science, the concept of risk refers only to negative outcomes, with particular reference to the hazards posed by modern technological developments in the offshore, petrochemical and nuclear power industries. Scientists and engineers in these industries seek to put numbers on risk through the calculation of probabilities and the use of databank information on component failures and reliability. These ideas of risk are not shared by social scientists, whose work has shown the difficulties involved in looking at risk as a one-dimensional concept when a particular risk or hazard means different things to different people in different contexts (see, for example, Douglas, 1978; Douglas and Wildavsky, 1982; Slovic, 1991). Risk is about perception and there are, therefore, no right or wrong answers. And I have already referred to the more recent emergence of the idea of risk as blame.

Having acknowledged that there is a debate about the idea of risk, let's start with a simple definition of risk as 'the chance of exposure to the adverse consequences of future events' (Scarff *et al.*, 1993:88). There are therefore three elements to be assessed in a risk: (i) the future event which may occur; (ii) the probability of the event occurring; and (iii) the adverse consequences if it does occur. Identifying the future event is the hazard identification process.

Hazard identification

If there are no right or wrong answers, and if different people do have different perceptions, it is important to ensure that a broad spectrum of opinion is adequately represented in the hazard identification exercise. So any hazard identification needs to be done by a group of people rather than by just one or two. Also, customers and local residents should be invited to participate as well as venue staff and personnel from any regulatory bodies.

There are two main types of hazard identification exercise; the strategic and the tactical. The strategic exercise considers the potential hazards arising from external threats and internal weaknesses. The tactical exercise looks at the hazards involved in the operational management of the venue. In this case the group undertaking the exercise needs to think of the venue as a system, broken down into zones, with each zone broken down into smaller areas. The exercise involves the group brainstorming everything that could go wrong in each part of the system.

For our worked example, I want to look at the playing-area zone in a football stadium, and in particular at the away-team bench, which is one area within that zone.

To keep things simple, we will assume that the group have identified four hazards, as follows:

1. A missile will be thrown at the away-team personnel on the bench;
2. The substitute players will obstruct the front of an advertising hoarding while they are warming up;
3. A spectator will shout verbal abuse at the away-team personnel on the bench;
4. The away-team personnel will shout abuse at the referee or linesmen.

So we have our list of hazards. Now we need to get an estimation of their probability and consequences.

Risk estimation process

Each hazard should be considered by the team who carried out the identification process and a collective judgement made about the probability of the risk occurring. The probability should be judged on a five-point scale ranging from none to low to low/medium to medium/high to high. A collective judgement should then be made about the potential adverse consequences if the hazard did occur. I would suggest that there are four types of adverse consequences to consider, namely:

1. For public safety and order;
2. For the profitability of the business (including its exposure to liability);

Table 13.2. Hazards register.

Ref.	Hazard	Proba-bility	Safety conse-quence	Profit conse-quence	Enjoy-ment conse-quence	Commu-nity con-sequence
A	A missile will be thrown at the bench	3	4	2	2	0
B	The subs will warm up in front of an advertising hoarding	2	1	3	1	0
C	A spectator will shout abuse at the bench	4	2	0	2	0
D	The bench will shout abuse at the referee	3	0	0	1	0

3. For the enjoyment of the spectators or participants; and
4. For the community and environment in the outside world.

All four types of consequences may be tackled in one exercise, or there may be a focus on just one type. However the exercise is approached, each type of consequence should also be judged on a separate five-point scale. Going back to our example, let's imagine that the estimation process has come out with a hazards register something like Table 13.2.

This shows how the different hazards can have different implications for the four different types of consequences. Such a hazards register should provide a substantial reference document to support the running of the venue. But the operator cannot reasonably be expected to tackle all the hazards, nor will it be cost-effective to try to do so. So we need to prioritize the hazards. This prioritization process is called risk evaluation.

Risk evaluation process

Having estimated probability and consequences, in however many dimensions, each risk in the hazards register should be plotted onto a five-by-five matrix. The distribution of the hazards on the matrix should then be evaluated by an appropriate forum, which may well be the Board of Directors of the company running the venue. The general principle governing risk evaluation is that risk should be reduced to a level which is as low as is reasonably practicable. In general terms,

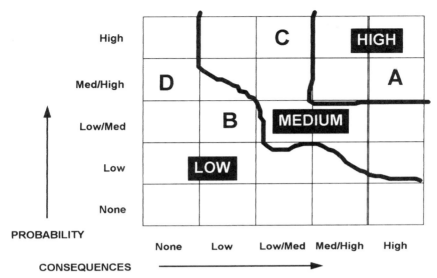

Fig. 13.2. Risk evaluation matrix.

those risk issues which have been judged to be of lower probability or consequences will be designated as 'Low Risk' and will be accepted as residual risks. At the other end of the scale, those risks which have been estimated as higher probability and consequences will be designated as 'High Risk' and therefore intolerable. These risks will have to become subject to remedial action, almost irrespective of cost, through the preparation of appropriate risk management plans. Where the boundaries fall between these two categories will be a question of management judgement, and, once decided, will determine which issues are designated 'Medium Risk'. These risks may require careful monitoring and incorporating into the risk management plans if appropriate, for example, where something can be done at a cost less than the benefit of the risk reduction.

The boundaries should then be added to the matrix. Since the demand for risk assessment is often safety related, I have only plotted the consequences for safety and order for the example in Fig. 13.2.

It can be seen that one of the hazards – the throwing of the missile – has been designated as High Risk, whilst one – verbal abuse by a spectator – is Medium and the other two are Low Risk.

The outcome of the risk identification, estimation and evaluation processes should then be reported as the formal risk assessment. This risk assessment documents which hazards have been identified as priorities and how and why those decisions have been made. So the risk assessment is an exercise in accountability.

Risk management process

In respect of each High Risk or relevant Medium Risk issue, an appropriate group of people should meet to consider what action can be taken to control the risk and reduce the probability and/or consequences to a tolerable level. The countermeasures defined, the resources assigned and the responsibilities allocated should be recorded. The outcome of the process will be the Risk Management Plan.

Taking the High Risk issue in our example we can ask ourselves what could be done to reduce the probability of a missile being thrown at the away bench. We might decide to sell the tickets in the surrounding area only to season-ticket holders or Family Club members. We would be able to vet applicants and would know who was in what seats in that area every game. Thinking about reducing the consequences for safety and order if a missile was thrown, we might decide to build a polycarbonate shelter around the bench and thus protect the occupants from harm. Turning to the Medium Risk, the verbal abuse, we might decide that the same ticketing policy would reduce the probability a little. We might also decide to locate a steward adjacent to the bench. This would have a modest opportunity cost but would ensure that a member of staff was available to nip any problems in the bud and so reduce the consequences of the abuse escalating into potentially harmful disorder. Thus the implementation of the countermeasures identified should result both in increased protection for our guests and customers and reduced exposure to liability for ourselves.

Risk monitoring process

However, the management of risk process is not a 'single shot' to be forgotten after it is completed. Regular monitoring is important to ensure that the risk implications of any changes are considered and appropriately acted upon. A formal review of the hazards, their estimated probabilities and consequences, tolerability and any risk management measures proposed should therefore be carried out at appropriate intervals, for example after major building work. The hazards register, risk assessment and risk management plan should be amended as appropriate and reissued accordingly.

Conclusion

The 'legislation by crisis' response to sports and leisure disasters has failed. There is still ample evidence of potential disasters, and near misses are a regular occurrence. The owners and operators of British sports and leisure facilities have a duty to care for the safety of their customers and need to be sure that their arrangements are capable of withstanding the closest public scrutiny. Proper management of risk offers one way of ensuring that duty of care is discharged through improved operational performance, thus keeping our sports and leisure venues enjoyable, profitable and, above all, safe for everybody.

Acknowledgement

The arguments in this chapter are set out in more detail in Frosdick, S. and Walley, L. (1997) (eds) *Sport and Safety Management*, Butterworth-Heinemann, Oxford. A previous version of the author's discussion on the failure of 'legislation by crisis' was also published in Frosdick, S. (1995) Organizational structure, culture and attitudes to risk in the British stadia safety industry, *Journal of Contingencies and Crisis Management* 3(1), pp. 43–57.

References

Canter, D., Comber, M. and Uzzell, D. (1989) *Football in its Place – An Environmental Psychology of Football Grounds*. Routledge, London.

Critcher, C. (1991) Putting on the style: recent aspects of English football. In: Williams, J. and Wagg, S. (eds) *British Football and Social Change – Getting into Europe*. Leicester University Press, Leicester, pp. 67–84.

De Quidt, J. and Chalmers, J. (1993) The Football Licensing Authority – progress report on licensing and safety. Seminar Presentation, *Football Stadia at RECMAN 93*, Football Stadia Advisory Design Council and the Football League. Wembley Exhibition Centre, 23 March 1993.

Department of Education and Science (1968) *Report of the Committee on Football (Chairman D.N. Chester CBE)*. HMSO, London.

Department of the Environment (1984) *Report of an Official Working Group on Football Spectator Violence*. HMSO, London.

Department of National Heritage (1997) *Guide to Safety at Sports Grounds*. HMSO, London.

Douglas, M. (1978) Cultural bias. Royal Anthropological Institute Occasional Paper No. 35. Reprinted in Douglas, M. (1982) *In the Active Voice*. Routledge and Kegan Paul, London, pp. 183–254.

Douglas, M. (1990) Risk as a forensic resource. *Daedalus*, 119(4), pp. 1–16.

Douglas, M. and Wildavsky, A. (1982) *Risk and Culture: an Essay on the Selection of Technological and Environmental Danger*. University of California Press, Berkeley, California.

Dunning, E. (1989) The economic and cultural significance of football. *Proceedings of Football into the 1990s*. Sir Norman Chester Centre for Football Research, University of Leicester, Leicester.

Football League, Football Association and FA Premier League (1995) *Stewarding and Safety Management at Football Grounds.*

Harrington, J. (1968) *Soccer Hooliganism: a Preliminary Report.* John Wright, Bristol.

Health and Safety Commission and Home Office (1993) *Guide to Health, Safety and Welfare at Pop Concerts and Similar Events.* HMSO, London.

Health and Safety Executive (1996) *Crowd Safety.* HSE, London (in press).

Home Office (1924) *Committee of Inquiry into the Arrangements Made to Deal with Abnormally Large Attendances on Special Occasions, Especially at Athletic Grounds – Report by the Rt Hon. Edward Shortt KC.* HMSO, London.

Home Office (1946) *Enquiry into the Disaster at the Bolton Wanderers Football Ground on 9 March 1946 – Report by R. Moelwyn Hughes KC.* HMSO, London.

Home Office (1972) *Report of the Inquiry into Crowd Safety at Sports Grounds (by the Rt Hon. Lord Wheatley).* HMSO, London.

Home Office (1985) *Committee of Inquiry into Crowd Safety and Control at Sports Grounds – Chairman Mr Justice Popplewell. Interim Report.* HMSO, London.

Home Office (1986) *Committee of Inquiry into Crowd Safety and Control at Sports Grounds – Chairman Mr Justice Popplewell. Final Report.* HMSO, London.

Home Office (1989) *The Hillsborough Stadium Disaster 15 April 1989 – Inquiry by the Rt Hon. Lord Justice Taylor. Interim Report.* HMSO, London.

Home Office (1990) *The Hillsborough Stadium Disaster 15 April 1989 – Inquiry by the Rt Hon. Lord Justice Taylor. Final Report.* HMSO, London.

Inglis, S. (1996) *Football Grounds of Britain*, 3rd edn. Collins Willow, London.

Law Commission (1996) *Legislating the Criminal Code: Involuntary Manslaughter.* HMSO, London.

Ministry of Housing and Local Government (1969) *Report of the Working Party on Crowd Behaviour at Football Matches (Chairman John Lang).* HMSO, London.

Priest, G. (1990) The new legal structure of risk control. *Daedalus* 119(4), 207–228.

Royal Society (1992) *Risk: Analysis, Perception and Management, Report of a Royal Society Study Group.* The Royal Society, London.

Scarff, F., Carty, A. and Charette R. (1993) *Introduction to the Management of Risk.* HMSO, London.

Scottish Education Department (1977) *Report of the Working Group on Football Crowd Behaviour.* HMSO, London.

Slovic, P. (1991) Beyond numbers: a broader perspective on risk perception and risk communication. In: Mayo, D. and Hollander, R. (eds) *Acceptable Evidence: Science and Values in Risk Management.* Oxford University Press, Oxford, pp. 48–65.

Stevens, A. (1991) Stadia of the future – the pros and cons! In: *Panstadia: A Comprehensive Guide to Stadium Newbuild and Management.* Executive Publications (Holdings) Ltd, Harrow, pp. 17–19.

Taylor, I. (1991) English football in the 1990s: taking Hillsborough seriously? In: Williams, J. and Wagg, S. (eds) *British Football and Social Change – Getting Into Europe.* Leicester University Press, Leicester, pp. 3–24.

Wilmot, D. (1993) *Policing Football Matches.* Greater Manchester Police, Manchester.

Quality Management in Public Leisure Services

14

Leigh Robinson

Leisure Management Unit, University of Sheffield, Hicks Building, Houndsfield Road, Sheffield S3 7RH, UK

Introduction

Quality as a distinct concept has gained momentum in the service industry over the past two decades as increasing demands from the general public have led to a growing emphasis on the concept of quality management and the delivery of quality services (Peters and Waterman, 1982; Pfeffer and Coote, 1991). Commercial service organizations realized that organization survival and competitive edge depended on the provision of a top-quality service and set about providing this. Inevitably, as demands for quality services began to be both recognized and met within the private sector, customer attention turned to providers of local authority services.

It can be argued that, as a result, innovative local authority managers considered the claims of cost reduction and service improvements made by quality proponents (Deming, 1986; Wille, 1992) and began to adopt the quality approach to management that had been popular in the commercial sector. The importance of the concept of quality in local authorities was later highlighted by the Association of County Councils who claimed:

> Quality has a role to play in helping local authorities to provide the right services at the right time, in the right place to the right people (and for the right price). It has a role in not only ensuring local government's survival but also in strengthening it.
>
> (Association of County Councils, 1992)

Given the relative newness of the quality approach in local authority management it will be some time before the full ramifications of quality management become clear and as such local authority managers are reliant upon evidence from the private sector and academics which indicates that quality management has a variety of advantages to offer those who choose to pursue it.

Gaster (1992) and Wille (1992) have noted the concept of 'right first time' which is inherent in quality management, leading to decreased wastage and increased efficiency. Increased customer satisfaction is also a consequence of quality management given the need for a customer focus (Clarke and Stewart, 1987). Sellers (1989), Carson (1990) and MacNeil (1994) have all provided evidence as to how increased customer satisfaction leads to increased revenue as satisfied customers continue to make use of the services provided. They have also outlined how dissatisfied customers fail to return, leading to decreases in revenue. There has also been evidence of increased productivity from staff and a corresponding increase in staff morale (Peters and Austin, 1984; Sanderson, 1992) as internal communication, consultation and training are all contained in the concept of the internal customer which is integral to quality management (Dale, 1994; Navaratnam and Harris, 1994). A more direct influence on staff morale is highlighted by the Local Government Training Board (1987) who have argued that morale will increase because services will be better, causing less complaints and leading to a decrease in labour turnover and absence rates. Thus, it appears that quality management leads to increased customer satisfaction, decreased costs and improved service delivery by front-line staff.

However, there has been no systematic research carried out to assess the extent of, and the reasons for, quality management within local authorities. This chapter seeks to explore these issues, using empirical evidence for the case of sport and leisure facilities provision by local authority leisure services. As the provision of quality has been managed historically through the use of quality programmes, the research on which this paper is based identifies the extent to which quality management programmes are used in public leisure facilities and seeks to generate an understanding of why they are used.

It has been suggested by Sanderson (1992) that quality programmes should be viewed as a combination of working practices and appropriate procedures that ensure that the provision of quality is 'built in' to the organization's activity. The use of quality programmes has been documented by frequent items in the professional journals regarding local authorities which are committed to, or have obtained, externally accredited quality programmes, such as ISO9002 (Melhuish, 1991; Faithfull, 1992; Wilson, 1994). These items, alongside articles relating to quality issues in general (Goodall, 1994; Sheppard and Studd, 1994; Courteen,

1995), appear to indicate that the use of quality programmes has become an important issue for managers of local authority leisure facilities.

There are three main reasons why the management of service quality is an issue for managers of sport and leisure facilities. Firstly, in this period of financial constraint local authority leisure services have the ability to contribute to the finances of local authorities. Secondly, the management of these facilities is subject to Compulsory Competitive Tendering (CCT) with requirements to monitor contractors' achievements. Finally, there is an aspect of 'choice' for customers of these facilities, so the service is provided in a market setting. A brief discussion of these reasons is necessary before the empirical evidence is considered.

Financial constraint

Since the mid-1970s local authorities have faced ongoing financial cuts implemented by central government. Although there is little evidence to indicate that leisure services have suffered disproportionately as a result of these cuts (Taylor and Page, 1994) the role of leisure services in contributing to local authority income is likely to place emphasis on the need for quality provision. As trading services, leisure services are in a better position than other local authority services to improve finances by affecting direct income as well as controlling costs. The ability to increase revenue and the ability to decrease costs are both claimed benefits of quality management and quality programmes.

Compulsory Competitive Tendering

CCT has the dual aims of trying to improve the quality of services and to cut costs of service provision (Audit Commission, 1989). Introduced into the management of sport and leisure facilities as an extension of the Local Government Act 1988, CCT required local authorities to put the management of these facilities up to competitive tender. In effect, local authorities became the clients of the contractors who managed their contracts and local authority staff only remained as managers of their facilities if they won the contract. Although initial contracts had to be awarded on the basis of price, contractors were required to have regard for the quality of the service they were guaranteeing to offer and therefore quality management is an issue for contract managers.

Choice

Many local authority services have no aspect of choice – for example, refuse collection. Residents have little or no choice in who provides the service or when and how it occurs. In contrast, the service provided by sport and leisure facilities involves several aspects of choice. Firstly, customers can choose whether or not to use the service; secondly, they can choose what aspects of the service they wish to use; and thirdly, within certain constraints, they can choose when to use the service. Finally, they have a choice between leisure alternatives provided by both the public and the private sectors. As a result, managers of sport and recreation facilities have to ensure that the service they offer is acceptable to existing customers and is attractive to potential customers. Therefore, the management of the quality of service is important.

These three factors make the management of service quality in sport and leisure facilities a key management task and it has been claimed that the use of quality management through quality programmes will lead to both service improvements and financial improvements. The empirical evidence discussed below aims to test these claims and to establish the reasons for the use of quality programmes in the management of sport and leisure facilities.

Methodology

The public leisure industry incorporates a wide number of activities and facilities. It was felt that to be of use to practitioners the research needed to focus on one aspect of service provision and as a result respondents were asked about the sport and leisure centres within their local authorities. This term was correctly interpreted by respondents to mean those multi-purpose facilities that provided active leisure within the local authority. In addition, this research aimed to investigate the use of all types of quality programme within local authority sport and leisure facilities. Therefore, the research considered externally assessed programmes such as Investors in People (IiP) or ISO9002 and internally developed programmes such as Total Quality Management (TQM). It is important to note that although the research focuses on sport and leisure facilities, the findings are transferable across most aspects of public leisure provision such as libraries, museums and countryside amenities.

In order to gain a comprehensive picture of the use of quality programmes in sport and leisure facilities it was considered necessary to survey all local authorities via a self-completion postal questionnaire, containing quantitative and qualitative questions. After piloting on a sample of the Institute of Sport and Recreation Management members the questionnaire was sent to Chief Leisure Officers in 488 UK local authorities in May 1995. The results presented here are based on

Table 14.1. Use of quality programmes in local authority sport and leisure facilities in the UK.

	Number	Percentage
Use quality programmes	155	65
More than one	(70)	(29)
Do not use programmes	85	35
Total	240	100

240 valid responses (a 49% response rate) which with a random sample would have a margin of error of 5.6%. It can be argued that the sample was not random as those with an interest in quality programmes would be more inclined to return the questionnaire than those with no interest. However, analysis of respondent characteristics (population size, political orientation, type of local authority and number of facilities) shows a reflection of the population as a whole and at face value it would appear that the sample reflects the population. The response rate for specific findings regarding the value of quality programmes is based on 155 local authorities, approximately one-third of all local authorities in the UK.

Results

These results include local authorities which were still in the process of obtaining accreditation to externally assessed programmes. However, to be included in these results accreditation had to be sought within three months of responding. It was felt that any local authority leisure provider this close to seeking accreditation was likely to be managing service quality through the use of the quality programme.

Overall picture

Table 14.1 shows that 155 local authorities (65% of respondents) were using or intended to use quality programmes in the management of their sport and leisure facilities. Just under half of these (70) use or are intending to use more than one quality programme.

These results indicate that a significant proportion of local authority leisure providers are committed to the use of quality programmes within the management of these facilities. They support the claims that the use of quality programmes is relatively common throughout local authority leisure services.

At this point it is important to consider the proportion of non-respondents and what the implications of these are for the research findings. Half of the local authorities in the UK did not respond to the questionnaire and it is possible to suggest that this lack of response was due to a lack of interest in the questionnaire as they were not using quality programmes in the management of their sport and leisure facilities. While it is unlikely that all non-responses were for this reason, even if the majority were not using quality programmes, the results show that a minimum of one-third of all local authorities were using quality programmes in the management of their facilities. As a consequence, the conclusion above is still valid.

Programmes used

Table 14.2 shows the relative popularity of different quality programmes used in the management of sport and leisure facilities and at this point it may be helpful to make clear the difference between Total Quality Management as a quality programme and the use of such quality programmes as BS EN ISO9000 in providing a quality service.

TQM is concerned with developing a culture within the organization that ensures that quality is integrated into all operations. Oakland (1993) outlines the need for organization planning to enhancing TQM while Dale (1994) highlights the need for wholehearted staff commitment. The emphasis of TQM is on developing a quality culture while quality programmes have their emphasis on working practices and procedures (Sanderson, 1992).

Although the difference may appear to be simply semantics, it is the focus on conformance to organizational procedures that is the differentiator between TQM and most quality programmes. Other quality programmes tend to address specific aspects of the organization and, although they contribute significantly to the process of quality management, they do so through quality assurance. TQM is a management philosophy, based on a continuum of quality improvement, encompassing all aspects of the organizations. Therefore, in the simplest of terms TQM is an organizational culture committed to improving the service continually, whereas quality programmes demonstrate commitment to the attainment of standardized procedures.

Table 14.2 shows that IiP was the most commonly used quality programme in public leisure facilities with 91 local authorities claiming a commitment to IiP. Given the human-resource and staff-development focus of IiP, which is essential in a people-based industry such as leisure, the fact that it was a popular quality programme was not unexpected. IiP can also be considered to be a relatively inexpensive quality programme to implement, given the support that is available from Training and Enterprise Councils for those committing to IiP.

However, what was unexpected about these results is that IiP was more commonly used than ISO9002. Most of the reports, articles and

Table 14.2. Quality programmes used in managing local authority sport and leisure facilities in the UK.

Programme	Number	% of those with programmes	% of all respondents
Investors in People	91	59	38
ISO9002 (BS5750)	64	41	27
Charter Mark	30	19	13
Total Quality Management	30	19	13
Other	32	21	13

Note that throughout this report ISO9002 will be used to refer to BS5750 accreditation as well as BS EN ISO9002 accreditation.

discussion on quality programmes in the leisure industry have been focused on ISO9002. However, this research has indicated that with 64 local authorities committed to ISO9002, it was only two-thirds as popular as IiP. One explanation for the apparent past success of ISO9002 may be due to its availability before other accredited quality programmes such as IiP or the Charter Mark. Indeed, if this research had been carried out 2 years earlier, it is likely that ISO9002 would have been the most commonly used quality programme.

In addition, this programme has been used as a means of guaranteeing quality in CCT specifications by having been written into contracts as an objective which will have had the effect of increasing its popularity. Now that it has been deemed anti-competitive to insist that contractors achieve a named quality programme, it is likely that future research will find a further loss in the popularity of ISO9002.

It was perhaps surprising that only 30 local authorities use the Charter Mark given that this quality programme was developed specifically for the public sector (HMSO, 1991). However, this is likely to be explained by the limited number of annual awards available and its association with the Conservative Government. In addition, it is a relatively 'new' quality award which may gain in popularity in future research.

As TQM programmes are aimed at the organization as a whole, this may have prevented local authorities from choosing to use TQM as their initial quality programme. This, alongside a lack of external recognition, is likely to account for the relatively lower popularity of using TQM programmes to manage quality.

Other programmes mentioned were primarily Customer Care programmes or Customer Charters with 25 local authorities using this type of programme in the management of their sport and leisure facilities. Other programmes mentioned were the UK Quality Award, the Northern Ireland Quality Award and other British Standards Institute (BSI) quality marks.

Table 14.3. Reasons for using quality programmes in local authority sport and leisure facilities.

Reason	Number	Percentage of those with programmes
To improve services	97	63
To improve efficiency	39	26
To meet contract requirement	35	23
For staff involvement and development	34	21
To follow a council directive	29	19
To increase competitiveness	25	16
To increase accountability	25	16
Other	32	22

Respondents could give more than one reason.

Reasons for using quality programmes

Proponents of quality programmes have claimed their ability to improve both service quality and the financial situation of organizations, through decreased costs and improved efficiency. Table 14.3 suggests that local authority leisure providers have subscribed to these claims, as the main reason for the use of quality programmes was to improve the services offered. This, alongside reasons of increased efficiency, increased accountability and staff involvement, indicates that local authority leisure providers chose to use quality programmes for the same reasons as managers in other industries.

However, what needs further investigation is the role of CCT in encouraging local authority leisure services to implement quality programmes. As mentioned earlier, the need to obtain certain quality programmes has been a requirement of some CCT contracts. In addition, the need to meet contract requirements was the third most common reason for implementing a quality programme, particularly to reduce the costs of, and aid with, the monitoring of these contracts. This indicates a direct influence of CCT upon the use of quality programmes.

Twenty-five local authorities use quality programmes to increase competitiveness, and qualitative answers indicate that this was primarily to win CCT bids. One respondent outlined that quality programmes were '. . . used to compete successfully with the private sector and more easily meet the challenge of CCT' (North Down Borough Council). Another respondent suggested that: '. . . quality programmes will make the DSO more competitive in the CCT context' (Metropolitan Borough of Wirral).

This, alongside the fact that the expressed objectives of CCT are to improve services and improve efficiency – the two most common reasons for using quality programmes – indicates that CCT has been a major influence in the promotion of the role of quality programmes. This argument is supported by the following comments from respondents: 'TQM was implemented in the run-up to CCT to give staff a focus for improving service quality' (Worthing Borough Council) and 'to ensure when facilities are subject to CCT, the competition will be competent contractors' (Banbridge District Council).

This role is likely to become more significant in future given the 1994 Secretary of State ruling that local authorities can consider the quality of CCT tenders when awarding the next round of CCT contracts (LGMB, 1994).

Having outlined some of the reasons for using quality programmes, it is now worth considering the actual impact of quality programmes upon operations as perceived by respondents. Assuming supporters of the introduction of such systems are right, there should be a resultant positive effect on service delivery in terms of customer satisfaction and management effectiveness through improved management practice. Table 14.4 shows that most respondents felt that they were unable to comment on the effect that quality programmes had on the management of their facilities. The majority of respondents felt that it was too soon to assess their impact, which is a reflection of the relatively recent popularity of quality programmes in public leisure services.

However, those that felt they could, indicated benefits in terms of customer service, improved management, staff motivation and assistance. This supports the claims that quality programmes improve service quality. Please note that the assessment of improved service was made by managers who may not be the best people to make this judgement. However, piloting of the survey indicated that this judgement could be made by considering decreases in customer complaints and through consideration of market research. However, this is an area for future research.

Respondents were less positive about the financial advantages of quality programmes. TQM programmes were felt to have a strong improving effect on both costs and revenue and ISO9002 was felt to decrease costs and to have some effect on increasing revenue; however, respondents were divided on the financial benefits that ISO9002 offered. The results for ISO9002 are likely to be due to the ongoing costs of accreditation of ISO9002, which does not occur with TQM programmes.

IiP was deemed to have caused decreased costs but not improved revenue and the Charter Mark did not have a positive effect on either. In addition, only IiP and TQM were felt to increase user numbers. It is possible that over time the financial advantages of quality programmes will become more apparent. However, at present the research neither supports nor reflects the claim that quality programmes have both service and financial advantages.

Table 14.4. The effect of quality programmes on the management of local authority sport and leisure facilities.

	Yes (%)	No (%)	Do not know (%)	Too soon to tell (%)
Improved service to customers				
Investors in People	29	1	3	67
ISO9002	55	1	8	36
Charter Mark	55	0	0	45
Total quality management	67	0	14	19
Increased usage				
Investors in People	13	6	15	66
ISO9002	19	19	18	44
Charter Mark	18	14	23	45
Total quality management	38	10	23	29
Improved management				
Investors in People	34	3	3	60
ISO9002	67	0	0	33
Charter Mark	50	0	9	41
Total quality management	67	0	10	23
Reduced costs				
Investors in People	14	6	10	70
ISO9002	25	17	10	48
Charter Mark	4	27	23	46
Total quality management	43	19	5	33
Increased revenue				
Investors in People	4	16	10	70
ISO9002	16	14	18	52
Charter Mark	14	23	18	45
Total quality management	38	6	23	33
Assisted staff				
Investors in People	40	0	1	59
ISO9002	69	0	0	31
Charter Mark	36	9	14	41
Total quality management	72	0	5	23
Improved motivation				
Investors in People	33	0	4	63
ISO9002	51	12	4	33
Charter Mark	50	5	0	45
Total quality management	58	5	14	23
Increased communication with customers				
Investors in People	26	5	6	63
ISO9002	52	12	4	32
Charter Mark	5	55	0	40
Total quality management	67	5	5	23

Table 14.5. Reasons for not using quality programmes in local authority sport and leisure facilities.

Reason	Number	Percentage
Lack of resources	30	35
Other priorities	29	34
Manage quality in other ways (user panels, performance indicators)	21	25
Appraisal under way	14	17
Programmes are of debatable value	12	14
Does not meet the needs of the department	8	9
Other	13	15

Respondents could give more than one reason.

From these findings it would appear that, according to managers implementing quality programmes, TQM has the most positive effect on all aspects of management, and therefore is the most appropriate programme for the management of public leisure facilities. It would appear that ISO9002 and IiP are the most appropriate externally assessed quality programme in terms of improved service and financial benefits. However, future research may produce different results as more respondents feel they can comment on the effect of their chosen quality programme.

Reasons for not using quality programmes

The main reasons for not using quality programmes (Table 14.5) were related to the perceived resources necessary to use quality programmes, with 59 responses relating to this area. Although it can be argued that the financial costs of quality programmes are recouped through increased efficiency or compensated by improved service provision, quality programmes are inherently resource intensive, particularly in terms of staff time (Robinson, 1996). Therefore, even local authorities who support the concept of improving service quality will choose not to use quality programmes if resources are scarce and other priorities are deemed more important.

However, only 12 respondents queried the value of quality programmes, which suggests that managing the quality of service in local authority leisure services is an uncontroversial issue even for those who are not committed to quality programmes. This was also supported by the findings that 35 local authorities are managing quality in other ways by the use of performance indicators and customer panels or are in the process of appraising the quality programmes available to public leisure providers, with the intention of implementing these in future.

Conclusions

From the research findings it is difficult to determine what is the most effective quality programme for use in the management of public leisure facilities. IiP is the most commonly used quality programme, but it is difficult to assess the impact of this upon management.

It would appear that, on the whole, there are no immediate financial advantages to the use of quality programmes in public leisure services. However, we can conclude that quality programmes are valuable in terms of improving services to customers through direct service improvements and through improved management and motivated staff. As a consequence it is likely that the above benefits will, in the longer term, lead to financial gains for the managers of local authority sport and leisure facilities.

This research indicates a clear need for further work in this area which should concentrate on two issues. Further investigation is necessary, firstly, to establish exactly what is meant by 'improved services and increased efficiency' and secondly, on the actual impact of quality programmes. However, the research outlined in this paper is a first stage for this future research by confirming that quality management is playing an important role in the delivery of public leisure services.

References

Association of County Councils (1992) *Signposts to Quality – Local Authority Case Studies.* ACC, London.

Audit Commission (1989) *Sport for Whom?* HMSO, London.

Carson, J. (1990) The keys to quality. *Managing Service Quality*, November, pp. 19–21.

Clarke, M. and Stewart, J. (1987) The public service orientation. *Local Government Policy Making* 13(4), March, pp. 34–40.

Courteen, D. (1995) Constructive criticism. *Fitness*, June, pp. 86–87.

Dale, B. (1994) *Managing Quality*. Prentice Hall, London.

Deming, W.E. (1986) Introduction. In: Gitlow, H.S. and Gitlow, S.J. (1987) *The Deming Guide to Quality and Competitive Position*. Prentice Hall, London.

Faithfull, P. (1992) Standard treatment. *The Leisure Manager*, April, pp. 25–26.

Gaster, L. (1992) Quality in service delivery: competition for resources or more effective use of resources? *Local Government Policy Making* 19(1), July, pp. 55–64.

Goodall, E. (1994) Quality Control. *Museums Journal*, January, pp. 22–25.

HMSO (1991) *The Citizen's Charter*. HMSO, London.

Local Government Management Board (LGMB) (1994) *Guidance on the Assessment of Quality in the Application of CCT to White Collar and Professional Services*. LGMB, Luton.

Local Government Training Board (1987) *Getting Closer to the Public*. LGTB, Luton.

MacNeil, D. (1994) *Customer Service Excellence*. Mirror Press, USA.

Melhuish, T. (1991) Quality, contracts, service. *Leisure Management*, April, pp. 63–64.

Navaratnam, K. and Harris, B. (1994) Customer service in an Australian award-winning public sector service industry. *International Journal of Public Sector Management* 7(2), 42–49.

Oakland, J.S. (1993) *Total Quality Management*. Butterworth-Heinemann, Oxford.

Peters, T. and Austin, N. (1984) *A Passion for Excellence*. Collins, Glasgow.

Peters, T. and Waterman, R. (1982) *In Search of Excellence*. Harper and Row, New York.

Pfeffer, N. and Coote, A. (1991) *Is Quality Good for You? – A Critical Review of Quality Assurance in Welfare Services*. Social Policy Paper, No. 5. Institute for Public Policy Research.

Robinson, L. (1996) *Quality Management – An Investigation into the Use of Quality Programmes in Local Authority Sport and Leisure Facilities*. ISRM, Melton Mowbray.

Sanderson, I. (1992) *Management of Quality in Local Government*. Longman, Essex.

Sellers, P. (1989) Getting customers to love you. *Fortune*, 13 March, pp. 26–33.

Sheppard, M. and Studd, S. (1994) *Quality in Perspective*. Sports Council, London.

Taylor, P. and Page, K. (1994) *The Financing of Local Authority Sport and Recreation – a Service under Threat?* ISRM, Melton Mowbray.

Wille, E. (1992) *Quality: Achieving Excellence*. Century Business, London.

Wilson, J. (1994) Quality control. *Recreation,* July/August, pp. 21–22.

15

Application of the SERVQUAL Model to the UK Leisure Industry: Are they Servicing the Service rather than Servicing the Customer?

Christine Williams

Lancashire Business School, University of Central Lancashire, Preston PR1 2HE, UK

Introduction

This research was carried out over a 2-year period at six leisure-related research sites – museum, art gallery, theatre, leisure centre, amusement park and a golf course – to investigate the development and integration of quality management systems into the operational management procedures. It explores whether or not service delivery has improved in terms of external customer satisfaction, when an accredited or non-accredited quality system has been introduced.

The decision to investigate this topic was due to comments and questions from leisure industry practitioners at ISO9002 workshops (Dale, 1994). The author deduced that some practitioners had very little understanding of the concept of quality management systems. The impressions found by the author were that some delegates felt that ISO9002 would either enable financial targets to be met or act as a cost-cutting exercise. Other practitioner perceptions were that a Total Quality Management (TQM) culture – as advocated by many including Crosby (1979), Deming (1982) and Juran (1988a) – would be achieved throughout their organizations after registration by an accreditation body, or a confusion that frequently occurred was that ISO9002 was as prescriptive as other British Standards Institute (BSI) standards with which they were familiar and would provide the 'recipe' for achieving excellent service delivery.

Methods and Models

SERVQUAL model

Quantitative research was carried out on the application of the SERVQUAL model. The scores subsequently generated gave direction to a second phase of qualitative research.

In most organizations the outputs of the management process are required to be expressed as a numerical value – performance indicators – a process driven by amongst others, the Audit Commission (1988) and Osbourne and Gaebler (1992) who state 'What gets measured gets done.'

The SERVQUAL model has been applied for over 11 years in the USA financial sector (Parasuraman *et al.*, 1985) and subsequently available to the remainder of the service sector. In related fields, Saleh and Ryan (1991; 1992) adapted the model for application in the hospitality sector and Taylor *et al.* (1993) utilized recreational services in the USA to test its reliability.

In the UK service sector a number of major companies have used SERVQUAL as a vehicle for improving service quality, including East Midlands Electricity (Chandlin and Day, 1993) and the Midland Bank (Buttle, 1996). Hutton and Richardson (1995) describe instances of its use in private sector healthcare, and Chaston (1994) carried out research into the National Health Service. Prior to this, Chaston (1993) researched the service delivery process for internal customers in the UK manufacturing sector.

The model consists of measuring the service quality gaps (see Fig. 15.1) over five dimensions. Whilst previous researchers, including Normann (1991), identified that service characteristics can be classified into two distinct groups, Tangibles and Intangibles, Zeithaml *et al.* (1990) found that the intangibles can be segmented into Reliability, Assurance, Empathy and Responsiveness. Knutson *et al.* (1990) and Babakus and Mangold (1992) confirm this.

Measurement of the gap scores is by three questionnaires, one for each response group of customers, managers and operations staff. The customer's questionnaire tests expectations and perceptions via two instruments, each comprising a series of 22 items (see Table 15.1) on a seven-point Likert scale (see Appendix 1).

The manager's questionnaire also tests for customer expectations using the same 22-item instrument as well as the antecedents of the service quality gaps (see Table 15.2). The operational staff are only surveyed on gap antecedents. The SERVQUAL gap scores are calculated by applying the formulae shown in Appendix 2.

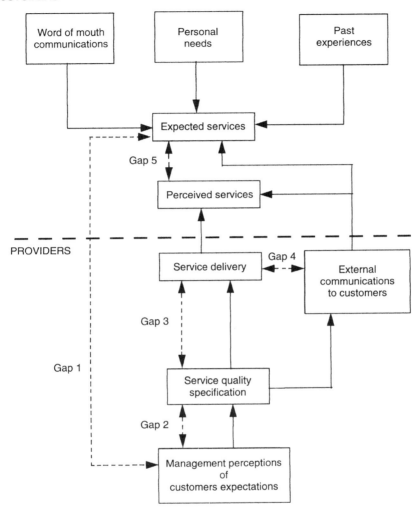

Source: Zeithaml *et al.* (1990).

Fig. 15.1. Concept model of service quality.

The use of three questionnaires enables comparisons to be made across the response groups and yields the gap scores. After calculating the SERVQUAL gap scores, the model continues by giving a diagnostic checklist (see Fig. 15.2) to allow organizations to implement changes to facilitate closure of the service quality gaps.

Table 15.1. SERVQUAL dimensions.

Dimension	Definition	Items in scale
Reliability	The ability to perform the promised service dependably and accurately	5
Assurance	The knowledge and courtesy of employees and their ability to convey trust and confidence	4
Tangibles	The appearance of physical facilities, equipment, personnel and communications materials	4
Empathy	The provision of caring, individualized attention to customers	5
Responsiveness	The willingness to help customers and to provide prompt service	4

Source: Buttle (1996).

Research methodology

All the managers and operational staff, at each of the six sites, were given questionnaires for self-completion, whilst the author's fieldwork comprised of an exit survey at five of the sites.

At the sixth site, the theatre, an exit survey was inappropriate due to the seasonal nature of their programme. Therefore, a postal survey was undertaken with 400 people chosen at random from the theatre's 25,000 mailing list.

The statistical package for the Social Science computer software was utilized to compute the SERVQUAL gap scores from the data sets. This gave customer SERVQUAL scores for all five dimensions, as well as gap 5 customers' expectations and perceptions. It allowed a comparison to be made between managers' perceptions of customers' expectations (gap 1). Gap 2, 3 and 4 scores were also calculated for both managers and operational staff.

Utilizing both negative and positive scores for all five gaps, comparisons were made with Zeithaml *et al.*'s diagnostic checklist (see Table 15.2). This acted as a catalyst for semi-structured interviews with key personnel, both managers and operational staff.

Therefore, a research site gaining the highest or lowest score at gap 1, appertaining to market research, would indicate that the person responsible for marketing within the organization should be interviewed. The development and implementation of quality initiatives into the operational management procedures were also explored with the interviewees.

It should be noted that it was not the author's intention to analyse and compare the data across the six sites, as the sites had been especially chosen for their diversity of management cultures and services (Table 15.3).

Table 15.2. Constructs hypothesized to influence service quality gaps within providers' organizations.

Constructs influencing gap 1

Market research orientation (MRO). Extent to which managers make an effort to understand customers' needs and expectations through formal and informal information-gathering activities.

Upward communication (UC). Extent to which top management seeks, stimulates and facilitates the flow of information from employees at lower levels.

Level of management (LOM). Number of managerial levels between the top-most and bottom-most levels.

Constructs influencing gap 2

Management commitment to service quality (MCSQ). Extent to which management views service quality as a key strategic goal and allocates adequate resources to it.

Goal-setting (GS). Existence of a formal process for setting quality-of-service goals.

Task standardization (TS). Extent to which technology and training programmes are used to standardize service tasks.

Perception of feasibility (POF). Extent to which managers believe that customers' expectations can be met.

Constructs influencing gap 3

Teamwork (TEAM). Extent to which all employees pull together for a common goal.

Employee–job fit (EFIT). Match between the skills or employees and their job.

Technology–job fit (TFIT). The appropriateness of the tools and technology that employees use to perform their jobs.

Perceived control (PC). Extent to which employees perceive that they are in control of their jobs and that they can act flexibly.

Supervisory control system (SCS). The extent to which employees are evaluated compensated on what they do (behaviour) rather than solely on output quality.

Role conflict (RC). Extent to which employees perceive that they cannot satisfy all the demands of all the individuals (internal and external customers) they must serve.

Role ambiguity (RA). Extent to which employees are uncertain about what managers and supervisors expect from them and how to satisfy those expectations.

Constructs influencing gap 4

Horizontal communication (HC). Extent to which communication and coordination occur between different departments that have contact with and/or serve customers.

Propensity to overpromise (PTO). Extent to which the firm feels pressure to promise more to customers than can be achieved.

Source: Zeithaml *et al.* (1990).

Table 15.3. Summary of research sites for service quality.

Research sites		Art gallery	Museum	Amusement park	Leisure centre	Golf course	Theatre
Sector	Public	✓	✓		✓	✓	
	Commercial			✓			
	Voluntary						✓
Management	Board of trustees	✓	✓				✓
	Councillors				✓	✓	
	Family			✓			
	ISO9002				✓	✓	
Quality initiative	Investors in People	✓	✓	✓			
	Citizen's Charter	✓	✓				

Research Site Case Studies

Art gallery

This site is part of a central government-funded public sector organization, operating under a Board of Trustees on seven associated sites. The organization had gained the Investor in People (IiP) Award (Employment Department, 1990) and is submitting a Citizen's Charter application (Buswell, 1993; Cabinet Office, 1995). The centralized Personnel Department recently benchmarked with the Post Office Quality Department.

A small number of respondents at this site objected to being referred to as customers. When asked how they perceived themselves, most liked the use of the word visitor, one described himself as a Patron of the Arts. The word customer seems to have been perceived by the visitors as a person who receives a service only when a fee is paid at point of use.

Museum

The museum is part of the same central organization that manages the art gallery but, unlike the art gallery, it has an admission charge for visitors. Researchers do not have to pay nor do customers only using the shop or the catering facilities. Unlike the art gallery, the museum is located within a popular tourism complex with many commercial attractions in direct competition.

Being part of the same centralized organization, this site and the art gallery gained IiP and applied for the Citizen's Charter Mark simultaneously. The organization's overall quality initiative is to work towards a TQM culture. Unless a full-time quality manager is appointed to drive the quality initiative, on behalf of the senior management, this will be difficult to achieve, especially with a fragmented organization located on seven sites.

Amusement park

This is in the private sector of the leisure industry, the parent company being family-owned. The amusement park leases land from the local authority but has a number of smaller owner-operated stalls within the boundary of its site. This has limited the organization's commitment to invest in new rides until the whole site can be leased. The amusement park employs 28 permanent staff, eight managers and 240 seasonal operations staff. Due to this influx of seasonal staff the organization has decided to gain IiP and is piloting the generic National Vocational Qualifications (NVQ) for amusement park operatives, having rejected ISO9002. They believe that ISO9002 is not flexible enough to cope with this site where a significant number of rides and ancillary facilities are not under their control but their customers believe they are. The responsibility for quality functions is with the personnel manager.

Out of the six research sites, this is one of two with free admission, but with a pay-as-you-ride system. It was also one of two weather-dependent sites, having only limited indoor facilities.

Leisure centre

A public-sector-provided facility funded by a metropolitan borough council. It is a dual-use site shared between the Leisure Services and Education Departments and located within the boundary of a school.

The leisure centre has both wet and dry facilities, and an athletic track is being constructed. The majority of the respondents who attend the centre swim (75%); a pattern of usage, according to a manager, that is reflected in the total admissions at the centre.

Being a dual-use facility, it is exempt from Compulsory Competitive Tendering regulations but operates within a similar framework in case the regulations should change. Catering and cleaning contractors work within the facility.

The leisure centre is registered to ISO9002 and has a quality manager as part of the central support staff. When negotiating access into the site, it was ascertained that there was not a division between managers and operational staff tasks; all staff to a greater or lesser extent carry out elements of both.

Golf course

This site is controlled by the same local authority as the leisure centre. The day-to-day management of the site has been put out to tender under the Local Government Act 1988 and has been retained by the Direct Service Organization (DSO). Under the original contract documents, all contractors had to have or be working towards BS5750 part 2. In the renewal documentation the need to be registered to ISO9002 if already a council contractor is not a requirement.

The author included the golf course as it has direct competition from the commercial and private club sectors. Also, the cultural changes that are taking place within local authorities tend to be polarized at golf courses, and in the majority of cases a true profit is being generated (CIPFA, 1994).

This course is unusual in that it does not have a clubhouse. The golf course café, whilst predominantly used by the golfers, is run as a facility for all park users. Even without a clubhouse there is a high number of repeat visits, with 65% of the 80 respondents playing at least once a week.

Theatre

This site was included because it was considering working towards the European Quality Award (EQA) (Jones,1995; European Foundation for Quality Management,1996), with consultative help from the Post Office Quality Team. As part of its EQA criteria Impact on Society, the Post Office gives free consultations to the voluntary sector.

The theatre is a charitable trust but unlike other voluntary organizations has no volunteer helpers: front-of-house staff are paid a nominal sum for their work.

Whilst a quality manager was not employed within the organization, the task was shared by the marketing managers who saw it as a positive step forward for the organization.

Quantitative Research Findings

Art gallery

Customers' SERVQUAL scores
Figure 15.2 indicates that the art gallery is in the negative zone in the five dimensions of service quality delivery. This indicates that service quality still needs to be improved even though the largest negative score is −1.007, when a maximum negative score of −6.0 is possible.

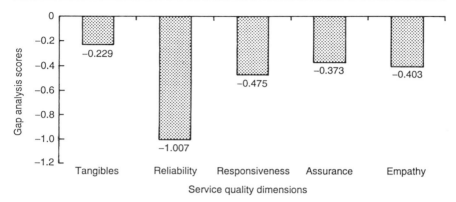

Fig. 15.2. Customers' SERVQUAL scores for the art gallery.

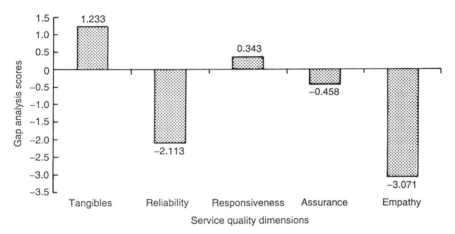

Fig. 15.3. Gap 1 art gallery – managers' perceptions of customers' expectations.

The two dimensions of Reliability and Responsiveness have the lowest scores and these relate to the organization's ability to perform the promised service dependably and accurately or the willingness to help customers and provide prompt service. This phenomenon was even more pronounced when the 38% of first-time visitors were deducted from the total of 60 respondents. This may be due to partial non-participation rather than poor service delivery. This issue is addressed on page 246.

Managers' SERVQUAL scores for gap 1
The service quality scores appertaining to gap 1 (managers' perceptions of customers' expectations) (see Fig. 15.3), demonstrate that the art

Table 15.4. Museum customers' score comparisons over the five dimensions of service quality.

SERVQUAL dimensions	All respondents	First visit only
Tangibles	0.146	0.161
Reliability	–0.610	–0.807
Responsiveness	–0.367	–0.375
Assurance	–0.004	–0.080
Empathy	–0.090	–0.050

gallery's employees have inaccurate perceptions of service quality compared with those of their customers, but again this has to be contextualized. In three dimensions – Reliability, Assurance and Empathy – the inaccuracy in their judgement is that the customers' expectations are lower than in reality; this should cause concern. The two scores for Tangibles and Responsiveness show that the managers' perceptions of the customers' expectations are higher than the reality.

Meeting a score higher than customers expect is a strategy advocated by many writers including Peters (1987) and Berry and Parasuraman (1994), but if services are performed to a lower standard than is expected, customers' gap 5 will increase. Parasuraman *et al.* (1991a) have suggested that customers have a zone of tolerance towards service quality, but the organization's performance could go below what is acceptable.

Museum

Customers' SERVQUAL scores
Table 15.4 illustrates that the museum site has a negative SERVQUAL score in four out of five dimensions. Reliability and Responsiveness are again the two lowest, with Tangibles being the only positive score. Visitors' comments indicate that the external environmental features of the museum's location, in an historic building complex with excellent views, contributed as much to the Tangibles positive score as the internal facilities.

The negative gap score was increased in three dimensions when the first-time visitors, a total of 47%, were deducted from the survey sample of 60 respondents. Comments from all categories of visitors were very complimentary about their leisure experience, so even slight negative values were surprising. Again, this may be caused by the same influence of partial non-participation as the art gallery.

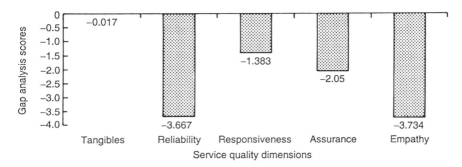

Fig. 15.4. Gap 1 museum – managers' perceptions of customers' expectations.

Managers' SERVQUAL scores for gap 1
The scores shown in Fig. 15.4 demonstrate that 43% of managers at the museum have inaccurate views of the customers' expectations of satisfaction with service quality.

In four dimensions – Reliability, Responsiveness, Assurance and Empathy – the inaccuracy in the managers' judgement is that the customers' expectations are again lower than in reality. The SERVQUAL scores for the Tangibles dimension is very similar to the customers' with only an inaccuracy of 0.017.

From the subsequent interviews it was found that staff are very critical of the service quality level expected by their customers. This judgement is based on the limited number of complaints they receive, yet they feel the service has reduced since the museum first opened. As this site has the highest percentage of first-time visitors, past experience of this facility will not be an element in their expectation scores.

Amusement park

Customers' SERVQUAL scores
The amusement park's largest negative score of −1.179 is for the Tangibles dimension, and is followed by Reliability (Fig 15.5). It was ascertained from the customers' comments that these two scores related to the physical environment, especially the conditions of the toilets and also to the fact that not all rides accept discount tickets. An overlap from one dimension to another may have occurred; this is considered on page 247.

Managers' SERVQUAL scores for gap 1
Managers are incorrect in their low perceptions of the Tangible aspects when judging customers' expectations, the remaining gaps indicate a

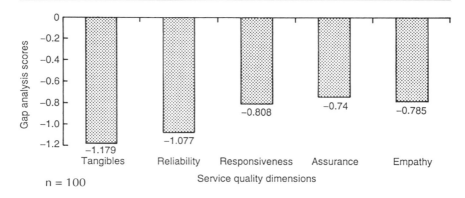

Fig. 15.5. Customers' SERVQUAL scores for the amusement park.

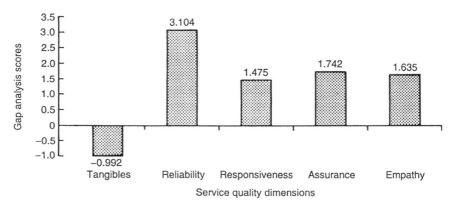

Fig. 15.6. Gap 1 amusement park – managers' perceptions of customers' expectations.

higher perception, especially the Reliability dimension at +3.104 (Fig. 15.6).

Managers at this site perceive the dimensions of Reliability, Responsiveness and Assurance to be fundamentals of health and safety and customer care, especially relating to the rides, whilst some customers do not have such expectations. As this site had the least first-time visitors (6%), the expectations of the majority of customers will reflect on past experiences; the customers' comments signified that they did not separate the tangible dimension from the reliability of service delivery.

Leisure centre

Customers' SERVQUAL scores
It is interesting that the customer SERVQUAL score for the Tangible dimension at this site is only slightly negative, at −0.538 (Fig. 15.7), when 25 respondents commented in the open-ended question no. 7 ('Do you have any further comments you would like to make about the leisure centre?') about the poor condition of the changing rooms and lockers. Whilst 75% of those surveyed used the changing rooms, only 41% go on to place their belongings in the lockers. The higher than expected Tangible SERVQUAL score could be reflected by the non-participation of the customers in many aspects of the facilities provided.

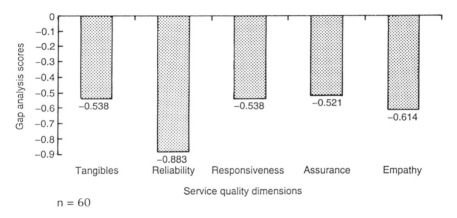

Fig. 15.7. Customers' SERVQUAL scores for the leisure centre.

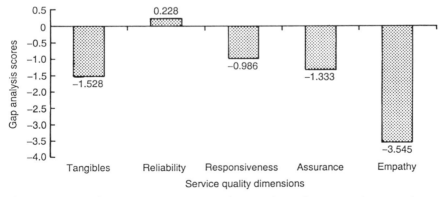

Fig. 15.8. Gap 1 leisure centre – managers' perceptions of customers' expectations.

Managers' SERVQUAL scores for gap 1

When calculating the SERVQUAL score for managers' perceptions of customers' expectations, Fig. 15.8 indicates that the Reliability dimension has the maximum inaccuracy on the managers' behalf, compared with the score of –0.883 from customers.

In the other dimensions the managers' perceptions are slightly lower than the reality, even though market research via focus groups and customers surveys are carried out on a regular basis to comply with ISO9002 documentation.

Golf course

Customers' SERVQUAL scores

Figure 15.9 illustrates that the golf course is quite poor in all dimensions. The negative score on the Tangibles dimension is a result of playing off winter tees in the summer, plus a range of other environmental issues such as flags missing, too many persons on the course, dress code not being adhered to.

One misconception at this site is caused by the golf course running at full capacity for most of the time. The staff perceive this as an indication of the excellence service they provide. The golfers feel that the staff are uncooperative and not empathic to them when they try unsuccessfully to make a booking; the staff see this as being totally outside of their control.

Managers' SERVQUAL scores for gap 1

The golf course managers' judgement of three dimensions – Tangibles, Reliability and Responsiveness – are lower than in reality (Fig. 15.10).

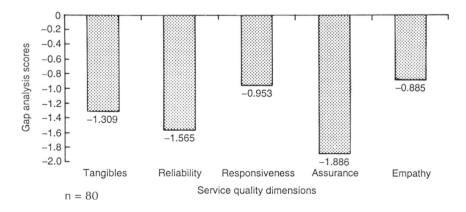

Fig. 15.9. Customers' SERVQUAL scores for the golf course.

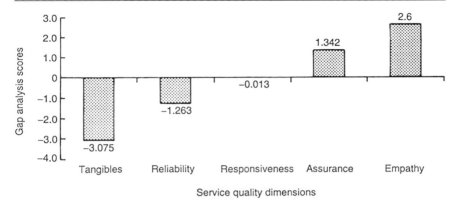

Fig. 15.10. Gap 1 golf course – managers' perceptions of customers' expectations.

The two remaining dimensions, Assurance (+1.342) and Empathy (+2.6), show that the managers' perceptions of the customers' expectations are far higher than in reality.

Very few of the customers use the full range of ancillary facilities and this factor will have significance to all of the scores generated by the instruments. It would seem that customers have opted out of the worst aspects of the service delivery such as the changing rooms and, whilst the course is now perceived by customers to be excellent, the staff still score the service from an holistic point of view.

Theatre

Customers' SERVQUAL scores
The theatre has been given negative scores in all dimensions (Fig. 15.11) with a maximum score of −0.739. From the comments written on the questionnaires, one factor that is producing slight negative readings over the dimensions of Reliability, Responsiveness, Assurance and Empathy is the time it takes to make telephone bookings or enquiries. Managers have instigated improvements to the booking system but these will only be experienced by the customers after the new season's mail shot.

Another factor that is being reflected in the negative Tangibles dimension score is that, even though the theatre complex has undergone a refurbishment programme, only a minority use the café (12% of the respondents) when attending a performance. Most customers' complaints relate to the tangible aspects of this area.

Managers' SERVQUAL scores for gap 1
Positive scores in Tangibles, Reliability and Responsiveness show that the managers feel that the customers have higher expectations than

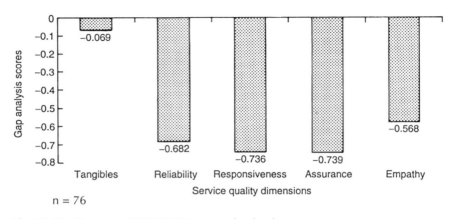

Fig. 15.11. Customers' SERVQUAL scores for the theatre.

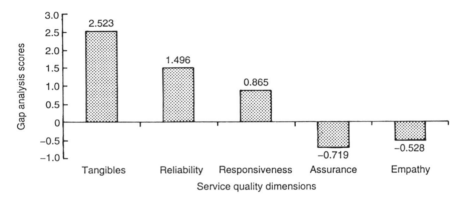

Fig. 15.12. Gap 1 theatre – managers' perceptions of customers' expectations.

they actually do, and on the other two dimensions, Assurance and Empathy, the inaccuracy is in the opposite direction (Fig. 15.12).

Zeithaml *et al.*'s (1990) SERVQUAL model indicates that three factors – word of mouth, personal needs and past experiences – affect the customers' expectation levels. With the present design of the instrument it is not possible to tell whether the customers' lower expectation scores for the Tangibles, Reliability and Responsiveness dimensions are based on current operational practices of this theatre or others.

Managers' and operational staff gap scores – gaps 2–4

The SERVQUAL scores for gaps 2, 3 and 4 were calculated using the formulae of Zeithaml *et al.* (1990) (see Appendix 2). The resulting gap scores are displayed in Tables 15.5 and 15.6. The research sites gaining the highest and the lowest SERVQUAL gap scores of the six data sets (an indicator of the quality of the service delivery processes in place), were selected for further investigation in the qualitative phase of the project.

Personnel from all six sites were interviewed regarding gap 1, because market research and upward communications, the specific antecedents of this gap, indicate how customer-orientated the organization is.

Qualitative Research Findings

Art gallery and museum

These two sites are in an excellent position culturally to implement any accredited quality system. The original Civil Service culture of the managing organization was very much in keeping with a mechanistic process, whereby each site has a clear set of aims and objectives that are acted upon. Even though an atmosphere of competitive tendering and income generation prevails, it is not allowed to deflect from the core service delivery. IiP and Citizen's Charter Initiatives are only extensions of this organization's existing procedures, but the main obstacle to continuous improvement is the lack of a full-time quality manager. This indicates a lack of commitment and understanding of quality management by senior management.

Amusement park

The amusement park is trying to give good value for money and a high level of service quality within a difficult environment. The organization is family-owned, which has advantages in that decisions are made quickly, but the disadvantage is that many senior positions are not available outside of the family group. There is the potential for motivational and retention problems with non-family staff.

Due to the multiple occupancy of the site, the organization has decided not to try to achieve ISO9002, as too many factors are outside of their control, but to concentrate on the human resource issues and gain IiP. Maynard (1995) validates this type of approach.

IiP is relatively inexpensive (£500 for a sample of employees) unlike ISO9002, and together with the generic NVQs, which also attract grant aid, an influx of seasonal staff can be accommodated in a cost-effective manner. Generally, a better-trained individual carries out their

Table 15.5. Summary of SERVQUAL gap scores for art gallery, museum and amusement park.

Gap no.	Possible causes	Art gallery		Museum		Amusement park	
		Managers' scores	Operational staff scores	Managers' scores	Operational staff scores	Managers' scores	Operational staff scores
1.	Market research	5.036		4.438		5.750 H	5.443
	Upwards communications	3.906 L		4.350		6.333 H	5.042
	Levels of management	4.375		3.000 L		6.000	3.833 L
2.	Committed to service quality	4.643		4.350		4.917 H	4.219
	Absence of goal settings	4.250		5.800 H		5.333	3.638
	Task standardization	4.188		5.300 H		4.833	4.750
	Perception of feasibility	3.708		3.467 L		4.222	4.887
3.	Teamwork	5.686	5.000	4.520 L	4.300	6.067	5.443
	Employee–job fit	5.143 L	6.500 H	5.900	4.364	5.833	5.042
	Technology–job fit	5.375	6.500 H	6.000 H	4.083	4.333 L	3.833 L
	Perceived control	3.857 L	3.875 L	4.350	4.021	4.875	4.219
	Supervisory control system	4.250	3.167 L	3.333	3.788	5.167 H	3.638
	Role conflict	3.750 L	5.625 H	4.100	3.650	5.250	4.750
	Role ambiguity	4.257 L	4.400	5.000	4.109	5.867	4.887
4	Horizontal communications	3.571 L	2.500 L	4.550	3.205	5.875	N/A
	Propensity to overpromise	4.500 L	2.750 L	3.300 L	3.750	4.333	N/A

Key: H, the highest score of the data sets, i.e. the smallest gap.

L, the lowest score of the data sets, i.e. the largest gap.

N/A, it was felt by the Park that these questions were not applicable for the operations staff to answer.

Table 15.6. Summary of SERVQUAL gap scores for leisure centre, golf course and theatre.

Gap no.	Possible causes	Leisure centre Managers' scores	Leisure centre Operational staff scores	Golf course Managers' scores	Golf course Operational staff scores	Theatre Managers' scores	Theatre Operational staff scores
1.	Market research	4.833		4.250 L		4.750	
	Upwards communications	4.917		5.875		5.350	
	Levels of management	5.333		7.000 H		6.000	
2.	Committed to service quality	4.250 L		4.720		4.563	
	Absence of goal setting	4.500 H		2.750 L		4.100	
	Task standardization	3.167 L		4.000		5.300 H	
	Perception of feasibility	4.167		5.833 H		4.867	
3.	Teamwork	5.733		6.700	5.500	6.100	6.243H
	Employee–job fit	6.083		7.000 H	6.500	6.000	6.423
	Technology–job fit	4.833		5.500	6.500 H	5.400	4.154
	Perceived control	4.000		5.000 H	3.875 L	4.500	4.250 H
	Supervisory control system	3.000 L		4.500	3.167 L	3.750	4.030 H
	Role conflict	4.792		5.875	5.625 H	4.100	5.333
	Role ambiguity	5.333		6.100 H	4.400	5.050	5.738 H
4	Horizontal communications	3.917		4.375	2.500 L	5.150	4.341H
	Propensity to overpromise	4.250		4.500 H	2.750 L	4.000	3.667

Key: H, the highest score of the data sets, i.e. the smallest gap.
L, the lowest score of the data sets, i.e. the largest gap.
NB. Due to the job descriptions of all Leisure Centre Operational Staff it was felt that they all had managerial responsibilities to a varying degree throughout their shifts, therefore scores for operations staff were omitted.

job more effectively and efficiently thus leading to a better service delivery to the customers (Deming, 1986).

The scenario illustrated at this research site is repeated throughout the leisure industry, i.e. is it worthwhile to train seasonal or part-time staff as the retention rate is poor? IiP must be a foundation on which organizations can start to improve quality of staff training and, in time, service delivery, resulting in improved customer retention and profitability.

Leisure centre

The multitude of services that the leisure centre delivers are far more diverse than at any other site, and it has the added problem of having to accommodate the sole use of the school for a major part of its daytime opening hours.

Meeting externally-set financial targets are paramount for the management of the centre as they are constantly monitored. Whilst participation targets are tentatively set for the activities programme, the generation of income takes priority over everything else.

The other priority area that was frequently mentioned was the compliance to Health and Safety Legislation. The root of this culture stems from the cost of litigation or compensation rather than customers' service delivery.

Many of the important decisions about the nature and scope of the service are not made by the centre's managers. Decisions are taken by elected members; stakeholders who are often quite remote from the operational management of the service, although they are ultimately accountable for the financial management. This situation does not occur at the other sites; there, management's 'accountability' extends far more deeply into the day-to-day work.

From the research at this site, it was found that the documentation preparation for both tendering procedures and ISO9002 are not dissimilar. Full understanding of operational procedures and monitoring of processes are common to both sets of documents. This is achieved by task standardization and conformance. The two documents not only complement each other, but ISO9002 also provides an external check, however tenuous, on suppliers; a matter which is a major priority to local authorities. This does not mean that service delivery qualities are necessarily those which the customers want or require.

Golf course

The culture of public sector management decision-making is equally relevant to this site as to the leisure centre. A golf course is a very specialized facility to provide: it is a single core service, mirroring the museum with its specialist collection, unlike the leisure centre where many activities can be programmed.

The golf course always exceeds every financial target that it is set by the local authority. The consequence of this is that the revenue and capital budgets are at acceptable levels, and are channelled into the continuous improvement of the core service, the course. The condition of the playing surface takes precedence over any other service delivery factor at this site.

The impact of the ISO9002 quality system on this site is minimal; the customers are not surveyed but conformance is achieved by unsolicited letters of praise. It is interesting that whilst registration is seen as an added administrative burden with very little benefit by the operations staff, it is reflected in the new tender documents. Registration to ISO9002 has not been seen as a necessary prerequisite for any existing contractor re-tendering for their existing contracts. The existing contractor now knows that it has won the new contract and is not renewing its ISO9002 registration. This would seem to justify some of the critics of ISO9002, including Juran (1993), when they say that it is just a seal of approval rather than a means of continuous improvement or a stepping stone to a TQM culture.

Theatre

After researching at the site for approximately a year, the author was very disappointed to see that the concept of a TQM culture has disappeared.

The quality of the service delivery process is not addressed from a total-organization approach. Senior management concentrate on how to improve service from the front-of-house areas and are continually revisiting these areas with consultants, whilst the creative side of the organization is left. The needs of the front-of-house staff as internal customers of the creative side of the organization are never addressed. Juran (1988b) states that 20% of non-conformance is in operators' hands and 80% is in the managers'.

This site is heading for stagnation rather than moving forward: this seems very unhealthy. The author sees that the introduction of an accredited quality system will act as a catalyst for change (e.g. ISO9002 or a quality award). Whilst everything is internally validated the fundamental problems can be ignored.

Unless the concepts of quality management are completely embraced by all of the senior management team, success in any terms will not be achieved (Crosby, 1979).

Conclusions

Critique of the SERVQUAL model

Whilst Saleh and Ryan (1991) and Chaston (1994) have found the SERVQUAL model adaptable to the UK service industry, especially the commercial sector – and recently Donnelly *et al.* (1995) have stated that SERVQUAL is an appropriate vehicle for the UK public sector – the author has found that this is not always the case.

Questionnaire design
The vehicle of two instruments to test expectations and perceptions is not only tedious, but the respondents get embarrassed at frequently choosing numeric seven for the expectations of an excellent facility. Buttle (1996) suggests that measuring expectations is unnecessary but when Parasuraman *et al.* (1993) were responding to criticism from Cronin and Taylor (1992) and Brown *et al.* (1993) they defended the two-part instrument as giving more accurate diagnostic information but suggested that the questionnaire length could be reduced by rating expectations and perceptions on scales in adjacent columns.

Non-participation in the service
The author found that comments from most visitors were very complimentary in their responses to the open-ended question 'Do you have any comments you would like to make about the [name of the site inserted]?', but slight negative values were being achieved. A reason for these negative results is due to respondents not having a problem for them to test the organization's systems.

If a respondent strongly agrees with a statement in part 1 of the SERVQUAL expectations questionnaire they will mark the value seven: in the third part, if they had not needed to test the organization, they will mark the neutral point, the numeric four. This has the effect of creating a three-point SERVQUAL gap score.

Berry and Schneider (1994) state that participation in the service is a requirement for the SERVQUAL model but these visitors have in effect become partial non-participants. One way to overcome this is to only sample customers who have had a problem, but an excellent service delivery organization may have very few respondents; their very nature is to deliver an excellent service that is problem free.

Respondents using public sector facilities
Respondents at the golf course (when they were filling out the customers' questionnaires) suggested that they did not expect to receive an

excellent service from a public sector organization, making comments such as 'they do the best they can in the circumstances', and 'well, it isn't a private course'.

The author can only conclude that a score of seven against an item on the perceptions instrument for a public sector facility may not necessarily equate to a seven for excellent service awarded to the commercial sector. Public sector practitioners, if not aware of this phenomenon, may not continue to seek improvements.

Reeves and Bednar (1994) have cited a number of researchers who have questioned the application of the model without 'industry-specific adjustments', but Parasuraman *et al.* (1993) address this issue by saying that the SERVQUAL instrument is the basic 'skeleton' underlying service quality that can be supplemented with context-specific items when necessary. They go on to point out that in Para-suraman *et al.* (1991b) guidelines to do this were given.

The reliability of the instrument may be brought into question if practitioners deviate too much from the SERVQUAL model.

Dimensions
Buttle (1996) writes that 'Critics have raised a number of significant and related questions about the dimensionality of the SERVQUAL scale. The most serious are concerned about the number of dimensions, and their stability from context to context.' The author found that the Tangibles and Reliability dimensions impinge on each other at the amusement park, and at the theatre the scores for the four dimensions other than the Tangibles were interrelated.

State of quality culture in the six research sites

There is very little evidence to suggest that any of the organizations researched for this project totally embrace the philosophy of a quality leisure experience for their customers. Compromise seems to be the constant theme running through all of the organizations' management strategies, with short-term financial implications taking precedence.

The organizations know what their customer needs are but are deflected away from their long-term aims to cope reactively with external factors, especially statutory regulations. The introduction of quality processes into operational procedures was carried out when looking for a solution for regulation compliance.

The philosophy of continuous improvement (Feigenbaum, 1983) and long-term success in whatever criteria the organization wishes to be judged is lacking, especially in senior management. The lack of a quality manager in the majority of these organizations indicates that commitment is limited. The organizations tended to focus quality initiatives on what the author sees as the easier, well-defined organizational management aspects where less-specialized staff are employed, and left the more difficult areas (such as curators or artistic staff) to have a choice of personal participation or not. It is impossible for a customer-orientated organization to emerge from this strategy.

At present simplistic, very mechanistic quality approaches have been initiated, but without the impetus coming from senior management more sophisticated holistic approaches to service quality delivery cannot be introduced successfully.

The sub-title of this paper is 'Are they servicing the service rather than servicing the customer?' The author has to conclude that the answer is yes, and that improvements to service quality for the customer come about as a by-product of addressing external pressures.

Future work

Ways to monitor service quality delivery still require future investigation, both quantitative and qualitative. This needs to include research into whether there is a generic model that can be used for numerically monitoring service delivery. This could provide the industry with a management tool similar to Statistical Process Control in manufacturing (Shewhart, 1931).

The current models (SERVQUAL, LODGESERV and Cronin and Taylor's SERVPERF, 1994) are said to require adaptations but major differences have not been addressed. These differences are the type of services that are being delivered, the sector in which the delivery organization is operating and the culture of the society receiving the service.

A trend which is gaining momentum is the use of quality awards criteria as a monitoring device. Investigation into the type of research methodology used for submitting data could highlight a move away from quantitative evidence of compliance to more qualitative methods.

References

Audit Commission (1988) *Performance Review in Local Government. A Handbook for Auditors and Local Authorities.* HMSO, London.

Babakus, E. and Mangold, W.G. (1992) Adapting the SERVQUAL scale to hospital services: an empirical investigation. *Health Services Research* 26(6), 767–786.

Berry, L.L and Parasuraman, A. (1994) Lessons from a ten year study of service quality in America. In: Scherring, E.E., Edvardsson, D., Laciness, D. and Little, H.C. (eds) *Quality in Services.* International Service Quality Association.

Berry, L.L. and Schneider, B. (1994) Lessons For Improving Service Quality – A Customer's Perspective. Unpublished conference papers, Managing Service Quality Conference, Manchester Business School.

Brown, T.J., Churchill Jr., G.A. and Peter, J.P. (1993) Research note: improving the measurement of service quality. *Journal of Retailing* 69(1), 127–139.

Buswell, J. (1993) *Customer Charters in Leisure Services*. ILAM, Reading.

Buttle, F. (1996) SERVQUAL: review, critique, research agenda. *European Journal of Marketing* 30(1), 8–32.

Cabinet Office (1995) *Make Your Mark: Charter Mark Awards 1995. Guide for Applicants*. HMSO, London.

Chandlin, D.B. and Day, P.J. (1993) Introducing TQM in a service industry. *Quality Forum* 19(3), 132–142.

Chartered Institute of Public Finance and Accounting (CIPFA) (1994) *Leisure and Recreation Statistics 1994–95 Estimates*. CIPFA, London.

Chaston, I. (1993) Internal customer management and service gaps within the UK manufacturing sector. *International Journal of Operations and Production* 14(9), 45–56.

Chaston, I. (1994) A comparative study of internal customer management practices within service sector firms and the National Health Service. *Journal of Advanced Nursing* 19, 299–308.

Cronin Jr., J.J. and Taylor, S.A. (1992) Measuring service quality: a re-examination and extension. *Journal of Marketing* 56, July, 55–68.

Cronin Jr., J.J. and Taylor, S.A. (1994) SERVPERF versus SERVQUAL: reconciling performance-based and perceptions-minus-expectations measurement of service quality. *Journal of Marketing* 58, January, 125–131.

Crosby, P.B. (1979) *Quality is Free*. McGraw-Hill, Maidenhead.

Dale, B.G. (1994) Quality management systems. In: Dale, B.G. (ed.) *Managing Quality*, 2nd edn. Prentice Hall, London.

Deming, W.E. (1982) *Quality, Productivity and Competitive Position*. MIT, Cambridge, Massachusetts.

Deming, W.E. (1986) *Out of the Crisis*. MIT, Cambridge, Massachusetts.

Donnelly, M., Wisniewski, M., Dalrymple, J.F. and Curry, A.C. (1995) Measuring service quality in local government: the SERVQUAL approach. *International Journal of Public Sector Management* 8(7), 15–20.

Employment Department (1990) *Investor in People*. HMSO, London.

European Foundation for Quality Management (1996) *Self-assessment Based on the European Model for Total Quality Management 1996*. EQFM, Brussels.

Feigenbaum, A.V. (1983) *Total Quality Control*. McGraw-Hill, Maidenhead.

Hutton, J.D. and Richardson, L.D. (1995) Healthscapes: the role of the facility and physical environment on consumer attitudes, satisfaction, quality assessments and behaviours. *Health Care Management Review* 20(2), 48–61.

Jones, B. (1995) Quality Awards. *Quality World*, February, pp. 85–91.

Juran, J.M. (1988a) *Planning for Quality*. The Free Press, Chicago, Illinois.

Juran, J.M. (1988b) *Juran's Quality Control Handbook*, 4th edn., McGraw-Hill, Maidenhead.

Juran, J.M. (1993) Juran's message for Europe. *European Quality* 1(1), 18–25.

Knutson, B., Stevens, P., Wullaert, C., Patton, M. and Yokoyama, F. (1990) LODGSERV: a service quality index for the lodging industry. *Hospitality Research Journal* 2, 277–284.

Maynard, R. (1995) Investor in people: quality through people. *Quality World*, October, pp. 697–702.

Normann, R. (1991) *Service Management: Strategy and Leadership in Service Business*, 2nd edn. Wiley, New York.

Osbourne, D. and Gaebler, T. (1992) *Reinventing Government*. Addison-Wesley, Wokingham.

Parasuraman, A., Berry, L.L. and Zeithaml, V.A. (1985) A concept model of service quality and its implications for future research. *Journal of Marketing* 49(4), 41–50.

Parasuraman, A., Berry, L.L. and Zeithaml, V.A. (1991a) Understanding customer expectations of service. *Sloan Management Review*, spring, 39–48.

Parasuraman, A., Berry L.L. and Zeithaml, V.A. (1991b) Perceived service quality as a customer-based performance measure: an empirical examination of organizational barriers using an extended service quality model. *Journal of Human Resource Management* 30(3), 335–364.

Parasuraman, A., Berry, L.L. and Zeithaml, V.A. (1993) Research notes: more on improving service quality measurement. *Journal of Retailing* 69(1), 140–147.

Peters, T. (1987) *Thriving on Chaos*. Pan, London.

Reeves, C.A. and Bednar, D.A. (1994), Defining quality: alternatives and implications. *Academy of Management Review* 19(3), 419–445.

Saleh, F. and Ryan, C. (1991) Analysing service quality in the hospitality industry using the SERVQUAL model. *The Service Industries Journal* 11(3), 324–343.

Saleh, F. and Ryan, C. (1992) Conviviality – a source of satisfaction for hotel guests? An application of the SERVQUAL model. In: Johnson, P. and Barry, T. Mansell (eds) *Choice and Demand in Tourism*. Mansell, London.

Shewhart, W.A. (1931) *Economic Control of Manufactured Product*. Van Nostrand, London.

Taylor, S.A., Sharland, A., Cronin Jr., J.J. and Bullard, W. (1993) Recreational service quality in the international setting. *International Journal of Service Industry Management* 4(4), 68–86.

Zeithaml, V.A., Parasuraman, A. and Berry L.L. (1990) *Delivering Quality Service, Balancing Customer Perceptions and Expectations*. Free Press, Chicago, Illinois.

Appendix 1. SERVQUAL questionnaire – expectation items.

Source: Zeithaml *et al.* (1990).

At . . . . insert generic name for the site

		Strongly disagree				Strongly agree		
1.	Excellent . . . . will have modern looking equipment.	1	2	3	4	5	6	7
2.	The physical facilities at excellent . . . . will be visually appealing.	1	2	3	4	5	6	7
3.	Employees at excellent . . . . will have a neat appearance.	1	2	3	4	5	6	7
4.	Materials associated with the service will be visually appealing in an excellent	1	2	3	4	5	6	7
5.	When excellent . . . . promise to do something by a certain date, they will do so.	1	2	3	4	5	6	7
6.	When a customer has a problem, excellent . . . . will show a sincere interest in solving it.	1	2	3	4	5	6	7
7.	Excellent . . . . will perform the service right the first time.	1	2	3	4	5	6	7
8.	Excellent . . . . will provide their services at the time they promise to do so.	1	2	3	4	5	6	7
9.	Excellent . . . . will insist on error-free records.	1	2	3	4	5	6	7
10.	Employees in excellent . . . . will tell customers exactly when services will be performed.	1	2	3	4	5	6	7
11.	Employees in excellent . . . . will give prompt service to customers.	1	2	3	4	5	6	7
12.	Employees in . . . . will always be willing to help customers.	1	2	3	4	5	6	7
13.	Employees in excellent . . . . will never be too busy to respond to customers' requests.	1	2	3	4	5	6	7
14.	The behaviour of employees in excellent . . . . will instil confidence in customers.	1	2	3	4	5	6	7

15.	Customers of excellent . . . . will feel safe in their transactions.	1	2	3	4	5	6	7
16.	Employees in excellent . . . . will be consistently courteous with customers.	1	2	3	4	5	6	7
17.	Employees in excellent . . . . will have the knowledge to answer customers' questions.	1	2	3	4	5	6	7
18.	Excellent . . . . will give customers individual attention.	1	2	3	4	5	6	7
19.	Excellent . . . . will have operating hours convenient to all their customers.	1	2	3	4	5	6	7
20.	Excellent . . . . will have employees who give customers personal attention.	1	2	3	4	5	6	7
21.	Excellent . . . . will have the customer's best interests at heart.	1	2	3	4	5	6	7
22.	The employees of excellent . . . . will understand the specific needs of their customers.	1	2	3	4	5	6	7

Appendix 2: SERVQUAL gap score formulae.

Gap 5: customer perceptions minus customer expectations of service delivery quality

Perceptions score	– Expectations score	= Dimension score
Items ((1+2+3+4)/4)	– Items ((1+2+3+4)/4)	= Tangibles
Items ((5+6+7+8+9)/5)	– Items ((5+6+7+8+9)/5)	= Reliability
Items ((10+11+12+13)/4)	– Items ((10+11+12+13)/4)	= Responsiveness
Items ((14+15+16+17)/4)	– Items ((14+15+16+17)/4)	= Assurance
Items ((18+19+20+21+22)/5)	– Items ((18+19+20+21+22)/5)	= Empathy

To find the organization's score for the individual dimensions across all the respondents, add all the scores together and divide by the total number of respondents. Scores are within a range of –6 to +6; negative scores indicate that the quality of the service delivery process needs improving.

Gap 1: managers' perceptions of customers' expectations

Utilizing managers' data sets calculates the scores for each dimension.

Estimated customers' expectations score	Dimension
Items ((1+2+3+4)/4)	Tangibles
Items ((5+6+7+8+9)/5)	Reliability
Items ((10+11+12+13)/4)	Responsiveness
Items ((14+15+16+17)/4)	Assurance
Items ((18+19+20+21+22)/5)	Empathy

To ascertain the average score for each of the five dimensions, add all managers' scores together and divide by the total number of managers.

To calculate gap 1 (the difference between the managers' perceptions of customers' expectations and the actual value of customer expectations), for each dimension subtract the managers' score from the customers' expectations scores.

Measurement of antecedents of gaps 1, 2, 3 and 4 (see Table 15.7)

Managers (gaps 1–4) and operational staff (gaps 3–4) indicate on a seven-point Likert scale their perceptions of the extent of the gaps.

Table 15.7. Antecedents of service quality gaps.

Gap no.	Possible causes	Statements in questionnaire
1	Market research	4
	Upwards communications	4
	Levels of management	1
2	Committed to service quality	4
	Absence of goal setting	2
	Task standardization	2
	Perception of feasibility	3
3	Teamwork	5
	Employee–job fit	2
	Technology–job fit	1
	Supervisory control system	3
	Role conflict	4
	Role ambiguity	5
4	Horizontal communications	4
	Propensity to overpromise	2

Source: Zeithaml *et al.* (1990).

The statement scores relating to each antecedent are added together and divided by the number of statements. The mean average for all the managers or operatives is calculated to give the organization's overall score for each antecedent in the four gaps. The higher the average score the smaller the service quality gap.

16

Up the Wall: the Impact of the Development of Climbing Walls on British Rock Climbing

Dan Morgan

Bolton Business School, Deane Road, Bolton BL3 5AB, UK

Commonly regarded as a minority activity, rock climbing is attracting increasing levels of attention from the media and is experiencing a noticeable increase in the number of activists. It is extremely difficult to quantify this number but estimated figures from the BMC (British Mountaineering Council) suggest that the climbing population has increased from 60,000 in 1984 to 100,000 in 1995 (source: interview with BMC General Secretary). In the context of other sports struggling to attract participants there appears to be something strangely ironic about the capacity of a sport which is traditionally regarded as a 'nutter's activity' to become so popular.

No satisfactory explanation has been proffered to explain this phenomenon. This chapter proposes that the accelerated provision of artificial climbing walls over the past 10 years has contributed substantially to this growth. It further discusses a number of issues which have caused consternation in the climbing community as a result of this development. The chapter essentially offers an initial attempt to realize the role that climbing walls have in the future direction of rock climbing.

This study is derived from a number of contributory sources. Firstly, the author is a climber of some 20 years' standing and has experienced first-hand many of the effects of the growth in the climbing population. Secondly, a number of interviews have taken place with significant individuals and organizations involved in the development and management of climbing walls. A number of climbers with considerable experience and differing views have contributed their ideas in an informal manner. Finally, a selection of novice climbers have been interviewed

© CAB INTERNATIONAL 1998. *Leisure Management: Issues and Applications*
(eds M.F. Collins and I.S. Cooper)

to reveal their motivations to climb and how they were attracted to the sport.

The chapter begins with establishing the role of climbing walls in the context of the historical development of the sport for training. It recognizes the initial peripheral role of walls as an artificiality and their function, regarded as a 'means to an end'. The role of outdoor education is pinpointed as a determinant of the provision of climbing walls, allied to the commissioning of architects to design the walls, which constitutes an early example of outside intervention in the sport. The apparent need to regain control of the activity is expressed in the way in which climbers have asserted themselves in the design, management and usage of walls to fulfil their perceived needs. The dynamics associated with this climbing-wall industry are located in the wider context of rock climbing and reveal the contest between 'sport climbing' and 'adventure climbing'. Finally, an assessment is made of the impact of the growth of the climbing-wall industry on the rock-climbing community by identifying significant trends amongst wall users.

The early climbers' enthusiasm for movement in the vertical plane, although principally exercised on the crags of upland Britain, was also evident in the way they ascended man-made structures such as buildings and towers. As well as the rustic barns of the countryside, ascents of the university towers of Oxford and Cambridge are well documented.

It is alleged that the first wall created specifically for climbers was at Leeds University; it was designed and created by Don Robinson, utilizing an existing wall in a corridor, and comprised chipped and cemented holds. Don Robinson later formed a company dealing with the construction of walls. However, his arrival in the market was too late to affect the development of many walls which were built during the boom in sports centre construction during the 1970s and 1980s. These were designed by architects with little awareness of what climbers actually wanted, and consequently they were soulless edifices with an accent on architectural function rather than aesthetics and usability (Sports Council, 1988:5,10–11).

The principal motive for the construction of walls was to provide a wet-weather alternative for climbers and also an accessible venue for those not living within easy travelling distance of crags. The majority were built in sports centres and were provided as a public facility. Additionally, many schools were provided with walls, offering a medium to practise the skills required of an increasingly important outdoor education component on the curriculum.

During this phase of wall construction the climbing community's involvement was relatively passive. Climbers concentrated upon the natural crags, climbing in all weathers to pursue their sport. The period up to the 1970s is characterized by the 'hardness' of British climbing, as captured in the biographies of prominent climbers of the era (Brown, 1967; Gray, 1970; Whillans and Ormerod, 1971). As walls began to appear, and the climbing population gradually grew, increasing attention was given to the design of the walls, and their potential to improve strength and technique began to become evident. Tales began to percolate through the climbing community of the use of walls by some prominent climbers to improve their climbing grades.

There has always been a healthy amount of competition for new routes in climbing, and climbers soon recognized the limitations of existing walls in offering what they regarded as challenging situations. Consequently, they began to adapt the existing walls by chipping holds and making additional features. At this stage, they were still primarily focused on the use of walls to assist their performance on the 'real thing', but it was becoming apparent that some individuals preferred the conviviality, comfort and the element of competition which they experienced at the walls. During the late 1970s and early 1980s enthusiastic climbers would visit walls on 2 nights of the week and occasionally at the weekend if the weather was bad. The initial response from climbing-wall managers was muted: they showed little appreciation for the potential market and did nothing to promote their facilities despite the increasing usage, which was particularly evident in the better-regarded walls with good access. Figure 16.1 reveals the significant growth in climbing walls since the late 1980s when climbers began to exert some control over their design and the commercial potential of walls became apparent.

Although suppressed in its overt form by the amateur traditions of the sport, competition has had a role to play in the development of climbing, often in the race to claim a new route. In the sometimes intense atmosphere of the climbing wall, informal bouldering competitions also took place between climbers. The move by the UIAA (International Union of Alpine Associations), the European governing body for mountain activities, to accept formal climbing competitions (with the first event held outdoors at Bardonechia, Italy, in 1985) unlocked an ideological dam which saw the potential for climbing competitions on an international scale.

It soon became clear that outdoor events were unacceptable, due to pressure from environmentally minded climbers and those who felt that the encroachment of competitions would have a detrimental impact upon their involvement in the sport. Additionally, commercial opportunities were dampened by inclement weather. Consequently, attention turned to indoor climbing walls where a number of manufacturers now existed who were in a position to exploit this increased interest.

Parallel with the emergence of competitions was the gradual acceptance in Britain of a different style of climbing which centred upon

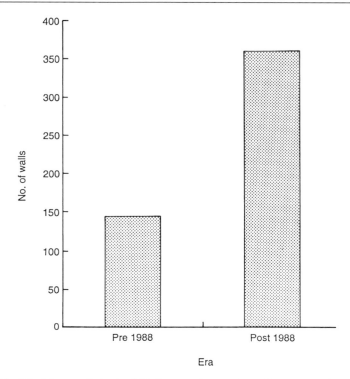

Fig. 16.1. Climbing walls in the UK. Source: Sports Council (1988) and UK Climbing WWW site (1996).

physical difficulty, eliminating any real danger by using expansion bolts which were drilled into the rock to provide safe anchors. This style of climbing became known as 'sport climbing' and met considerable resistance as it was regarded as cheating and contradicting an implicit component of climbing; that it should contain an element of risk. 'Sport climbing' seriously reduced that element of risk thus removing any adventure from the activity. However, this style was wholly compatible with climbing walls, where the tolerance of risk was much lower than outdoors, essentially because sports centre managers did not want injured or dead climbers littered around.

In Britain, although it was a further 4 years before the BMC relented to pressure and sanctioned the first competition in Leeds in 1989, there was already a growing market for walls and attention began to turn to the commercial opportunities. In 1992, the first commercially operated wall opened up in Sheffield: it was owned by a consortium of climbers who recognized the demand for a purpose-built facility and who had also worked out the profit potential.

The response from climbers was predictable; increasingly, they had turned to walls as a bad-weather alternative and recognized that they had something to offer in the form of exercise and a training facility. Walls became not only an alternative but a venue in their own right, offering a comfortable arena in which to socialize and train, and increasingly to compete in either informal or formal competitions.

The increased visibility of climbers on the competition circuit and in sports centres has presented the general public with an accessible view of the sport which has led to a certain amount of demystification. Where previously climbers were only to be seen at relatively isolated and difficult-to-access venues, now they could be seen operating in the comfortable and easier-to-comprehend environs of a sports centre. This has helped to locate climbing in the public eye and also present it in the intelligible form of competition. It has also, encouraged by a management which regards the wall as a cost centre, increased entrance to the sport through this medium. However, this perspective is restricted to a sanitized version of rock climbing with an emphasis on control, safety and accessibility, and does not reflect the philosophy of 'adventure climbing'.

The emergence of organized competition fuelled further interest in the use of walls. Competitions appeared at international, national, regional and local levels. They comprised of a variety of forms including bouldering and leading competitions held between teams and individuals and incorporating various categories based upon age and sex. This new form of structured climbing was also more accessible and understandable to the outside world, and the competition organizers attracted media interest and consequent sponsorship deals. Reebok, which had no previous interests in climbing, were enticed to sponsor the British team. The effect upon the sport as a whole was to attract further participants who have to some extent been satiated by the wall providers.

Currently, there are 24 purpose-built commercially orientated climbing walls, all built within the past 4 years, and this number looks set to increase. In addition, publicly owned sports centres, which have had to become more commercially inclined due to Compulsory Competitive Tendering (CCT), have identified the commercial potential of climbing and have marketed their products accordingly. Figure 16.2 reveals the current designation of climbing walls; the significant growth area is in the dedicated centres which are commercially run venues.

There is little, if any, planning or control of the growth of walls. The BMC has provided an advisory document (Sports Council, 1988) and has coordinated development and management briefing sessions in collaboration with the Institute of Leisure and Amenity Management (ILAM). It has also commissioned climbing-wall development plans for

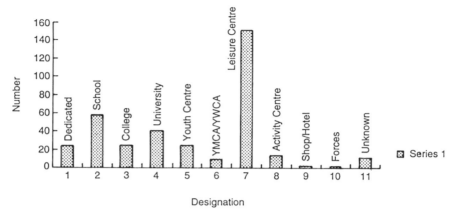

Fig. 16.2. Designation of climbing walls, 1996. Source: Based upon information from UK Climbing WWW site (1996).

each of the BMC areas, undertaken by local voluntary committees. However, the rationale behind these documents was less to do with providing a structured framework for the controlled development of walls and more to do with maintaining and securing funds for the BMC from the Sports Council. The Sports Council stipulates that the receipt of funds for governing bodies is dependent upon them producing sports development plans.

The position of the BMC is controversial here; its mandate is to represent the members, protect their freedom and promote their interests, and not to develop the sport. The contravention of this mandate in these circumstances is shrouded by the focus on climbing walls rather than on climbing *per se*. The distinction between the two, however, is not very clear-cut and there is significant evidence showing that climbing walls are themselves actively promoting climbing outdoors by offering transition courses exposing individuals introduced to climbing via walls to the crag environment. Indeed, the BMC has organized a number of 'first step' events designed to educate wall climbers to the outdoor crag.

This promotion of climbing, whilst couched under the rubric of climbing-wall development, is seen by some as a threat to the traditional form of 'adventure climbing'. Andy Macnae, the BMC's Information Officer, realizes this tension and perceives the solution to be in proactive wall management, which introduces beginners to the intricacies of adventure climbing via walls (The Climbing World Cup, 1995).

The manifestation of the competing ideologies of 'adventure' and 'sport' climbing has emerged in contests over the rock environment. A celebrated incident occurred in a previously innocuous quarry in Derbyshire which was prepared for 'sport' climbs by one party of climbers and later returned to its 'natural' or 'adventure' climbing state by another party, by removing the fixed equipment. This contest over the space to climb is a corollary to the competing ideologies, and it is argued that this situation is exacerbated by the climbing-wall mentality which seeks to reduce risk and make climbing more consumerist.

The frenzy of activity in the climbing-wall market has also been promoted by the emergence of an industry which currently has four major operators on a national and international scale. These have formed a trading group which seeks to maintain control over the quality of the walls' construction, as well as market their own products more profitably. Currently, these companies have strong links with the climbing community, although it is argued that they are more responsive to some elements of that community than others.

The notion that there is more than one climbing community reveals differences of opinion about the nature and structure of the activity. Peter Donnelly (in Ingham and Loy, 1993) has sought to present climbers as a subculture with their own definable characteristics. However, he also recognizes that climbing is not a homogenous entity and climbers are indeed heterogeneous in their understanding and practice of the sport. It is useful to regard the community as displaying a spectrum of values with regard to the role of 'sport climbing', competition and climbing walls. At one end are the 'fundamentalists' who oppose the principles of this triumvirate and regard them as undermining the traditions of British rock climbing. At the other end of the scale are the 'radicals' who embrace the competition culture and seek to promote 'sport climbing' without restriction, and identify closely with the physicality of the climbing-wall medium.

An undoubted feature of the development of climbing walls has been the increased involvement in the sport by young people and women. A number of walls offer clubs aimed at young persons and a number of 'youth festivals' have taken place which have attracted new activists. The content of these events has concentrated upon the competitive and physical exercise components of climbing, elements which are readily identifiable in 'sports climbing'.

There has been no research to discover why more women are now active in the sport. Excluding external factors which will no doubt have a bearing upon women's ability to participate, it is argued that 'sport climbing' has made climbing more accessible to women by considerably reducing the risk element. In addition, there has been a considerable de-masculinizing in climbing, particularly as females have asserted themselves by succeeding on some of the more difficult 'sport' and 'adventure' climbs. In short, it has been shown that women can compete at the highest levels with men in the sport.

It is argued in this chapter that the development of climbing walls has increased the democratization of rock climbing by making it more accessible and has also contributed to the challenge upon rock climbing's élitism which is premised upon a willingness to confront risk. However, it is also argued that in opening up climbing in this way it is reducing it to another 'incorporated' sport (Donnelly in Ingham and Loy, 1993). As well as the problems of overcrowding which are currently experienced at popular venues, there is a more insidious and damaging problem associated with 'incorporation'. This appears as climbing becomes vulnerable to a number of constraining mechanisms such as licensing, compulsory insurance, payment to climb and training. These factors are more easily recognizable in the quantifiable world of wall climbing. In essence, the activity of rock climbing may be in danger of returning to the conventions which the pioneers of the activity sought to escape.

References

Brown, J. (1967) *The Hard Years*. Gollancz, London.

Gray, D. (1970) *Rope Boy*. Gollancz, London.

Ingham, A.G. and Loy, J.W. (1993) *Sport in Social Development*. Human Kinetics, Champaign, Illinois.

Sports Council (1988) *Development, Design and Management of Climbing Walls*. Sports Council, London.

The Climbing World Cup (1995) *Official Programme*, November.

UK Climbing WWW site (1996) www.thebmc.co.uk/walls.intal

Whillans, D. and Ormerod, A. (1971) *Portrait of a Mountaineer*. Heinemann, London.

17

Evidencing the Sport–Tourism Interrelationship: a Case Study of Elite British Athletes

Guy Jackson[1] and Martin Reeves[2]

[1]Recreation Management Group, Department of Physical Education, Sports Science and Recreation Management, Loughborough University, Loughborough, Leicestershire LE11 3TU, UK; [2]Cheltenham and Gloucester College of Higher Education, Francis Close Hall, Swindon Road, Cheltenham GL50 4AZ, UK

Introduction

Sport and tourism have received considerable attention in the research literature, but until recently as separate spheres of activity. An international review of sports-tourism literature conducted by Glyptis and Jackson (1992) revealed that evidence of an interrelationship was in fact emerging. The work of *inter alia* Redmond (1991), Standeven and Tomlinson (1994) and de Knop and Standeven (1997) has identified that this 'symbiotic relationship' between sport and tourism is intensifying. As interest in this field grows, there is a clear need for empirical contributions to support initial desk research and to add data particularly on the volume and value of sports-related tourism.

As part of a wider programme of research into the sport–tourism interrelationship across a range of sports-tourism types, and as an exemplar from the more 'committed' end of this range, this chapter presents some initial results of a study of tourism resulting from élite competitive involvement in one sport. The reported study plots the travel profile, behaviour patterns and attitudes of a representative sample of élite track and field athletes, who have international honours at junior and/or senior levels. The data can be viewed as indicative of the level of sports tourism which results from élite-level participation in other sport types – which should clearly be studied in detail.

The research also provides a contribution towards the more detailed and systematic quantification of the significance of sport as a tourism generator, which cannot be effectively established from existing tourism statistics.

The development of understanding in terms of the links between sport and tourism requires a working definition in order to concentrate thought and, despite the scarcity of literature in this area, one of the most realistic definitions has been provided by de Knop (1997) and Standeven:

> . . . sport tourism comprises all forms of active and passive involvement in sporting activity, participated in casually or in an organized way, that depends upon travel, and where the aim is to improve physical fitness and mental well-being, form social relationships, or obtain results in competition at all levels.

Sports-related tourism and other elements of the leisure industry where sport and tourism interrelate are of significant scale and will continue to develop. Their importance, however, has not been matched with substantive research or literature specifically examining the links. This problem continues at least partly because of the responsibility for development planning, policy administration and resource allocation for sport and tourism being vested in separate agencies. There are relatively few examples of integration, particularly at an institutional level.

The evidence increasingly suggests, however, that they are inextricably linked. For example, according to Glyptis and Jackson (1992) over a quarter of holidays taken in the UK by Britons now have participation in a certain sport or series of sporting activities as the prime purpose for the trip. In addition to this, 'incidental' participation in sport (sport which is undertaken during the holiday but was not perceived as the prime motive at the outset) takes place in almost 50% of domestic holidays.

The lack of detailed research in the field is evidenced by wide variation in estimates of the volume and value of sports-related tourism. Smith and Jenner (1990) have estimated that by the end of the 1980s 'activity holidays', in which sport or a specific activity constituted the main purpose of the trip, accounted for around 10% of all holidays in Europe, and by 1995 this figure was predicted to escalate to 13%. The British Tourist Authority and the English Tourist Board (BTA/ETB, 1988) have estimated that 14% of UK domestic-holiday tourists engage in activity-based holidays. Leisure Consultants (1992) estimated that 7 million trips in the UK are activity orientated, with approximately half of these being primarily sport based. This equates to the generation of 3.5 million domestic sports activity holidays and £500 million in expenditure.

It is now well recognized that tourism demand is becoming more activity-orientated. This has been fuelled by tourism-industry supply response establishing more facilities which are not only sport-related but also increasingly sport-specific. Standeven and Tomlinson (1994) note that:

> . . . clearly the sport–tourism interaction has been a long established one. But it is now becoming more consciously developed and the interaction is now perceived more as an integrated, symbiotic relationship.

It is clear that in terms of both economic significance and participation volumes (and therefore social significance), the interrelationship is worthy of empirical investigation and analysis. The two leisure sectors of sport and tourism are participated in separately by large numbers of people from different socio-economic backgrounds, in different settings both at home and abroad, and additionally have significant economic implications. Except for a few sporadic analyses, what has until recently been overlooked, and remains under-recognized by the respective agencies responsible for sport and tourism, is the very large and increasing significance of the hybrid, sports tourism.

Research within the Recreation Management Group at Loughborough University attempts to synthesize and develop understanding in this area and contribute to policy development. The economic, social and environmental significance of the sport–tourism interrelationship is being reviewed in the ongoing work of a small team of researchers and includes three PhD-level studies. Early pioneering work (Glyptis, 1982) was followed by an international literature review commissioned by the Sports Council (Glyptis and Jackson, 1992) and more recent economic value estimates (Collins and Jackson, 1997, in press). These foundations are now being built upon by the development of empirical studies to further demonstrate the significance of the sport–tourism interrelationship. Work is currently being focused on collaboration with commercial sector providers to more clearly establish the volume and value of this growing sector of the leisure industry and to bring evidential material into the public domain.

The particular project from which one case study will be outlined is *inter alia* attempting to develop a conceptual framework for reviewing and understanding the sports-tourism sector, including analysis along a continuum from purely incidental sports participation whilst on holidays that have other primary purposes, through a range of sports-orientated tourism types to the dedicated and consistent sports tourist, whose tourism behaviour is driven, sometimes exclusively, by sports participation and/or spectating.

The wider empirical work within this broad study of the sport–tourism interrelationship is focused on a series of case studies of increasingly typical forms of sports-tourism provision and experience. These include, for example: the sports-orientated resort or centre-based holiday (monitoring projects are underway in collaboration with large-scale operators such as Butlins); outdoor-pursuits-orientated adventure, activity-centre holidays, traditionally operated by smaller commercial operators (we have an ongoing study monitoring activity-holiday behaviour in West Wales); and travel to sports events (large-scale spectator surveys were carried out at the recent Europa Athletics Cup in Birmingham and World Athletics Cup in London, to identify spectator travel behaviour for medium-scale, high-profile sports events, and further work with other sports is planned).

Another case study (reviewed in more detail here) concentrates on the committed-behaviour extreme of the sport–tourism continuum and examines the generation of tourism through élite-level sports participation, competition and training. It focuses on a group (n = 20) of athletes who have all represented Great Britain at junior and senior levels in track and field athletics. Within this cohort, a variety of age, experience and competitive success was sampled, and each athlete was interviewed by a researcher using a semi-structured interview schedule. The second part of data collection involved the athlete completing a 12-month calendar diary detailing travel behaviour for training and competition commitments within the UK and abroad, and any additional holiday and short-break tourism.

Methodology

The case-study approach appears pertinent to the provision of much-needed empirical data on the variety and significance of sports-tourism behaviour. Traditionally, the aim of such case-study research is to develop and widen understanding of the topic under investigation and to enable the researcher to obtain a holistic picture of the situation under scrutiny. In summary, the beneficial characteristics of case studies (see *inter alia* Eisenhardt, 1989) are, for example:

- effectiveness in explaining previously under-researched phenomena, testing theories and confirming findings from other studies;
- having the potential to enhance internal validity by the use of multiple studies; and
- providing a suitable context in which quantitative and qualitative methods can be combined.

Such non-experimental research where variables are neither controlled nor manipulated, and with the phenomenon under study analysed in its natural setting, facilitates the study of context, which is the aim in this case.

When more than one method of data collection is used, the process of cross-checking data becomes important, with the quantitative and qualitative methods allowing access to different levels of reality. Hence, the qualitative can indicate salient relationships and these can then be corroborated and reaffirmed by gathering data via quantitative methods. This has proved an invaluable approach in this present study.

The research for this case study of élite-level sports-tourism was conducted throughout spring 1996 in London and Loughborough. Many of the athletes lived, worked and/or studied at Loughborough University. The remainder of the sample were contacted during training evenings at Shaftesbury Harriers AC, or during the annual international invitation athletics match staged at Loughborough in May.

The first stage of the data collection involved a detailed tape-recorded interview, adopting a semi-structured format in five sections. The schedule began with background questions to compile a profile of the athlete including level of sports performance and representative honours. Section 2 sought information on the athletes' sports-related travel, including that for training and competition. Section 3 elicited information on recreational activities undertaken whilst the athlete was involved in travel for both training and competition. Section 4 attempted to differentiate travel for spectating and other purposes from that specifically linked to activity for training and competition. The final section of the interview examined the location and type of other holidays and travel undertaken, outside that which was related to their élite sports performance.

The qualitative data generated from these interviews was supplemented by quantitative information in the form of a time–space budget diary approach. A 12-month calendar on which all of the main athletics competitions were listed was given to each athlete to complete. The notation of the athletics competitions was found to be necessary to act as an *aide mémoire* to respondents, since most athletes' training and minor competitive activities and, in many cases, their work, domestic and recreational activities are structured around key competition dates. A colour scheme was used to separately identify time engaged in travelling to and from competition, to and from training in the UK and abroad, and travel for other purposes.

The composition of the sample was designed to represent a cross-section of élite-level athletes across a range of variables including age, sex, representative level and experience. The sample of 20 athletes covered 11 males and nine females. At the time of interview seven could be classified as senior international, eight were junior international and five were 'intermediate' internationals (not currently in the senior Great Britain athletics squad but with recent international experience).

Results

This chapter represents work in progress, and since further tourism profiles along the sport–tourism continuum are required, these results should be treated as preliminary. The initial results are presented to highlight some of the empirical work now being developed to evidence the nature and scale of the sport–tourism interrelationship.

The key finding of the research, and one the researchers hoped to demonstrate, was the significant level of travel generated by or resulting from participation in élite-level sport. The case study of athletics has proved a fertile area in this regard, for whilst the level of travel for competition on a domestic and international basis was expected, the volume of travel for week-to-week training and additional to travel for warm-weather training purposes exceeded expectations (see Box 17.1).

The selected quotes from the full transcripts of the qualitative interviews provide a good insight into the nature of activities undertaken by the athletes whilst training and competing. The profile of activity was found to be dominated by the requirements of their respective training and competing regimes, with the fear of injury whilst participating in other sports punctuating the interviews. The athletes noted that boredom could often be a problem when away on warm-weather training trips to otherwise attractive destinations. A relatively limited range of activities was open to them and so participation in non-sport activities was often appreciated. It was at these times that the athletes would become involved in sightseeing, eating out and fulfilling a profile more similar to that of a traditional holiday tourist (see Box 17.2).

The extent of travel is such that a certain amount of frustration was expressed by some athletes having to travel long distances frequently in order to keep in contact with their respective coaches and to attend National Squad training. This was accepted as an integral and inevitable part of an international athlete's lifestyle. It does, however, raise issues about the quality of experience. In addition to the volume of tourist travel generated by élite sport, which is the primary purpose of this case study, there are several other behavioural elements of interest involved in élite-level sports-tourism which have resulted. The motivational issues and severe pressures imposed on élite athletes by these training commitments alone are highlighted (see Box 17.3).

The types of activities undertaken whilst away in the UK for training purposes were, not surprisingly, fundamentally different to those observed when abroad. Training and quality time with coaches tended to fill more of the period away from home, with residual time devoted to quiet meals and early nights. The intensity of such periods dictates

Box 17.1. Frequency and location of warm-weather training.

'Generally warm-weather training starts in March carrying through to April. I usually go once a year, but ideally I would like to go twice a year if I can afford it.' (Mark Hylton)

'Ideally I would like to go [warm-weather training] twice a year. Once in December and then once in March.' (Sonia Bowyer)

'I've been to Uruguay, Holland, Lanzarote, Calahasi, California, Tenerife, Spain and most European countries; most of the hot countries such as Spain and Portugal and these types of places.' (Jackie Ageopong)

'You know you cannot predict the English weather, so you have to go somewhere where you know it will be hot.' (Jackie Ageopong)

Box 17.2. Activities undertaken whilst warm-weather training.

'We play anything to take the monotony out of athletics training all the time: you know, we might go cycling, swimming, just to get out. It can become a bit intense when you are just training; you tend to eat, breathe and talk athletics. So, for example, when I was in Lanzarote last January we went cycling, swimming or we went to play badminton, basketball and joined in with the aerobics. So just anything to take your mind off the athletics training.' (Jackie Ageopong)

'We go swimming quite a lot. We use it as a session. We play a bit of basketball, but I tend not to play too many other sports because your muscles are not used to it and there is a greater chance of sustaining an injury.' (Mark Richardson)

'I tend not to play other sports as I am usually too tired after my athletics training. There is also the injury risk. I do a bit of swimming, obviously, but really when I go I believe that I am specifically there to train. I try not to do other active things so that I can conserve my energy and put it into my training. I cannot risk getting injured.' (Angela Davies)

'Club La Santa was very good because you have all the facilities there to use. You get given a timetable and you can go along to the activities you want to. I actually went to a few stretch classes and that was all included in the price of the hotel.' (Angela Davies)

the very nature of any ancillary activity undertaken and some parallels can be drawn between these sports-tourists and business tourists. The experience is clearly very different from traditional domestic short breaks.

Box 17.3. Training commitments in the UK.

'Some of the training sessions are at Crystal Palace so I stay overnight either at a friend's house or cheap hotel near the track. I finish training, have a meal and then travel back in the morning.' (Emma Merry)

'I travel down to Crystal Palace from Loughborough twice a week for training and train at Loughborough four times a week.' (Emma Merry)

'I have to travel from Loughborough to meet up with the Gateshead team, so there is a lot more time spent travelling this year.' (Simon McAree)

'For the National Squad weekends you only have to pay for your travel; the Athletics Federation put you up in a hotel and pay for all of your food over the weekend.' (Angela Davies)

'I travel all over England to watch my family and friends compete in athletics. Some of these involve an overnight stay.' (Emma Merry)

Box 17.4. Other holidays taken by the athletes.

'The season basically specifies when you can go away, so by the time the season has finished you are talking about the September/October period.' (Paul Hibbert)

'When the season has finished places are starting to get a bit colder in the UK, so I go abroad and visit friends in places such as America.' (Graham Beasley)

'I do not take other holidays during the year, due to the expense of going to training camps.' (Anna Roze)

'I take proper holidays during the year, either once or twice a year or depending how much money I have left once I have paid for my warm-weather training. I go on holiday directly after the season has finished, mainly sun/sea destinations.' (Clare Raven)

'I do fancy skiing holidays, but the risk of injuries is so high that I would be worried about breaking a leg and missing a season.' (Spencer Newport)

Due to the enormous commitment on both time and finance imposed by élite-level athletics in this country, the athletes interviewed remarked how little time they had left to take other holidays both in the UK and abroad, or day visits (including spectating at other sports events) unless they were directly related to their athletics programme. This was also reflected by the fact that very few of the athletes travel to watch other athletics competitions and only tend to spectate at those at which close friends are competing. Other holidays taken by the athletes are fitted in around these training and competition commitments and normally occur at the end of the season before winter training commences.

Again, the type of activity engaged in whilst taking these holidays is seen to be restricted by the requirements imposed by élite-level performance in athletics. This was seen to be the case despite the fact that the season's training and competitive commitments had been satisfied (see Box 17.4).

The summarized results of the three time–space budget diaries which follow provide further evidence of some of the issues which have been identified here, and not least the significant time and financial commitment undertaken by these athletes over a period of 12 months. Whilst clearly these are individual experiences, they have been selected for their representativeness and are not untypical of the findings across the other élite athletes interviewed. In this research, we have treated day-return travel (e.g. for training) as sports-tourist activity in the same way as spectating at a football league match away from the home area can be conceived. This is, so long as it meets the accepted time and distance requirements for day-visit tourism, to be considered away from the area of residence. Even adopting the stricter view that tourism must involve an overnight stay, the travel profiles highlighted here evidence the large amount of travel involving an overnight stay that élite participation in athletics generates.

One case is provided for each of the three levels of performance and experience reviewed.

Case one. Angela Davies: senior international athlete

Training UK: 38 days
Competition UK: 24 days
Training abroad: 4 days
Competition abroad: 34 days (World Cup, Madrid, Spain and Olympic Games, Atlanta, USA)

Total commitment: 100 days
These results are illustrated in Fig. 17.1.

Angela Davies, aged 28, is a senior international athlete and represented Great Britain at the Olympic Games, Atlanta, and preparation resulted in a significant amount of time being spent in competition outside of the UK. Angela did most of her training at Loughborough where she was based, and hence did not need to travel and stay overnight, with the exception of National Squad training weekends. Her diary also included an intensive one-week training programme in the UK, for which she stayed with friends and family. All of the

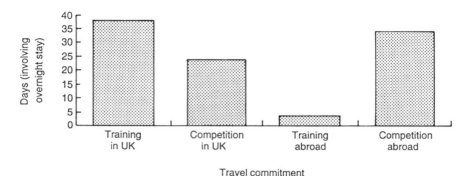

Fig. 17.1. Angela Davies: total days involving travel for training and competition in the UK and abroad (October 1995–September 1996).

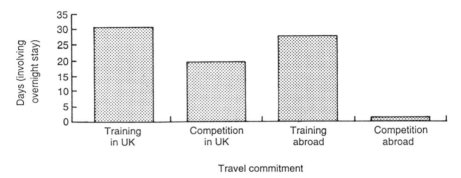

Fig. 17.2. Emma Merry: total days involving travel for training and competition in the UK and abroad (October 1995–September 1996).

domestic competitions attended involved travel over 20 miles and an overnight stay, either in paid accommodation or with friends and/or relatives.

Case two. Emma Merry: intermediate international athlete

Training UK: 31 days
Competition UK: 20 days
Training abroad: 28 days (warm-weather in Portugal and Spain)
Competition abroad: 2 days
Total commitment: 81 days
These results are illustrated in Fig. 17.2.

Emma Merry, aged 21, has risen through the junior ranks and made several competitive appearances for the senior Great Britain squad in competition both in the UK and abroad. Her diary for the 12-month

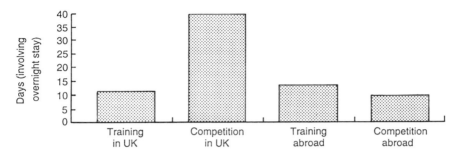

Fig. 17.3. Alasdair Donaldson: total days involving travel for training and competition in the UK and abroad (October 1995–September 1996).

period was dominated by training commitments on two levels: firstly, the frequent 300-mile round trip from Loughborough to Crystal Palace and attendance at National Squad training weekends; secondly, two periods of warm-weather training abroad. The first of these, in December, was to the Algarve, Portugal, and the second, in March, to Club La Manga, Spain. Her competitive commitments for the year have been mostly domestic, and these all involved travel over 20 miles and an overnight stay, except for the international invitation match in May, which was staged at Loughborough.

Case three. Alasdair Donaldson: junior international athlete

Training in the UK:	12 days
Competition UK:	40 days
Training abroad:	14 days (altitude training in Johannesburg, South Africa)
Competition abroad:	10 days (World Junior Championships, Sydney, Australia)
Total commitment:	76 days

These results are illustrated in Fig. 17.3.

Alasdair Donaldson, aged 19, has represented Great Britain at Junior International level and narrowly missed out on qualifying for the Atlanta squad for the 800 metres. The year for Alasdair was dominated by two separate intensive sports-tourism periods: the first, a 2-week warm-weather training camp near Johannesburg, South Africa, at Easter; and the second, 10 days of competition at the World Junior Championships in August, in Sydney, Australia. His coach is also based at Loughborough and therefore he did not need to travel for training, except for attendance at National Squad weekends at Crystal Palace and Oxford.

His domestic competitive commitments, during the study period, started with cross-country races in October, November and December. All of the competitions highlighted involved travel over 20 miles and an overnight stay.

Conclusions

This case study represents work in progress and a more detailed analysis is underway. As far as evidencing the sport–tourism interrelationship, the results already provide a useful illustration from the sports-committed end of the sport–tourism continuum of how far sport does generate travel and tourism.

In summary, the study has highlighted:

- the extent to which élite level participation in sport generates tourism;
- the duration and frequency of travel by athletes for both training and competition;
- the behaviour patterns of those tourists involved in travel associated with élite-level sport;
- the qualitative differences between travel for élite participation in sport and more traditional forms of participation.

This case study has also produced a series of further questions and opened lines for future research. The substantial level of travel and tourism, both domestic and international, which is clearly generated by this representative cohort of élite British athletes is significant in itself, and illustrates just for one sport the significance of sport to tourism at the élite end of the spectrum. To this has to be added the activities of less talented performers, coaches and administrators and spectators, particularly for the larger scale events. Beyond this study, it will be of enormous interest and value to research the patterns of travel generated by other sports and at other levels of participation and spectating.

The recent hosting of Euro 96, the European Football Championships, in England and the Olympic Games in Atlanta have again highlighted the level of travel and tourism generated by players, coaching staff, families and friends, officials, spectators, media and other interested professionals.

The interrelationship between sport and tourism continues to intensify, and there is more travel associated with sport at all levels of performance, and for spectating and a range of other purposes. This is fuelled by increasing market sophistication, greater expectations, improved communications technology and broader horizons. In a relatively short time span, this sector of sports-tourism has grown from the academic and commercial interest of a few into a significant area of academic and commercial endeavour. It remains imperfectly understood even in terms of volume and value estimates, and empirical work is rare. Several sports-tourism types remain unresearched. What we are attempting is to provide snapshot evidence, in both qualitative and quantitative terms, of the extent and significance of modern sport in generating tourism.

References

BTA/ETB (1988) *The Short Break Market.* BTA/ETB, London.

Collins, M.F. and Jackson, G.A.M. (1998) The economic impact of sport and tourism. In: de Knop, P. and Standeven, J. (eds) *Sport and Tourism: International Perspectives. Human Kinetics.* Champaign, Illinois.

de Knop, P. and Standeven, J. (eds) (1998) *Sport and Tourism: International Perspectives. Human Kinetics.* Champaign, Illinois.

Eisenhardt, K.M. (1989) Building theories from case study research. *Research Academy of Management Review* 14(4), 532–550.

Glyptis, S.A. (1982) *Sport and Tourism in Western Europe.* British Travel Education Trust, London.

Glyptis, S.A. and Jackson, G.A.M. (1992) Sport and Tourism: an International Literature Review. Unpublished report to the Sports Council. Recreation Management Group, Loughborough University.

Leisure Consultants (1992) *Activity Holidays: the Growth Market in Tourism.* Leisure Consultants, London.

Redmond, G. (1991) Changing styles of sports tourism: industry/consumer interactions in Canada, the USA and Europe. In: Sinclair, M.T. and Stabler, M.J. (eds) *The Tourism Industry: an International Analysis.* CAB International, Wallingford.

Smith, C.P. and Jenner, P. (1990) Activity holidays in Europe. *EIU Travel and Tourism Analyst.* Economic Intelligence Unit, London.

Standeven, J. and Tomlinson, A. (1994) *Sport and Tourism in South-east England: a Preliminary Assessment.* South-east Council for Sport and Recreation, London.

The Search for a Sport–Tourism Policy Network

18

Mike Weed[1] and Chris Bull[2]

[1]Centre for Leisure and Tourism Studies, The Business School, University of North London, Stapleton House, 277–281 Holloway Road, London N7 8HN, UK; [2]Centre for Tourism and Leisure Studies, Department of Geography, Canterbury Christ Church College, North Holmes Road, Canterbury, Kent CT1 1QU, UK

Introduction

In recent years many commercial providers have been quick to recognize and capitalize on the links between sport and tourism to which consumers appear to have responded positively. The tourism industry uses sport as a major element in promoting destinations, with over a quarter of holidays now having sport as a prime purpose of the trip. In addition, incidental participation in sport (on holidays where sport is not the prime purpose) occurs in almost 50% of domestic holidays (BTA/ETB, 1990). Inevitably, such high levels of activity have stimulated increasing interest from academics in the positive benefits of such links. Although the first works on the sport–tourism link appeared in the 1960s, it has been in the 1990s that academic activity in this area has grown.

Work by Glyptis (1982; 1991), Redmond (1990; 1991), Jackson and Glyptis (1992) and Standeven and Tomlinson (1994) is unanimous in identifying a complex, multi-faceted, symbiotic link between sport and tourism, with the main opportunities being:

1. The development of sport and tourism for economic benefits.
2. The development of sport and tourism for social benefits.
3. The generation of tourism through sport – particularly using sport as a means of spreading the tourism pound more widely.
4. The use of holidays as an introduction to sport and to sustain interest thereafter.

A common thread running through these and many other works in the field has been the focus on advocacy, seeking to justify linking sport

© CAB INTERNATIONAL 1998. *Leisure Management: Issues and Applications*
(eds M.F. Collins and I.S. Cooper)

and tourism and identifying the potential benefits to be gained from doing so. In 1992 the most detailed work in this area to date was produced when the Sports Council commissioned Loughborough University to conduct an international review of literature on sport and tourism. The report represented a watershed in the examination of the sport–tourism link, drawing together over two decades of research and development in the field. The authors concluded that:

> . . . there is sufficient evidence from a world-wide trawl of published English language literature to confirm the very real and potential mutually beneficial links between sport and tourism which agencies administering policies for sport and tourism in the UK could gain through increased cooperation.
>
> (Jackson and Glyptis, 1992)

With the positive nature of the sport–tourism link confirmed, this chapter now seeks to move on from the simple advocacy of earlier works, attempting to take a preliminary step towards examining the attitudes and practices of policy makers and providers and how they seek to satisfy consumer demand, prior to embarking on substantial empirical research.

The chapter briefly reviews earlier work on the national and regional strategies of the sports and tourist agencies in England (Weed and Bull, 1997). Following this, the types of relationships that exist between the sport and tourism policy communities and their importance to the establishment of a sports-tourism policy network are examined. Several areas of influence on these relationships are identified, as is their potential impact on the sports-tourism policy process.

The Regional Agencies

Overall responsibility for both sport and tourism in Britain lies with the Department of National Heritage (DNH) which delegates policy formulation in England to the Sports Council and English Tourist Board respectively. These in their turn operate through a further tier of regional bodies which liaise independently with key resource providers such as local authorities. It is these regional bodies that are the focus for attention here.

The Regional Tourist Boards (RTBs) came into being when the 1969 Development of Tourism Act enabled the English Tourist Board to create a structure of regional tourism organizations. Currently there are 11 Boards which are tripartite entities, jointly funded by the English Tourist Board, local authorities and the commercial sector. The boards are non-statutory and thus vary in their aims and objectives, but most include increasing tourism volume and expenditure in their region as a central area for attention (Robinson, 1994).

In contrast to the RTBs, the Regional Councils for Sport and Recreation (RCSRs) were set up by delegated legislation in 1976 with the following aims:

> To provide a forum at regional level for consultation among local authorities and a wide range of user and other affected interests in relation to sport and recreation.
> To promote in the region the general development of public participation in sport and physical recreation; and of appropriate provision to meet the growing demand for informal outdoor recreation.

(DoE, 1976)

The RCSRs have no resources as such and their secretariat is provided by the Sports Council through its regional offices. The government review of the Sports Council announced in July 1994 contained proposals to revoke the statutory status of the RCSRs, alongside an enhanced role for Sports Council regional offices. At the time of writing, the RCSRs are to be replaced by smaller forums; but the consequences of these proposals for the future of the Sports Council remain unclear.

One of the statutory requirements of the RCSRs is to draw up regional recreation strategies, the third generation of which were completed in 1994 following the publication of the Sports Council's strategy *Sport in the Nineties – New Horizons* (Sports Council, 1994). The RTBs also produce regional strategies although, as there is no statutory requirement to do so, they vary greatly in their regularity and scope. Through analysing these strategies, the regional agencies' awareness of, and commitment to, linking sport and tourism can be gauged.

The Regional Strategies

In analysing the regional strategies it is important to make the distinction between sport-tourism activity that is promoted unilaterally by the agencies, and true examples of multilateral sport-tourism initiatives between the Tourist Boards and the Regional Councils. The review reveals that, in many cases, when the agencies get involved in sport-tourism activity they do so independently of their regional partner agency. With this in mind, seven areas of interest were identified:

1. The need for partnership.
2. Trends affecting sport-tourism.
3. Use of sport/tourism in promotional activity.
4. Sporting fixtures and major events.
5. Facility issues.

6. Access to countryside resources.

7. Prospects for integration.

The need for partnership

Although most agencies state the need to work with their regional partner, in very few cases are there any formal mechanisms for doing so. Three regions have set up 'regional leisure forums', but the terms of reference are often unclear, and in one case meetings only take place once a year. Motives for liaison vary, but the most common amongst the RTBs is 'to ensure that tourism is recognized in the Regional Council's activities', a view that is perhaps a little one-sided if trust and shared understanding are to be promoted. There is a need for partnership, but it is essential that it is genuine partnership taking into account the aims and aspirations of both partner agencies. Unfortunately, it appears that this is the case in very few instances.

Trends affecting sport-tourism

The growing interest in the links between sport and tourism has already been identified, but what has prompted this interest? The Southern Tourist Board is typical of many others in identifying a 'growing interest in health and sport which affects tourism' (STB, 1991:7). Societal forces are facilitating interest in sports holidays, and many of the RTBs are aware of these forces. However, what most RTBs do not seem to accept is the need to collaborate with RCSRs on these matters.

In the South-west, such a need has been recognized in the form of a joint policy statement (WCTB/SC(SW), 1992). The South-west Council for Sport and Recreation recognizes that:

> the value of tourism in the South-west needs to be considered in any
> discussion about sport and recreation . . . as more people are employed in
> tourism-related industries than in any other part of Britain.
> (SWCSR, 1994:9)

It was originally expected that liaison in coastal areas would be greater because tourism is a particularly important element in coastal economies. However, the collaboration in the South-west is not matched in other coastal tourism areas such as the South or East Anglia.

Use of sport/tourism in promotional activity

With the RTBs making use of sport in promoting tourism, and the RCSRs similarly making use of tourism, it is strange that there is little in the way of joint marketing campaigns between the agencies. The sports sector uses tourism as part of the 'case for sport', quoting sport's effect on tourism as a justification for sport's claims for funding and resources, whilst many RTBs see sport as a linking theme that improves the tourism profile of an area. Aspects of the sport–tourism relationship are marketed – the North-west Tourist Board identifies 'sport as an area of strength – enhanced by the Olympic bids' (NWTB, 1992:8) – but only rarely do these campaigns involve inter-agency activity. Considering the agencies' self-professed need for partnership, joint marketing campaigns focusing on a region's sport–tourism strengths would seem to be an ideal starting point for further liaison.

Sporting fixtures and major events

Virtually all the RCSRs see major events as having a role in 'raising the sporting profile of the region', whilst the RTBs are aware of the capacity of sports events to attract tourists. Agencies are aware of both the increasing competition to host major events and the need to encourage add-on stays and return visits by those attending these events. The Heart of England Tourist Board, for example, identifies major events as a tourism opportunity, but adds that these 'would mainly have to be won from elsewhere' (HoETB, 1989:22). Collaboration with the West Midlands CSR would seem to be essential in bidding to win these events, but neither the WMCSR or any other sports body is identified as a partner for this purpose. Therefore, as with other areas of the sport–tourism link, agencies promote and support staging major events independently of each other, when the need is for increased cooperation.

Facility issues

Mixed developments combining tourism, leisure, shopping, office and residential developments are one of the leisure industry's major growth areas, and are identified as such by the RTBs. However, Standeven and Tomlinson (1994) warn of the need for development to be in tune with the needs of the local community, suggesting that regional centres giving specialist advice on the scale and quality of planned provision be developed. Whilst mixed leisure developments proliferate, no examples of partnerships providing such regional centres were found.

The dual use of facilities has the potential to benefit both the sports participant and the tourist. Along the same lines as community use of school sites, tourist-based facilities could be opened up to the local community in the off-season or at slack times, whilst in rural areas the tourist market can make facility provision feasible where it would not otherwise have been so. With the West Country Tourist Board (1992) suggesting that local involvement in tourist activity helps to alleviate antagonism, dual use of tourist sports facilities seems to provide a natural opportunity to achieve this.

Access to countryside resources

The countryside is one situation where the needs of the tourist and the sports participant are virtually indistinguishable. Both groups are facing problems over access to land (Sports Council, 1992; ETB/CC, 1993), and the tourist industry and the sports lobby both campaign for continued and improved access. However, there were no examples of joint lobbying on this issue. The recent outlawing of mountain-biking in some National Parks may indicate a current trend in designated countryside areas, thus making sustaining access an enduring issue; joint lobbying surely is an important element to effectively advancing this cause.

Prospects for integration

Whilst this analysis paints quite a gloomy general picture of the prospects for liaison on sport and tourism, in two regions – the South-west and, in particular, the South-east – there is considerable liaison and forward thinking on the sport–tourism relationship. The South-east CSR commissioned a report on sport and tourism in the region (Standeven and Tomlinson, 1994) which saw the Channel Tunnel making the English Channel a frontier rather than a barrier to sporting contact, opening up the possibility of cross-channel leagues and twinning by local teams. It also recognizes that if the Tunnel is to spread wealth throughout the region rather than direct wealth through it, then a strong sporting identity separate from that of London needs to be developed to attract visitors. This stance is supported by the South-east England Tourist Board through the Southeast Regional Leisure Forum.

The Southeast CSR provides an insight into what a greater exploitation of the sport–tourism link could achieve given greater integration by national and regional agencies. Unfortunately, the strategy review shows that, against a backdrop of increasing sport-tourism activity there is currently very little in the way of integration between the regional agencies.

The Policy Communities for Sport and Tourism

This analysis provides no obvious explanation as to why liaison exists in some regions but not in others. It was originally thought that there might be greater liaison in coastal areas where sport would be forced to consider the large tourist volume, or in regions with large conurbations where sport may be a large factor in urban tourism, especially in places with experience of bidding for major games. Furthermore, it was thought that the more recent tourism strategies might better recognize the contribution of sport. However, the anticipated patterns all failed to emerge, as did any other fruitful insights.

Therefore, in seeking an explanation for these piecemeal liaisons, it would seem to be necessary to look beyond the more obvious explanations to a deeper examination of the policy processes for sport and tourism. In this respect, the concept of the policy community (Houlihan, 1991) may be a useful tool.

The theory of the policy community stems from several different longstanding areas of research, many of which have survived considerable academic scrutiny. Organizational sociologists comment on the concern of organizations with 'the requirements of organizational maintenance and enhancement' (Wilson, 1973) and their occupancy of 'policy space' (Downs, 1967) which Jordan and Richardson (1987) likened to the concept of 'territory'. Group theorists see public policy as the product of the interaction of clusters of interest groups identified with particular policy areas, which reflect the contemporary balance of influence but which also exhibit a degree of stability over time (Richardson and Jordan, 1979).

Combining these two areas of research, it is possible to view policy making as taking place inside an arena where the policy process tends to fragment into relatively autonomous sectors. It is in conceptualizing these sectors that the idea of the policy community has emerged.

There is considerable confusion over what comprises a policy community as the range of actual and potential actors with an interest in a particular policy area may be enormous. Wright's (1988) broad definition is of a policy community comprising: 'those actors and potential actors in a policy arena who share a common identity or interest'. However, because this is so broad, and because not all community members will be active in considering every issue, Wright also conceives of a 'policy network'. A policy network contains actors involved with specific issues or processes and is a particularly useful idea because it enables the identification of networks where membership is drawn from two different communities (Wright, 1988).

The concept of the policy community and the related idea of a policy network is particularly useful in examining policy development in sport-tourism, allowing as it does a focus on recurring relations between members; the nature, extent and source of value consensus; and how far issues are dealt with by identifiable groups of actors (Wistow and Rhodes, 1987).

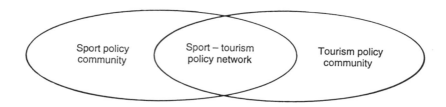

Leisure policy universe

Fig. 18.1. Sport–tourism relations.

The sport and tourism policy communities exist within a leisure policy universe that has been given a stronger collective identity of late by the creation of the Department of National Heritage. Figure 18.1 shows that the area where the sport and tourism policy communities overlap is where a sport-tourism policy network should emerge. There is, however, a third dimension to this diagram because the membership of a particular network need not come exclusively from within the policy universe (Wright, 1988). Thus it is conceivable that an interest in the sports-tourism policy network may come from, for example, the economic development or foreign affairs policy communities.

Several issues concerning the effective operation of policy networks can be identified as pertinent to sports-tourism. The problem of leadership is one such; Rhodes (1986) claimed that leadership is normally centred around government departments, which in the case of both sport and tourism would be the Department of National Heritage (DNH). However, the government takes a liberal-pluralist view of sport, believing that it should not be a formal part of government, rather a consensus developed among voluntary actors (Gruneau, 1982); hence policy making is devolved to the Sports Council. In addition, tourism is viewed mainly as a commercial concern where market forces, rather than direct government intervention, set the tone for future policy development, hence the existence of the respective tourist boards. Thus, rather than policy leadership coming from a unified government department, the main protagonists in the sport and tourism policy communities are the Sports Council and English Tourist Board respectively. Both these organizations appear to be reluctant to take a lead on sport-tourism issues. Furthermore, if either were to do so, it would no doubt meet with objections from the other who would feel its 'policy space' was being invaded. Thus, it would seem that the only way forward for a sport-tourism policy network would be some sort of joint initiative between these two organizations and their regional subsidiaries.

A second issue is that of resource control. There are two types of resources that affect an actor's ability to take part in the policy process; physical and financial resources such as facilities and grant in aid, and resources of expertise and knowledge (Rhodes, 1988). Whilst the Sports Council and the English Tourist Board have expertise and knowledge in complementary areas relevant to sport-tourism, neither agency seems willing to commit staff time or financial resources to such partnerships. This may be a symptom of the sectorized nature of the policy arena, with both the Sports Council and English Tourist Board believing that their resources are for the development of their sector alone, and are not to be diverted to other sectors of the leisure industry. This has been emphasized by the government directing the Sports Council away from any health-related issues, unlike in many overseas countries.

Finally, legitimacy is an important issue in a policy network. It refers to the ability to speak authoritatively on behalf of a group of interests, as well as acknowledgement of the right to be consulted on, or to participate in, policy discussions (Houlihan, 1991). One of the major problems for a sport-tourism policy network is that there are many organizations who, quite justifiably, feel they have a right to be consulted on developments, but no one organization with the capacity to represent or, as highlighted earlier, lead the network.

These various problems led Houlihan to state:

> . . . while every policy sector will generate a policy community this is no guarantee that a policy network will emerge to deal with particular issues. Some communities may lack the necessary value consensus or strength of mutual interests to provide the basis for the formation of a network.
>
> (Houlihan, 1991)

The review of the respective agencies' regional strategies shows that this is most certainly the case with sports-tourism. The agencies act independently, perhaps due to a lack of value consensus or perceived mutual interest across the two policy communities, and so no sport-tourism policy network emerges. The reasons for this may be uncovered by exploring the nature of relationships within and between the sport and tourism policy communities.

Relationships between the Sport and Tourism Policy Communities

Houlihan (1991) identifies seven types of relationships which he sees not as fixed but as evolving in terms of their intensity and nature (see

Table 18.1. Sport–tourism relations.

Relationship	Basis of relationship
Bureaucratic	Convention, legislation
Formal professional	Shared expertise and ideology
Technical	Requirements of plan
Informal professional	Shared interests and problems
Informal consultative	Information transmission
Formal consultative	Information exchange
Party political	Broadly common ideology

Source: Houlihan (1991).

Table 18.1). At the present time limited bureaucratic links exist between sport and tourism bodies such as the cross-representation on regional agencies or those that exist as a consequence of their co-location in the DNH. In addition, there may be some technical links concerning specific projects. The most productive links to date have been informal/professional, the best example being between the Southeast Council for Sport and Recreation and the Southeast England Tourist Board.

However, Houlihan's analysis is somewhat flawed in that he fails to recognize that these relationships may be negative or antagonistic. Such antagonism is particularly likely to occur in more formal relationships where people are required to communicate with each other. It is perhaps the case that negative relationships arise out of an implementation gap (Lipsky, 1980) where policy makers feel that liaison should occur, but where the implementors of those policies are opposed to such links, or vice versa. Whilst antagonistic relationships do at least mean that there is some form of contact occurring, they are unlikely to lead to a clear value consensus or perception of mutual interest.

Regardless of the shape or form of these relationships, it is certainly the case that to date they have not been strong enough for a discernable sport-tourism policy network to emerge. Therefore, it is necessary to examine the influences on the strength and extent of these relationships.

Influences on Sport–Tourism Relations

Examining the various aspects of sport–tourism relations poses a number of questions. What factors influence the nature of relationships within and between policy communities? What dictates whether relationships will be positive or negative? What influences the development of closer relationships that would encourage an identifiable sport-tourism policy network to emerge? From examining a wide range of literature, the following areas of influence were identified:

- ideology (political and professional);
- government policy;
- organizational structure;
- organizational culture; and
- key staff.

Obviously these individual areas do not exist in a vacuum, but can influence each other – for example, government policy is influenced by political ideology and key staff, whilst organizational culture is influenced by ideology, the structure of the organization and key staff. The influence of each of these will now be examined and their effect on the sport-tourism policy process evaluated.

Ideology

Political ideology
The ideological justification for the provision of leisure – whether this be sport, community arts or tourism (particularly day-tripping and urban and rural tourism) – has been redefined from being seen as a right of citizenship in the early 1970s, to that of a central area for combatting urban/youth problems in the late 1970s to mid-1980s, to an area where good (commercial) management practices should be established in the late 1980s (Henry, 1993).

The social-democratic consensus that emerged in British politics after the Second World War was sustained for around 30 years until the mid-1970s. During this time, leisure was seen by both political parties as enhancing the quality of life and thus was a natural extension of the Welfare State.

However, as the social-democratic consensus began to break down it was replaced with an 'authoritarian populism' which emphasized a reduced welfare state expenditure promoting social order and fostering self-reliance on the part of the individual, the family and community groups (Hargreaves, 1985). As a result, state spending on leisure shifted towards community recreation in the inner-city where it was hoped it would help maintain social order. This shift in leisure spending represented a move away from social consumption and towards social expenses, with leisure being seen as having the potential to be employed as 'soft-policing'.

Towards the end of the 1980s, however, state expenditure on sport and recreation in the inner-city was again changing in its emphasis. The relative distance from the urban riots of 1981 and 1984 and the conviction that social regeneration largely depended on economic regeneration saw the government reducing expenditure and directing funding towards regeneration schemes, and attempting to expose the leisure sector to commercial management practices (Henry, 1993).

Leisure is now cast in an active role in image marketing, aiding the attraction of business investment/relocation. It is assumed that the new service industries will locate in areas where the cultural infrastructure is capable of attracting and retaining people in the geographically and socially mobile core workforce, such as financial services and information technology personnel.

Since the breakdown of the social-democratic consensus there has been an inevitable tension between those who still believe leisure is an end in itself and the prevailing political belief in recent years that leisure should be seen as a means to achieve other policy goals. All too often in the recent past, leisure has become subservient to other, more pressing, political matters. Despite its quasi-autonomous status, grants to the Sports Council have been earmarked for schemes to combat deprivation in the inner-city, whilst the Tourist Board has promoted several schemes with urban regeneration as its goal.

Political ideology engenders party-political relationships which will always be inconsistent regarding leisure while the prime motivation for leisure provision is related to other policy areas (Houlihan, 1991). Although many sport-tourism-related projects in urban areas such as Manchester, Sheffield and Glasgow have benefited from recent government funding, this may prove to be transitory as currently there is no mechanism to develop and articulate sport-tourism interests as political objectives for leisure change in the future. In an underdeveloped policy area such as sport-tourism such party-political relationships, although based on a broadly common ideology, will rarely be capable of helping to develop a sustainable policy network when pressures prevail from other more influential policy areas.

Professional ideology
The roots of a leisure profession can be traced back to the creation of the British Travel Association in 1929 and the Central Council for Recreative and Physical Training (later the Central Council for Physical Recreation) in 1937. However, an identifiable leisure profession – albeit dealing mainly with sport, arts, parks and countryside issues – largely emerged as a result of the 1974 local government reorganization which resulted, under the guidance of the Bains report, in a large number of unified leisure departments (Henry, 1993). Five years later in 1979, a number of fragmented bodies joined together to form the Institute of Leisure and Amenity Management (ILAM) which provided a further focus for the development of the leisure profession.

The sports/arts/countryside threads of the leisure profession originally developed in the mould of liberal welfare professions (such as social work, teaching, planning, etc.) where the emphasis is on service. However, whilst the tourism thread developed in a more *ad hoc* manner and included some elements of liberal welfarism, the major emphasis, not surprisingly, was commercial. The change in political thinking on leisure in the late 1980s resulted in an influx into all leisure sectors from the industrial professions (such as accounting, banking, surveying, etc.) who also subscribed to a more commercial ideology.

This creates an inevitable tension, analogous to the tension between ends and means in the political arena, over the direction in which the leisure profession should develop. The nature of sport dictates that leisure professionals subscribe to the liberal welfare ideology of service to clients. However, the tourism sector, because of its economic potential, tends to attract industrial professionals with a more commercial outlook. Thus the ideological tension within the leisure profession can be reduced, in this context, to one between the sport and tourism sectors. Such tension will do little to encourage formal professional relationships, which need a degree of shared ideology between the agencies. However, the problems of a particular region, or shared interests in particular projects, may result in individuals forming informal professional relationships. Limited preliminary evidence to date suggests that such relationships may provide the most likely route to a policy network in this area.

Government policy

Government policy is the manifestation of political ideology. Whilst political ideology is a set of values that guides thinking on the problems of society (Hall, 1982), government policy represents the specific, and possibly transient, framework within which society must operate. It is also the case that the ideology of an organization or individual could conflict with current government policy, creating various tensions. The general thrusts of government policy in recent years have been of centralization and commercialization in which leisure has been cast in an active role – central government has attempted to use it to regenerate local economies through Urban Development Corporations (UDCs), whilst it has been employed locally by the left wing in political and cultural resistance to domination by the centre. The early 1980s saw several government attempts, through various pieces of regulation and legislation, to control local government spending. However, this range of measures failed to suppress local authorities' spending plans as they used increasingly unorthodox methods to raise funds, such as selling mortgage debt and lease-back arrangements.

It was during this period that the Greater London Council and various Metropolitan Counties pursued highly publicized programmes which brought leisure into the mainstream of local political thinking.

In its opposition to governmental attempts at centralization, the Greater London Council used leisure to promote a positive image of socialist authorities and used cultural events such as the London Marathon to provide publicity for policies such as 'London for Jobs' and the 'Fares Fair' subsidy of local transport (Bianchini, 1987).

The government response to these initiatives was the Local Government Act 1985 which abolished one tier of local government, the particularly troublesome Greater London Council and Metropolitan Counties. Centralization increased in 1987 as the number of Urban Development Corporations was increased to ten, all in Labour-controlled areas.

Increased commercialization of leisure was achieved in the late 1980s when local authorities were required to submit the management of a large range of leisure services to market discipline through competitive tendering. Compulsory Competitive Tendering (CCT) meant that either a private contractor would manage a local authority's leisure facilities, or the authority itself would form a Direct Services Organization (DSO) to bid for its own contract. In either case, CCT would radically alter the philosophy and structure for delivering local authority leisure services.

Therefore, government policies produced a set of bureaucratic relationships required by convention and legislation. These policies, as outlined above, can create tensions in restricting organizations' ideological freedom. For example, although several UDCs have grant-aided sport-tourism initiatives, the antagonism such organizations create in local authorities as they invade their 'policy space' means that relationships between the tiers of the policy network come under strain. Thus, as suggested earlier, more formal, bureaucratic relationships within the policy network tend to be negative. However, the increasingly commercial and competitive nature of leisure may mean that new technical relationships across all spheres will appear, as competitive bids are required to be submitted for contracts, resources and grant funding.

Organizational structure

How an organization is structured affects how it operates and how it interacts with the outside world. Henry Mintzberg (1979) in his detailed analysis of organizational structure, which remains a useful typology today, identified five fundamental parts of organizations:

1. *The operating core* is at the heart of every organization comprising the workers who carry out the basic work concerned with the production of goods and services.
2. *The strategic apex* is at the opposite end to the operating core, and

contains the people charged with overall responsibility for the organization; the chief executive and other top-level managers along with their secretaries and assistants.

3. *The middle line* connects the operating core to the strategic apex through a chain of middle managers who act as information filters in addition to performing a role delegated from the chief executive in relation to their unit.

4. *The technostructure* comprises the analysts, removed from the operating work flow, who serve the organization by standardizing the work of others. Work study analysts standardize work processes, planning and control analysts standardize outputs, and personnel analysts standardize skills.

5. *Support staff* exist to enable and sustain the main operating flow of the organization and are often self-contained units with their own operating core. Examples, at various levels of the hierarchy, include public relations, research and development, reception and the cafeteria.

Each of these parts exerts a pull on the organization towards a particular structural form. The strategic apex exerts a pull towards centralization so that it can fully control the decision-making process. It achieves this through direct supervision and a *simple structure* emerges. From the technostructure comes the pull to standardize work processes, resulting in the emergence of a *machine bureaucracy.* Members of the operating core try to minimize the power of administrators and thus exert a pull to professionalize through standardizing their skills and training from outside agencies. This results in the operating core being left to work autonomously and a *professional bureaucracy* emerges. The middle line also seeks autonomy which it must draw up from the operating core and down from the strategic apex resulting in a pull to Balkanize and the emergence of a *divisionalized form.* Finally, the influence of the support staff is maximized when their collaboration is required in decision making as a result of their expertise. The organization becomes structured into work units coordinating between themselves through mutual adjustment, resulting in an *adhocracy.*

Although these five structures are ideal types, and in practice some form of hybrid emerges, although one part of the organization and consequently one particular structure does tend to be dominant. The structures each give rise to different relationships – for example, the professional bureaucracy will tend towards formal and informal professional relationships with other organizations, whilst a machine bureaucracy will tend to form technical relationships. It can be reasonably assumed that the national and regional agencies for sport and tourism experience a pull to professionalize, through the knowledge and expertise located in their operating cores. However, it is also reasonable to

assume that central and local government experience a pull to standardize work processes and thus operate in a more mechanistic bureaucratic
manner. This may create various problems in establishing a coherent
basis for relationships between these sets of organizations within a
policy network.

Tensions within organizations can exist between the principle of
hierarchy and the need to maximize the use of expertise (Gouldner,
1954). Because expertise (if only based on greater knowledge through
delegated responsibility) resides primarily in the lower ranks there is
an inevitable conflict between authority based on expertise and authority based on hierarchy. This may result in some of the more informal
relationships, based on shared interests and problems, being formed
between people and units at the lower end of the hierarchy which may
undermine the more formal relationships being formed at the top. This
realization led to the concept of an 'implementation gap' (Lipsky, 1980)
mentioned earlier, with policies being modified as they move from the
strategic apex to implementation.

Finally, some structures may have difficulty in accommodating
new relationships within their present formulation, the prime example
being a machine bureaucracy where control is through standardized
procedures and outputs. The technical nature of the machine
bureaucracy means that new relationships outside the immediate
policy community (such as those required in a sport-tourism policy
network) will struggle to establish themselves because they are not
provided for within its standard procedures.

Organizational culture

Organizations are moulded by forces that infringe upon their structures
and stated goals (Selznick, 1949). Each organization attempts to utilize
its members to achieve its ends. However, the members tend to resist
being treated as means and act to bring their own special problems and
purposes to bear upon the organization. Strategic Contingencies Theory
(Crozier, 1964) recognizes that organizations are power structures in
which structural features interact with and are affected by factors
which make some participants more powerful than others, regardless of
the formal hierarchy. Mayo (1933) found that inter-personal relationships determined work behaviour in a way that formal organizational
rules in no way anticipate.

An organization's culture is a quite intangible phenomenon which
has attracted academic analysis since the early part of the century. It
develops as an ethos created and sustained by social processes, images,
symbols and rituals, which means that organizations exist as much in
the heads and minds of their members as they do in concrete sets of

rules and regulations (Morgan, 1986). Organizational culture can be expressed as a function of the interaction between the organization's structure and the humanistic effect of its members, and thus often cliques and patterns of clientism emerge as an informal structure alongside the formal one (Dalton, 1959).

Various power relations and cultural aspects within an organization can conspire to keep certain issues from ever being discussed. This 'mobilization of bias' (Schattschneider, 1960) is a process that confines decision making to safe issues and is referred to by Bachrach and Baratz (1962) as non-decision making. Non-decision making differs from negative aspects of decision making – such as deciding not to act and deciding not to decide – in that non-decision making prevents issues from ever being discussed: 'The most effective and insidious use of power is to prevent . . . issues from emerging in the first place' (Lukes, 1974).

Bachrach and Baratz (1962) argue that non-decision making is not neutral but operates to the disadvantage of persons and groups seeking a reallocation of resources and values. Therefore it is quite possible that there could be a mobilization of bias against the various relationships that would result in the formation of a sport-tourism policy network.

Cooke (1987) identifies 12 organizational culture constructs – humanistic, affiliative, approval, conventional, dependent, avoidance, oppositional, power, competitive, perfectionistic, achievement, and self-actualizing – which conspire to form an organization's style as either: *constructive, passive/defensive* or *aggressive/defensive*. Organizations with a defensive style are most likely to jealously guard their 'policy space' and thus will rarely be open to new initiatives such as sport–tourism relations, whereas an organization with a more constructive style may seek ways in which it can accommodate in its activities relationships with organizations outside its immediate policy community. It may be that the current political climate of increasing commercialism and tight fiscal control encourages organizations to become more defensive in their outlooks.

Key staff

Reviewing the influence of key staff on an organization can be regarded as examining the influences previously discussed at a micro level. The attitudes, previous experiences, employment history, educational background and personal contacts of key staff can affect an organization's relationship with the outside world although, as outlined above, its culture can also affect the individual workers. The previous employments and education of staff will have partly shaped their outlook as a result of the various cultures, structures and policies they have experienced.

The conflicts that can arise when an organization's ideology is in conflict with government policy have already been examined. Similarly, an individual within an organization may not share some or all of the ideology of that organization, and thus further tensions emerge which can greatly affect the relationships that the organization and the individual both form with the outside world. Therefore, any new policy direction, such as sport–tourism links, that is imposed on an individual is liable to lead to the negative or antagonistic relationships described earlier.

Key staff are not necessarily those at the top of the organization. As the analysis of structure has shown, specialist knowledge or long experience often locates influence in the middle line or operating core. Delegation of any task results in the subordinate gaining greater knowledge of that task (Gouldner, 1954), if only through familiarity, resulting in the tension between hierarchy and expertise outlined earlier. Easton (1965) identifies the importance of 'gatekeepers' in regulating the flow of demands on an organization; thus, people with the ability to restrict access to other staff or information can exert a major influence on an organization's direction. Analogous to Schattschneider's (1960) theory of 'mobilization of bias', the personal assistant to a chief executive officer can stifle consultative links by restricting access to him/her, whilst a press officer, as the first port of call, is able to shape the nature of any potential new external relationships that may develop.

Summary – the Role of Professionals

Various tensions have been identified in each of the five areas outlined above; ideology, government policy, organizational structure, organizational culture and key staff . Common to many of these is the predominance of the professional. Professionalism locates expertise in the operating core, aided by 'gatekeepers' who not only prevent the flow of information down, but also preserve the autonomy of the professional by preventing the flow of expertise up the hierarchy. The Department of National Heritage delegates responsibility to the Sports Council and English Tourist Board, creating a tension between the agencies' specialist knowledge (professionalism) and the system's hierarchy (Gouldner, 1954).

Tension is created both between professionals subscribing to divergent ideologies, and between the leisure profession and prevalent political thinking. Implementation gaps (Lipsky, 1980) arise from tensions between professionals and their superiors, whilst cultural tensions may be created by the professional's 'mobilization of bias' (Schattschneider, 1960). Finally, key staff are influenced as much by the culture of their profession as by the culture of the organization in which they work. The predominance of professionals in policy communities and policy networks is further reflected in the work of Houlihan (1991) who quotes Sharpe (1985) and Laffin (1986) in support of his view that 'The significance of professional groups is that they constitute a potentially cohesive and influential lobby within a policy community.'

Conclusion

The review of regional strategies identified a general lack of genuine liaison and partnership between the regional agencies responsible for sport and tourism policy. The related concepts of the policy community and policy network appear to provide some potentially productive insights into the reasons for this. Five areas – ideology, government policy, organizational structure, organizational culture and key staff – and the predominance of professionals within these areas, appear to exert considerable influence on the relationships within and between policy communities.

As described in the introduction, the analysis above provides a preliminary exploration of the reasons for a lack of partnership on sport and tourism. The next stage of research is to substantiate these speculations through empirical investigation. Areas for further examination include: the stability of party-political relationships relating to leisure, the extent of the tension between sport and tourism professionals, how far the government alienates sport and tourism professionals, the full impact of organizational culture on sport–tourism relations, the tensions caused by professionals within an organization's structure, and the impact of key individuals on sport–tourism relations.

Further research on these issues should contribute significantly to future policy making in sport and tourism through recommendations relating to setting an appropriate division of responsibility for policy-making agencies at national, regional and local level, including suggestions for adopting of mechanisms through which sport and tourism can be most effectively linked for mutual benefit.

Acknowledgements

The authors would like to thank Jayne Hoose for her comments on early drafts of this paper.

References

Bachrach, P. and Baratz, M.S. (1962) Two faces of power. *American Political Science Review* 56.

Bianchini, F. (1987) GLC–RIP: cultural policies in London 1981–1986. *New Formations* 1.

British Tourist Authority/English Tourist Board (1990) *The UK Tourist: Statistics 1989*. BTA/ETB, London.

Cooke, R. (1987) *The Organizational Culture Inventory*. Human Synergistics Incorporated, Illinois.

Crozier, M. (1964) *The Bureaucratic Phenomenon*. University of Chicago Press, Chicago.

Dalton, M. (1959) *Men Who Manage*. Wiley, New York.

Department of the Environment (1976) *Regional Councils for Sport and Recreation. Circular 47/76*. HMSO, London.

Downs, A. (1967) *Inside Bureaucracy*. Little Brown, Boston.

Easton, D. (1965) *A Systems Analysis of Political Life*. Chicago University Press, Chicago.

English Tourist Board/Countryside Commission (1993) *Principles for Tourism in the Countryside*. ETB/CC, London.

Glyptis, S.A. (1982) *Sport and Tourism in Western Europe*. British Travel Education Trust, London.

Glyptis, S.A. (1991) Sport and tourism. In: Cooper, C.P. (ed.) *Progress in Tourism, Recreation and Hospitality Management*, vol. 3, Belhaven Press, London, pp 164–183.

Gouldner, A.W. (1954) *Patterns of Industrial Bureaucracy*. Free Press, Chicago, Illinois.

Gruneau, R. (1982) Sport and the debate on the state. In: Cantelon, H. and Gruneau, R. (eds) *Sport, Culture and the Modern State*. University of Toronto Press, Toronto.

Hall, S. (1982) *Conformity, Consensus and Conflict*. Open University Social Sciences Foundation Course (Units 21 and 22). Open University, Milton Keynes.

Hargreaves, J. (1985) From democracy to authoritarian populism. *Leisure Studies* 4(2).

Heart of England Tourist Board (1989) *Quality First: a Tourism Strategy for the Heart of England into the 1990s*. HoETB, Worcester.

Henry, I.P. (1993) *The Politics of Leisure Policy*. Macmillan, London.

Houlihan, B. (1991) *The Government and the Politics of Sport*. Routledge, London.

Jackson, G.A.M. and Glyptis, S.A. (1992) Sport and Tourism: A Review of the Literature. Report to the Sports Council, Recreation Management Group, Loughborough University. Loughborough. Unpublished.

Jordan, A.G. and Richardson, J.J. (1987) *British Politics and the Policy Process*. Allen and Unwin, London.

Laffin, M. (1986) Professional communities and policy communities in central–local relations. In: Goldsmith, M. (ed.) *New Research in Central–Local Relations*. Gower, Aldershot.

Lipsky, M. (1980) *Street-Level Bureaucracy.* Russell Sage, New York.

Lukes, S. (1974) *Power: a Radical View.* Macmillan, London.

Mayo, E. (1933) *The Human Problems of an Industrial Civilization.* Harvard University Press, Massachusetts.

Mintzberg, H. (1979) *The Structuring of Organizations: a Synthesis of the Research.* Prentice Hall, Englewood Cliffs.

Morgan, G. (1986) *Images of Organization.* Sage, London.

North-west Tourist Board (1992) *Building on Success: the Strategy for Tourism in the North-west.* NWTB, Wigan.

Redmond, G. (1990) Points of increasing contact: sport and tourism in the modern world. In: Tomlinson, A. (ed.), *Sport in Society: Policy, Politics and Culture.* LSA Publication No. 43. Leisure Studies Association, Eastbourne.

Redmond, G. (1991) Changing styles of sports tourism: industry/consumer interactions in Canada, the USA and Europe. In: Sinclair, M.T. and Stabler, M.J. (eds) *The Tourism Industry: an International Analysis.* CAB International, Wallingford.

Rhodes, R.A.W. (1986) *The National World of Local Government.* Macmillan, London.

Rhodes, R.A.W. (1988) *Beyond Westminster and Whitehall.* Unwin Hyman, London.

Richardson, J.J. and Jordan, A.G. (1979) *Governing Under Pressure.* Martin Robertson, Oxford.

Robinson, K. (1994) Anniversary celebration: the changing administration of tourism. *Leisure Management* 14(4), 22–26.

Schattschneider, E.E. (1960) *The Semi-Sovereign People.* Holt, Rinehart and Winston, New York.

Selznick, P. (1949) *TVA and the Grass Roots.* University of California Press, Berkeley.

Sharpe, L.J. (1985) Central coordination and the policy network. *Political Studies* 33(2).

Southern Tourist Board (1991) *Sharing the Challenge: A Tourism Strategy for the Southern Region for the 1990s.* STB, Eastleigh.

South-west Council for Sport and Recreation (1994) *Visions into Reality: the Regional Strategy for Sport and Recreation.* SWCSR, Crewkerne.

Sports Council (1992) *A Countryside for Sport.* Sports Council, London.

Sports Council (1994) *Sport in the Nineties – New Horizons.* Sports Council, London.

Standeven, J. and Tomlinson, A. (1994) *Sport and Tourism in South-east England: a Preliminary Assessment.* SECSR, London.

Weed, M.E. and Bull, C.J. (1997) Integrating sport and tourism: a review of regional policies in England. *Progress in Tourism and Hospitality Research* 3(2), 129–148.

West Country Tourist Board (1992) *Spreading Success: a Regional Tourism Strategy for the West Country.* WCTB, Exeter.

West Country Tourist Board/Sports Council (South-west)(1992) *Tourism and Sport: a Joint Policy Statement.* WCTB/SC(SW), Exeter/Crewkerne.

Wilson, J.Q. (1973) *Political Organizations.* Basic Books, New York.

Wistow, G. and Rhodes, R.A.W. (1987) Policy Networks and Policy Process: the case of care in the community. Paper, PSA Annual Conference, Aberdeen.
Wright, M. (1988) Policy community, policy network and comparative industrial policies. *Political Studies* 36(4).

Author Index

Subject Index

WORLD LEISURE AND RECREATION ASSOCIATION

WLRA: Who Are We?

WLRA is a world-wide, non-governmental membership organisation, dedicated to discovering and fostering those conditions best permitting leisure to serve as a force for human growth, development and well-being.

WLRA addresses, primarily at the world level, a wide range of concerns including tourism, park and recreation services, the arts and culture, sport and exercise, health, recreational media, theme and entertainment centres, and children's play. The goals of the Association are:

1. To encourage research addressing the full range of leisure phenomena.
2. To provide a forum for the analysis and critique of knowledge and practice.
3. To disseminate knowledge of the universal significance of leisure for improving quality of life.
4. To act collectively to raise the quality of leisure experiences for all, regardless of social category.

How do we do it?

- We provide FORUMS: biennial World Congresses, regional conferences, seminars and workshops, print and electronic media

- We work with PARTNERS: The United Nations and other world bodies, regional and national leisure and recreation associations

- We deliver PROGRAMMES: graduate education, consultation, international experiences for students

- We celebrate SUCCESS: excellence in leadership

- We promote STANDARDS: sustainable and meaningful leisure

- We ADVOCATE: the right to leisure experiences in sustainable contexts

For Details and Membership Information:

On the Internet: Web site: www.worldleisure.org
E-mail: wlra@hg.uleth.ca
By fax/voice mail: 1(0)403 381 6144

Or, by writing to: WLRA Secretariat
                              3 Canyon Court West
                              Lethbridge AB T1K 6V1
                              Canada

Leisure is Life Worthwhile .... get involved!

DATE DUE